BUILDING
small

A TOOLKIT
FOR REAL ESTATE
ENTREPRENEURS,
CIVIC LEADERS,
AND GREAT
COMMUNITIES

JIM HEID, FASLA

**Urban Land
Institute**

About the Urban Land Institute

The Urban Land Institute is a global, member-driven organization comprising more than 45,000 real estate and urban development professionals dedicated to advancing the Institute's mission of shaping the future of the built environment for transformative impact in communities worldwide.

ULI's interdisciplinary membership represents all aspects of the industry, including developers, property owners, investors, architects, urban planners, public officials, real estate brokers, appraisers, attorneys, engineers, financiers, and academics. Established in 1936, the Institute has a presence in the Americas, Europe, and Asia Pacific regions, with members in 80 countries.

The extraordinary impact that ULI makes on land use decision-making is based on its members sharing expertise on a variety of factors affecting the built environment, including urbanization, demographic and population changes, new economic drivers, technology advancements, and environmental concerns.

Peer-to-peer learning is achieved through the knowledge shared by members at thousands of convenings each year that reinforce ULI's position as a global authority on land use and real estate. In 2020 alone, more than 2,600 events were held in cities around the world.

Drawing on the work of its members, the Institute recognizes and shares best practices in urban design and development for the benefit of communities around the globe.

More information is available at uli.org. Follow ULI on Twitter, Facebook, LinkedIn, and Instagram.

Recommended bibliographic listing:
Heid, Jim. *Building Small: A Toolkit for Real Estate Entrepreneurs, Civic Leaders, and Great Communities.* Washington, DC: Urban Land Institute, 2021.

Urban Land Institute
2001 L Street, NW, Suite 200
Washington, DC 20036-4948

ISBN: 978-0-87420-468-1

Author

Jim Heid, FASLA
CRAFT Development
UrbanGreen Advisors

Collaborating Authors

Samantha Beckerman, Development Manager,
Brookfield Properties

Margaret O'Neal, Programs Director, Congress for
the New Urbanism

Adrienne Schmitz, Editor and Writer

Contributing Authors

Holly Bolton, FSMPS, CPSM, Owner, 3chord
Marketing

Brian Falk, Director, The Project for Lean Urbanism

David Farmer, PE, AICP, CEO, Metro Forecasting
Models LLC

Andrew Frey, Principal, Tecela

David Greensfelder, Managing Principal,
Greensfelder Real Estate Strategy

Howard Kozloff, President/Founder, Agora Partners

Lorenzo Perez, Cofounder and Principal, Venue
Projects

Alan Razak, Principal, AthenianRazak

Jay Renkens, Director of Planning and Design
Services, MIG

Reviewers

Liz Dunn, Owner, Dunn & Hobbes LLC

Andrew Frey, Principal, Tecela

Jeff Johnston, Principal, Cathartes

Howard Kozloff, President/Founder, Agora Partners

Edward T. McMahon, Senior Resident Fellow, Urban
Land Institute; Chair, National Main Street Center

Margaret O'Neal, Programs Director, Congress for
the New Urbanism

Alan Razak, Principal, AthenianRazak

Elizabeth (Libby) Seifel, President, Seifel Consulting

ULI Project Team

Catherine Gahres
Senior Vice President, Membership and Marketing

Cindy Chance
Senior Vice President, Product Councils

Trey Davis
Vice President, Marketing and Membership

David Mulvihill
Vice President, Professional Development (retired)

Edward T. McMahon
Senior Resident Fellow

James A. Mulligan
Senior Editor

Laura Glassman, Publications Professionals LLC
Manuscript Editor

Brandon Weil
Art Director

John Hall, John Hall Design Group
Book Design and Production

Craig Chapman
Senior Director, Publishing Operations

Lori Hatcher
Senior Vice President, Marketing (retired)

Patrick Phillips
Global Chief Executive Officer (retired)

CONTENTS

LEFT: The Orchard, Phoenix, by Venue Projects. *(©2020 Andrew Pielage)*

a few *small* words EDWARD T. McMAHON

AMERICA IS A BIG COUNTRY, founded on big ideals, with big ambitions and even bigger accomplishments. In the everyday world, this has often translated into a bigger is better approach to almost everything: big corporations, big stores, big cars, big meals, and big buildings. But bigger is not always better. Globalization, urban renewal, industrial pollution, the decline of family farms, and suburban sprawl are just a few examples of where

oversized approaches to business, land use, and community development have led to unintended and often negative consequences.

In his 1973 book, *Small Is Beautiful: Economics as if People Mattered,* British economist E.F. Schumacher championed human-scaled, decentralized approaches to technology and business. Considered one of the most influential books of the late 20th century, Schumacher's analysis led to what we today call the "sustainability" movement.

As I write this in summer 2020, the world is in the grip of both a global health crisis and a global economic crisis. Although pushed to the back of the headlines, it is also facing a global climate crisis. There has never, it seems to me, been a greater need for more thoughtful, more appropriate, more sustainable approaches to business and real estate

development. Now comes Jim Heid extolling the economic, environmental, and social benefits of building *small.*

For most of human history, the majority of buildings were relatively small in scale. Then two things changed: technology and economics. Until the mid-20th century, buildings taller than five or six stories were uncommon because it was impractical for inhabitants to regularly climb anything taller. The wider use of elevators and structural steel changed all that. So did economics. The growth of big corporations meant the decline of local banks and small businesses. The neighborhood pharmacy, the general store, and the local eatery were replaced by national chains, big-box retailers, and fast-food restaurants—fueled by big capital that only lends to development that could show the ability to attract credit tenants.

ABOVE: The United States is a country shaped by big ideas, big landscapes, and big buildings.

Today, the subtle differences between places have faded, and larger regional differences hardly exist. Now building materials can be imported from anywhere. Hills can be flattened and streams put in culverts. We can transform the landscape with great speed and build anything that fits our budget or strikes our fancy. Technological innovation, standardized codes and regulations that respond to capital and insurance requirements, and a global economy make it easy for building plans drawn up at an office in New York City to be applied over and over again in Phoenix, Philadelphia, Portland, or Prague.

What is more, the fundamental nature of development changed when real estate became an asset class. Like stocks and bonds, big development is now largely an investment business that demands predictable rates of returns and formulaic approaches to design, tenanting, and construction. A multifamily building in New England looks pretty much the same as one in the Pacific Northwest because maximizing returns requires the same proven layout and design.

Many young men and women got into the real estate development business because they wanted to build affordable housing, create walkable neighborhoods, or enliven their communities. Yes, they were interested in profitability, but also in placemaking, equity, and livability. Unfortunately, globalization has led to standardization and homogeneity in building and project typology, outdated codes and attitudes have dumbed down design innovation, and short-term investment returns overshadow long-term community value creation.

It is perhaps no surprise that a book on small-scale development has come from one of real estate's big thinkers. An active member of the Urban Land Institute for more than 35 years, Jim Heid has long been one of ULI's most popular and respected instructors in its professional development program. A real estate developer and strategic thinker, Jim has advised a wide range of companies, landowners, and government agencies on how to develop real estate assets that foster community improvement while generating appropriate economic returns. Known as both a visionary and a pragmatist, Jim is one of America's most articulate spokesmen for sustainable design and development.

Jim's new book is all about bringing back incremental, neighborhood, and community-relevant real estate. It shows why small-scale development is so important; how it can appeal to consumers and communities alike; and how it can further both eq-

> *This book is all about bringing back incremental, community-relevant real estate . . . and how it can further both equity and profitability in our cities, suburbs, and small towns.*

uity and profitability in our cities, suburbs, and small towns. It also shows how the development community can get back to building places that people love, that move the soul as well as the traffic. It makes you think about questions such as, "Would 10 five-story buildings with 10 different local owners be better for a community than one 50-story building with a single out-of-town institutional owner?" More than just raising questions, this book provides the tools and techniques that small developers can use to build more authentic and distinct buildings and places, and that civic leaders can use to change the trajectory of real estate development in their communities.

Often when I visit a city, I am more impressed by the vitality of neighborhoods with small-scale historic buildings than I am by the same city's downtown, which usually has seen far more investment and has far more big, new buildings. Neighborhoods like Fells Point in Baltimore or Elmwood Village in Buffalo or Over-the-Rhine in Cincinnati attract my attention, not just because they are historic, but also because they are typically walkable, diverse, vibrant, and interesting. What is more, researchers have found that such neighborhoods also have more women- and

minority-owned businesses, more locally owned businesses, and a greater variety of uses and housing types. These are also the areas where small-scale developers can get a start and where people know

cost-effective, and more resilient than putting all your eggs into one or two big projects. Jim is not an opponent of big projects or big buildings. He recognizes that they are appropriate and needed in "many sites, where a large, master-planned, multiphased project is the only solution." However, Jim also makes it clear that in "a range of settings and political climates," *small* can be a better option. Today, almost every city and town is littered with vacant

> ***Building small is harder and more time consuming than building one big thing. But it can also be less risky, more pragmatic, more cost-effective, and more resilient.***

their neighbors. As a preservationist, I am always asking, "What are we building today that will be worth preserving in the future?" Jim has helped me understand that if given a chance to develop and survive, small-scale buildings, whether new or old, can punch above their weight class in helping build stronger, more equitable local economies

In summary, this is a book about the power of *small*. Small steps, small businesses, small deals, and small developments can add up to big impact. Jim acknowledges that building small is harder, more time consuming, and less flashy than building the one big thing. But it can also be less risky, more pragmatic, more

lots, obsolete strip malls, disinvested neighborhood commercial areas, and opportunities for adaptive use of older buildings that could fill in the holes of the streetscape while creating new value and new vitality. Jim is asking us to think small in a big way. He suggests that it is more practical, more actionable and will result in more interesting places if communities would seek out many real estate singles, rather than just going for the grand slam.

Edward T. McMahon is a senior resident fellow at the Urban Land Institute and chairman of the National Main Street Center.

ABOVE: Creating neighborhood-relevant real estate and an active human-scaled public realm is a key outcome of building *small*. (©2016 David Delphs)

why this book?

WHEN I STARTED MY CAREER IN REAL ESTATE in the early 1980s, the state of the art was master-planned environments—big ideas and big sites in search of a vision and a plan that defined the future in excruciating detail. As both the market and regulating agencies sought ever-more-certain outcomes, strict design standards evolved, prescribing everything from paint color to building mass to curb design. Project war-room conversations focused on ever-increasing levels of control and detailed organizational charts to determine

who would review future submissions, who would manage the design process, and how to ensure that nothing untoward might interrupt the grand vision of perfection.

Two decades later, the conversation morphed from one of control to authenticity. It turned out that all those beige boxes lined up in Stepford harmony were leading to stilted and uninspired places. While a shrinking segment of the market still found them to be nirvana, an ever-expanding segment found them to be sorely lacking. What was once seen as certainty was turning into sterility—predictable, boring, lacking the sense of surprise and discovery that

comes from stumbling upon something interesting, something vital. These master-planned developments lacked the inspiration that helps us see the world differently, try something new, and find a moment of inspiration and delight.

What was once seen as certainty was becoming boring—lacking the sense of surprise and discovery that comes from stumbling upon something vital.

Fast forward to 2005. The first wave of millennials started to earn a real living and the baby boomers continued to downsize. In 2007, the iPhone was launched. These were harbingers of the changing

ABOVE: In the 1980s, real estate and design focused on creating certainty and consistency through strict design standards. What resulted has been less than inspiring to a new generation.

needs of the household and portended a different take on what a growing segment of the market wanted from the built environment. Where and how do members of these groups spend their dollars? Where and how do they want to work and live?

Reemerging main streets and smaller neighborhood commercial streets found new meaning, anchored by local food halls and food trucks as locally owned businesses took over low-cost storefronts to sell

development came a need for less prescriptive (and boring) square footage and more inspired, interesting, and unique environments.

As the trend watchers added up the data and the anecdotal results came in, something became clear: the leading edge of a growing market was choosing something that was not what developers had been building for the past five decades.

In the boardrooms and project offices, the conversation changed. Grit replaced greenfield. Conversations that would have been incomprehensible a decade earlier began to take place. Jürgen Krusche, lecturer and researcher at the Institute for Contemporary Art

> **The cool, vibrant, and economically resilient places are those that are quietly, stealthily, and continually evolving.**

artisanal goods, retro furnishings, and music on vinyl.

Coworking spaces began to replace the suburban office campus. Flexible, open floor plans began to emerge to accommodate the desired form of working, replacing the purpose-built rooms and cubicles of old. And lofts and townhouses, developed ground up or through the adaptive use of industrial buildings, replaced new single-family homes.

With the increasing focus on trying something new and a more evolving (and evolved) approach to

Research at Zurich University of the Arts, suggested in a 2012 debate that ugliness—"a word he uses to describe the chaotic, patchwork wildness or messiness that a city garners when it is left to fall apart slightly—is what enables vibrancy to happen. What's more, he argued that vibrancy is more important to quality of life than 'beauty,' which is often defined by cleanliness and order."[1]

The cool, vibrant, and economically resilient places are not those that were master planned and executed

---

ABOVE: Plaza Walls is a nonprofit that curates urban murals to brand an emerging neighborhood in Oklahoma City. **OPPOSITE:** *Top:* Melbourne, Australia's laneways are an interconnected network of 15-foot-wide alleys populated by small restaurants and cafés that have become part of the city's brand. *Bottom:* A casual eatery in Mount Pleasant, South Carolina, demonstrates *small* by creatively using outdoor space, found objects, and small buildings to provide a variety of experiences to accompany its food. *(All images ©2020 CRAFT Development)*

with precision, but those that are quietly, stealthily, and continually evolving—where no single developer has led the charge and no single plan has been created. Instead, entrepreneurs are investing in buildings, following their passion for great design, curating unique uses, seeing what happens, and then adjusting as the market self-defines—all the while creating valuable real estate. The natural outcome of this incremental approach to development is authenticity. Unique—and wonderful—places are emerging from the nooks and crannies of towns and cities of all sizes and economic stripes, not because it was prescribed by the code books to be authentic, but because it evolved organically and, hence, authentically.

The number of developers working at the incremental, evolutionary, and small scale is substantial. They are making an impact in a workmanlike manner, one building, one block, one neighborhood at a time, in a series of quiet, surgical strikes. This is the story that needed to be told, in hopes of inspiring and encouraging our industry and our leaders to know there is another way to build more enduring and vital communities. And that other way is building *small*.

ULI's Small-Scale Developer Forums

IN 2012, THE URBAN LAND INSTITUTE INVITED ME TO HELP EXPAND its professional development offerings. After some discussion it was recognized that a program targeted to small-scale, entrepreneurial developers was missing from ULI and the industry as a whole.

Shortly thereafter, ULI convened the first Small-Scale Developer Forum (SSDF) in San Francisco. The forum was envisioned to provide more than just instruction; it set out to create an opportunity for real estate entrepreneurs to gather in a setting that was collaborative, collegial, and inspiring. Since our first meet-up in 2012, I have led all 15 forums, in 15 different cities, bringing together more than 400 participants. Many of our attendees come back time and again because of the invaluable knowledge they gain, the extended network they are building, and because, as one participant put it, "After years of feeling alone in the *small* wilderness, I finally found my tribe."

Tours and discussion started in the major metropolitan markets of San Francisco, Seattle, and Washington, D.C., where *small* was riding a wave of success, fueled by the influx of millennial workers pursuing a more urban and vital lifestyle. After visiting these major markets, we began to wonder if the power of *small* was also being realized in less high-priced and cele-

brated markets. Moving on to Austin, Phoenix, Denver, and Oklahoma City, we witnessed the transformative power of *small* in emerging urban/suburban centers, where small development was creating unique third places—where people socialize most often, after the home and workplace—and at the same time changing real estate values along arterial strips and sprawling tract neighborhoods built in the 1960s and 1970s. Testing the thesis further, we then visited former industrial powerhouses that were being reborn, through small development that was repurposing great old building stock and a low cost of entry, into vibrant new urban neighborhoods throughout Pittsburgh, Baltimore, Indianapolis, and most notably Detroit.

In every city visited, we noted similar outcomes, regardless of the techniques or tools used. Universally, small, incremental development was enabling enterprising, creative, and dedicated real estate developers

ABOVE: SSDFs in Indianapolis *(top)* and Miami *(bottom)* combine active tours of the city, personal discussions with developers, and a chance to network with like-minded small developers. *(Jim Heid/ULI)* **OPPOSITE:** Organizations advocating for small, incremental development gathered in 2016 to share efforts and discuss common principles at the first annual Small Summit in Louisville, Kentucky. *(© Jim Heid)*

to transform their communities in positive ways that earlier generations of "big" developers could not.

Many of the observations, comments, and lessons shared on the pages of this book were inspired by—or came directly from—the SSDFs. In sharing these stories and emerging research supporting the value of *small*, I hope others will be inspired to become entrepreneurial developers, seek changes in their local codes to make small easier, or step up to invest in emerging projects in their communities so that the power of *small* can find its rightful place as a practical and effective tool for building great communities.

WHO ELSE IS THINKING SMALL?

Based on the success of the SSDFs, Andrew Frey, a small developer from Miami and active SSDF participant, reached out to peer organizations to evaluate whether there was interest in gathering and sharing what each is doing and learning in this arena. In September 2014, the first Small Scale Summit was convened in Louisville, Kentucky, as an adjunct to the National Trust for Historic Preservation's annual conference. Attending the one-day think session were leaders from ULI, the Congress for the New Urbanism, the Project for Lean Urbanism, Strong Towns, LOCUS | Smart Growth America, the National Main Street Center, Preservation Green Lab (now the National Trust for Historic Preservation's Research & Policy Lab), and the Incremental Development Alliance (IncDev Alliance). Since then, the annual gathering has brought in other thought leaders in this arena, including Massive Small, SuperNormal, and the American Institute of Architects.

Although each speaks to a different constituency, and may focus on a different facet, approach, or leverage point for making *small* more commonplace, we all came to recognize that *small* is a mutually shared value.

ULI SMALL-SCALE DEVELOPERS FORUMS, 2012–2019

Forum	Year	City	Theme
1	2012	San Francisco, CA	
2	2012	Washington, DC	
3	2013	New Orleans, LA	
4	2013	Seattle, WA	
5	2014	Austin, TX	Small Projects, Big Impact
6	2015	Miami, FL	Arts, Culture, and Small
7	2015	Phoenix, AZ	Small in the Suburbs
8	2016	Pittsburgh, PA	Reinventing the Rust Belt with Small
9	2016	Denver, CO	Health, Transit, and Small
10	2017	Detroit, MI	Coworking + Urban Manufacturing Meet Small
11	2017	Portland, OR	The Role of the Public Realm and Small
12	2018	Charleston, SC	Small Contemporary Design in an Historic City
13	2018	Indianapolis, IN	Active Transportation and Small
14	2019	Baltimore, MD	When Small Opportunity Abounds
15	2019	Oklahoma City, OK	Building Small Projects, Building a Small Firm

how to use this book

THIS BOOK IS WRITTEN TO BE ACCESSIBLE, INSPIRATIONAL, AND PRACTICAL. Depending on your interest in *small,* you can read it from front to back, or you can enter any section that is of immediate interest to you. *Building Small* is intended to be more than a one-time read—acting as both a source of inspiration *and* a resource that can be visited and drawn upon time and again to make *small* a bigger solution.

The book is written for two primary audiences:

- **Developers, designers, and investors:** For those desiring to direct their personal efforts toward small-scale development, as either a career or a hobby, this book provides practical tips, from-the-trenches anecdotes, and selected tools to illustrate how building *small* differs from larger, more conventional real estate development.

- **Civic leaders, public agencies, and their staff:** For this audience, the process of development is important to understand so the unintended

	FOR THE DEVELOPER AND ENTREPRENEUR	FOR CIVIC LEADERS, AGENCY STAFF, AND INTERESTED CITIZENS
what & why	**What defines *small*? Why is it important for communities?**	
	→ Why *small* is a meaningful career path → Why *small* builds stronger places, neighborhoods, and long-term value → How *small* brands and differentiates bigger projects	→ Why *small* should be a key element of your economic development strategy → How policy and planning decisions encourage—or preclude—*small*
how	**What makes *small* different from *big* to develop?**	
	→ Finding sites and testing feasibility → Legal tools to protect yourself → Uses that work in *small* → Financing approaches → Construction, design, market assessment, and approvals	→ How to become better partners to small developers, if that is what you want → The challenge of financing *small* and how communities can help → Added costs and risks that misaligned approval processes create for *small*
who	**What lessons have been learned from real projects and people building *small*?**	
	→ How successful small developers build their firms → Executing small projects: vision to opening → Lessons learned from operating mixed-use small projects → Creative financing strategies from real projects	→ How agencies changed their regulatory culture to encourage *small* → How nonprofits can also be successful small developers → How *small* is used by a state agency to help transform economically challenged communities

ULI SMALL-SCALE DEVELOPER FORUMS, CASE STUDIES, AND SUCCESS STORIES

2013 SEATTLE

Chophouse Row
SEATTLE, WA

2017 PORTLAND

Guerrilla Development
PORTLAND, OR

2012 SAN FRANCISCO

2016 DENVER

2018 INDIANAPOLIS

The Newton
PHOENIX, AZ

Office of Customer Advocacy
PHOENIX, AZ

2015 PHOENIX

2019 OKLAHOMA CITY

Pivot Project
OKLAHOMA CITY, OK

2014 AUSTIN

Midtown Detroit
DETROIT, MI

2017 DETROIT

MassDevelopment
BOSTON, MA

2016 PITTSBURGH

Small Change
PITTSBURGH, PA

AF Bornot Dye Works
PHILADELPHIA, PA

Oslo
WASHINGTON, DC

2018 BALTIMORE

2012 WASHINGTON, DC

Tomorrow Building
CHATTANOOGA, TN

2013 NEW ORLEANS

2015 MIAMI

- Small-Scale Developers Forum
- Success Story (Chapter 12)
- Case Study (Chapter 13)

---

consequences of well-meaning but burdensome regulations become more evident. The objective is not to place blame but to raise awareness of the barriers that exist in communities desiring more small-scale development. For this audience, the book offers leverage points where changes can be made to accelerate and encourage more small development. (See chapter 11 specifically, which identifies common barriers and emerging "hacks" to existing codes to increase the feasibility of *small*.)

The book is organized in three parts:

- **Part I: The What and Why of *Small*.** Chapters 1 and 2 help define many of the ideas, the rationale, and the growing body of evidence why *small* deserves elevated attention and industry focus.
- **Part II: The How of *Small*: the Toolkit**. Chapters 3 through 11 offer lessons, anecdotes, and

practical "how-tos" for developers embarking on small projects. For those working in the regulatory arena, reviewing plans, or writing policy, this section provides practical lessons and highlights pitfalls that should be addressed to make *small* easier to accomplish if that is your community's goal.

- **Part III: The Projects and People Building *Small*.** Chapter 12 shares the people and organizations—both public and private—that have been successful in advancing small development efforts. Chapter 13 features projects from which the reader can draw detailed information, including programming, design, entitlements, financing, and marketing, as well as lessons learned. Projects were selected to demonstrate *small*'s applicability across a range of use types; construction types (ground up and adaptive use); and rural, suburban, and urban settings across the United States.

Biergarten, San Francisco. *(©2020 Envelope A+D)*

the
what
and
why
of small

what is *small*?

building small is not a new idea. It is, in fact, quite old. *Small* is at the core of the places, cities, neighborhoods, and districts that we have come to love. But like many things we once knew about building high-quality human settlements, the virtues of *small* had been forgotten. There are many reasons for this amnesia, but over the past decade, a growing cadre of innovative developers have brought *small*'s potential back into the spotlight.

With the success of projects of all kinds, in settings across the country, small development is gaining more notice. *Small* presents a compelling option in an ever-increasing number of community discussions, offers big developers a new partner for creating more authentic places, and presents investors the opportunity for return *and* to create positive community impact.

Defining *small* is not easy. Whereas much of the real estate industry—its regulations, financing tools, and corporate capacity—has grown in its quest to execute ever-larger projects, small development has evolved in an almost skunk-works-like manner. Entrepreneurial developers—as well as people with no development experience—are stepping in to fill a void in their communities while fulfilling their passion to make meaningful change to the built environment and their community fabric.

At the same time, new evidence emerging through use of big data demonstrates that *small* is more than a quaint idea: it has real economic value, often surpassing the cost/benefit metrics of larger, institutional-scale development.

A primary goal of this book is to elevate small-scale development from its perceived "niche" status to its recognition as a scalable complement and important solution that parallels larger, institutional-scale development for building great communities. To succeed in that objective, the definition—or defining elements—of small-scale development must be articulated. As is the case with other planning jargon that defies simple, sound-bite definitions (i.e., *sustainability*, *urbanism*, *resilience*), it is best to talk about what small-scale development is *not* before talking about what it *is*.

Small-scale development is not just a matter of developing smaller real estate assets. A fast-food restaurant is arguably a small-scale real estate asset, but it is not *building small*.

Small is not dependent on location, and it is not formulaic. It is not determined solely by dollar value or square footage. It is also not real estate philanthropy—creating unreplicable real estate at below-market returns just for social good. Nor is it a hobby or avocation for people who "don't really understand real estate."

Small, as described in this book, provides an alternative approach to the shaping, harnessing, and directing of resources that go into buildings and the spaces between those buildings—together forming the built environment. For far too long

Small provides an alternative approach to harnessing the resources that go into buildings—and the spaces in between.

the real estate industry has placed its focus on big development—the result of a closely held cadre of institutional capital advisers, regulatory demand for highly prescribed long-range master plans, adversarial

---

ABOVE: Fast-food restaurants are small real estate, but they are not building *small*.

communities that try to stop change by "running out the clock" on a project's financial resources, and the institutionalization of real estate companies that require large projects to cover their overhead and expansive executive teams.

This book proposes that an alternative approach exists for the real estate industry to contribute to the built environment in a meaningful way. It also suggests there is a different career path for those who are interested in real estate but do not thrive in a corporate setting. This opportunity has been long overlooked because it is less formulaic, requires a more entrepreneurial attitude, and is—arguably—more disruptive (see sidebar).

Small-scale development (or incremental development, as it is also known) is first and foremost about the "grain" of development—how a diversity of building sizes, timing, and uses creates a more vital, interesting neighborhood. It is also about using disciplined real estate investment and execution to create more than just financial assets.

ABOVE: Piazza Hospitality worked with David Baker Architects to create three small hotels on a single street, carefully inserting them into the existing fabric of Healdsburg, California. The result is the operating and room efficiency of a 120-room hotel with the benefit of three different brands, a finer-grained streetscape, and phased buildout. This outcome contrasts greatly with what might have happened if parcels had been aggregated and cleared to accommodate a single, big 120-room hotel. *(©2020 David Baker Architects)*

The Opportunity of Small

SITTING IN A FORGOTTEN QUADRANT OF TWO INTERSECTING CONTINUUMS—project scale and development culture (see figure)—small development presents a unique opportunity more attuned to the needs of communities in transition, more responsive to market demand for authenticity, and more resilient to economic changes as markets continue to evolve.

With the exception of single-family homes, most of the real estate industry's intellectual energy, capital, and career-based skills have been directed toward institutional capital or merchant building, delivering on long-term design and planning processes that encompass many blocks (top right quadrant), because jurisdictions require highly prescribed master plans. These create long-term endeavors that are often out of step with the market by the time construction begins.

Other approaches (top left and bottom right quadrants) are misaligned in terms of capital and level of effort.

It is in the bottom-left quadrant where the potential of small-scale development becomes evident—for those with a more entrepreneurial skill set to direct "bootstrapped" capital toward creating innovative, incremental development. Although small-scale development can stand on its own or nest into a master plan framework, it is essentially about incrementalism and evolution. This means thinking about long-term value creation versus short-term returns—making it better aligned with community placemaking goals but at odds with most capital providers, who want a clear exit in three to five years.

WHAT ARE WE TALKING ABOUT?

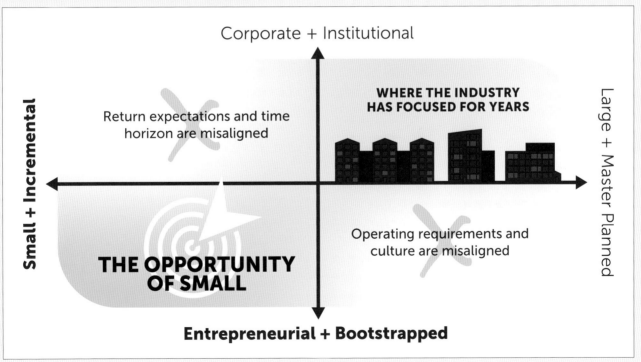

Source: ©2015 CRAFT Development.

ACTIVATION OF THE PUBLIC REALM

→ the hallmarks of *small*

SMALL-SCALE DEVELOPMENT IS BEST IDENTIFIED THROUGH A SERIES OF HALLMARKS, OR QUALITIES, RATHER THAN THROUGH A SINGLE DEFINITION.

BUILDING BETTER

MOVING TOGETHER

EMBRACING NATURE

SHARING FOOD

VALUES DRIVEN

SMALL:

→ emanates from a **clear sense of purpose** from its sponsor, who often takes a triple-bottom-line and long-term-hold view;

→ sees real estate development as a means to an end—the end being creation of great places that help with the **positive evolution of neighborhoods**, whether new, maturing, or those being rediscovered;

→ builds on, and contributes to, existing neighborhood assets—such as **fine-grained street character** and an iconic neighborhood element (like a theater or landmark restaurant or business)—rather than trying to create something insular as its own amenity;

ABOVE: *Top:* Piazza Hospitality's Spoon Bar activates the public sidewalk in Healdsburg, California. *(©2020 David Baker Architects/Bruce Damonte) Bottom:* Specialized Real Estate Group organizes its development around four key principles. *(©2020 SPREG)*

is generated by **entrepreneurial individuals** and organizations;

starts with a clear vision that generally cuts against customary underwriting of highest and best use, instead **seeking a contextual and best use** for the neighborhood and community;

is not easily classified singularly as residential, office, or retail and is the antithesis of build-to-suit, striving for **long-term agility and flexibility**, resulting in real estate that is adaptable, resilient, and more future-proof;

ADAPTIVE USE

can involve adaptive use or be built from the ground up, though the overall goal is to **transform the building or site into an economic asset** and generate a positive community outcome and returns to the sponsor;

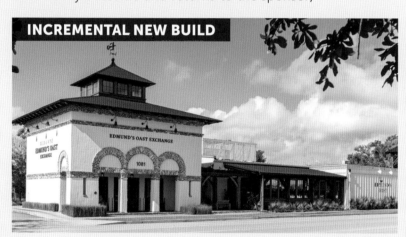

INCREMENTAL NEW BUILD

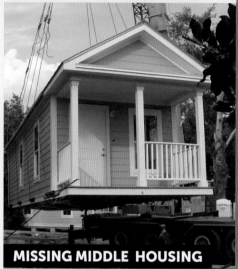

MISSING MIDDLE HOUSING

requires an especially **disciplined approach to capital and execution** and a commitment to wealth creation—for the sponsor and the community—with local economic development as an objective; and

requires more time and "emotional capital" per square foot than *big* because it seeks to be **contextually responsible, community responsive, and market differentiated**. This means capital, approvals, tenanting, and operations cannot be "off the shelf."

CREATIVE FINANCING

ABOVE: *Left:* Raven Cliff Company's Half Mile North used an incremental building approach to forge a new district from an obsolete industrial area in Charleston, South Carolina. *(© paulcheney.com) Top right:* Dunn & Hobbes adapted a vintage car dealership into the Melrose Market food hall in Seattle. *(©2018 Travis Gillett) Middle:* Redesigned modular homes were used to provide missing middle housing in Mississippi, post–Hurricane Katrina. *(© Bruce Tolar) Bottom:* Pivot Project used historic tax credits as part of a creative capital stack to revitalize the iconic Tower Theatre in Oklahoma City. *(© Pivot Project)*

RURAL

→ the geography of *small*

***SMALL* IS NOT JUST URBAN**. It works just as well in a city as it does in a suburban strip shopping center or on a rural main street because its success depends on form and function within its context, rather than a location-dependent highest and best use of a property.

For these reasons, *small* in its many forms is gaining relevance as a valued mode of development. During the economic expansion after the 2008 recession, the towns and neighborhoods that people love—as shown

(SSDFs) have been in forgotten, transitioning, or placeless shopping strips. This is because third places are more desperately needed in these settings than in mature urban zones where density and older buildings already create an intrinsic sense of place. For entrepreneurial developers, the suburban milieu also presents more opportunities at a lower cost of entry than does the urban core. *Small* can be either a much-needed change agent

> **Small *can be a much-needed change agent for banal suburbs or a simple refinement to existing urban neighborhoods dulled through years of disinvestment.***

by rising real estate values—consistently benefited from the patina of time and the fabric of *small*.

In some ways, the most transformative projects witnessed through ULI's Small-Scale Developer Forums

for transformation of banal suburbs or a simple stroke to polish an existing urban neighborhood that already has great strength and structure but has been dulled through years of disinvestment.

RURAL

SUBURBAN

SUBURBAN

URBAN

URBAN

OPPOSITE AND ABOVE, RURAL: Modern General created a third place on the rural edge of Santa Fe. *(Both images: ©2020 CRAFT Development)*
SUBURBAN: The Newton and Windsor have helped revitalize aging suburban corridors in Phoenix. *(Both images: ©2020 Andrew Pielage)* **URBAN:** Chophouse Row helped pioneer regeneration of urban Seattle's Capitol Hill neighborhood. *(Left: ©2015 Andrew JS; right: ©2016 Lara Swimmer)*

why

build *small*?

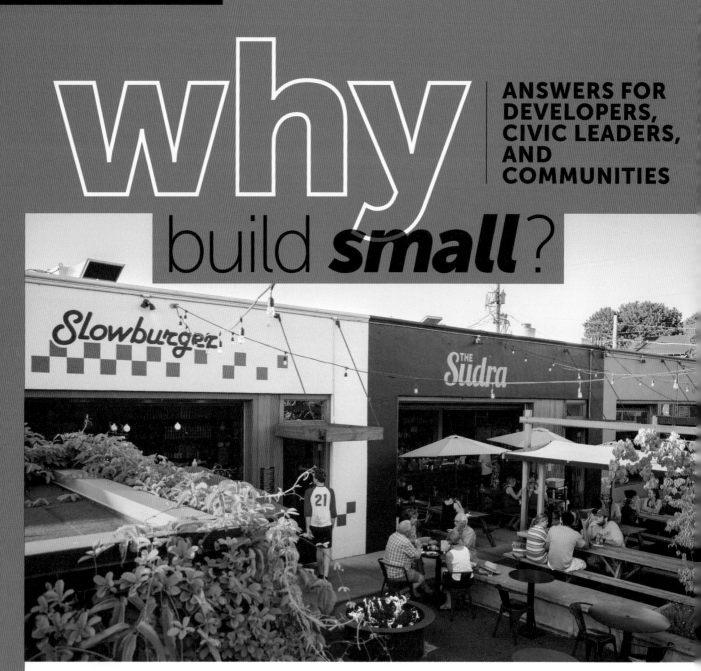

he list of reasons *not* to build *small* is long.

Innumerable factors conspire to make building *small* harder, more time consuming, and more emotionally taxing than its bigger sibling. So, why should entrepreneurial developers and the communities in which they work try to overcome the myriad industry and jurisdictional obstacles that beset small projects?

WHY *SMALL* MATTERS

There are many reasons to build *small*. It makes great cities even greater and helps second- and third-tier cities elevate their game. It provides a cost-effective technique for transforming homogeneous suburban strips into magnets of ongoing investment and economic activity. It polishes the unique qualities of small towns to make them even more livable. It creates local economic ecosystems that are more durable in the face of external shocks.

Building *small* promotes the type of growth that builds wealth over time and makes a place better with age. Streets with smaller and rehabbed older buildings have more value per acre than streets built using suburban development patterns, such as big-box stores and car-centered suburban strip malls.

IS *SMALL* BETTER THAN *BIG*?

To promote building *small* is not to villainize big development. There are many sites where a large, master-planned, multiphased project is the only solution. It would be impossible to develop New York City's Hudson Yards by building *small*: it cost more than $1 billion just to deck over the railyards before any new structure could be built. In other settings, large-scale financing schemes are needed to acquire the site, carry out environmental cleanup, navigate lengthy and expensive legal agreements, and perhaps survive contentious entitlement battles. In such situations, working at a large scale is appropriate and necessary.

But in a growing range of settings and political climates, *small* is an equally effective option that needs to be elevated and discussed in city hall and community gatherings. There are far more fallow corner gas stations and bank sites, obsolete strip malls, and low-density single-family homes amid urbanizing neighborhood commercial streets than sites like Hudson Yards. Through small-scale projects, these holes in the urban fabric can be made productive economic

contributors to the local economy while helping flesh out the public realm and improve its walkability, vitality, and identity. Sometimes, even larger sites can benefit from a component of small development to create authenticity and local appeal and provide a better contextual response to its surroundings. (See "Why *Big* Needs *Small*," later in this chapter.)

OPPOSITE: The Ocean by Guerrilla Development repurposed an obsolete auto repair complex as a series of small restaurants, thereby bringing vitality to an underserved neighborhood corner in Portland, Oregon. *(©2020 Brian Foulkes)* **ABOVE:** There are far more vacant corner gas stations *(bottom)* and small infill parcels in need of redevelopment than there are large shovel-ready sites. Small interim uses such as casual dining help usher in longer-term redevelopment once a market is established, as here in Hyde Park, Boise, Idaho *(top)*. *(Both images: ©CRAFT Development)*

→ the argument for *small*

SMALL PROJECTS OFFER ENTREPRENEURIAL DEVELOPERS a way to get into the game. For experienced developers, *small* can provide a career path that harnesses their years of experience, while creating something more interesting and catalytic than the "institutional" projects that may have dominated their earlier career.

For localities, the case for small development is both intuitively simple and inordinately complex. The primary arguments are:

- ***Small* creates better cities and towns** that are more authentic, human-scaled, and interesting places.
- ***Small* creates more value**—and tax base—per acre than large-scale development.
- ***Small* is more resilient**—better able to withstand external shocks and recover more quickly afterward.
- ***Small* creates a healthier local economy,** in part by attracting the kinds of talent, and hence the kinds of employers, cities and towns want.

As explained later in this chapter, the country is amidst a coalescing of economics, market desire, and changing demographics that sets the stage for the long awaited return to small-scale development. *Small* will not replace *big*, but it can become an important partner—or alternative strategy—for building great places in many communities across the country.

MORE AUTHENTIC, HUMAN-SCALED, AND INTERESTING PLACES

The best-known proponent of *small* was urban writer and activist Jane Jacobs. Although her seminal book *The Death and Life of Great American Cities* was published more than 50 years ago, her wisdom and poetic insights into what makes great neighborhoods could easily be the content of a current blog or podcast on urban placemaking and how to build great cities.

When *Death and Life* was published in 1961, Jacobs lived in Greenwich Village, a neighborhood on the Lower East Side of Manhattan known for its streets and alleys lined with 19th-century townhouses. It was a mix of commercial, residential, and industrial uses, and she wrote of the ways in which this diversity promoted and preserved the cultural vitality of the area. Jacobs made a direct connection between neighborhood safety and "eyes on the street." Those eyes belong to those who run their businesses or live in the area, and those who come to the neighborhood for errands and pleasure. "The buildings on a street equipped to handle strangers and to ensure the safety of both residents and strangers, must be oriented to the street," she wrote. "They cannot turn their backs or blank sides on it and leave it blind."[1]

Jacobs also emphasized the importance of having a substantial number of stores and other public places sprinkled along the sidewalks of a district. These enterprises must have customers at all times of the day and night for the sidewalks outside to be in continuous use, so eyes are always on the street in sufficient numbers to provide safety.

Jacobs describes a successful city as one where the intricacy of sidewalk use and its constant succession of eyes is like a dance—"intricate ballet in which the individual dancers and ensembles all have distinctive parts which miraculously reinforce each other and compose an orderly whole. The ballet of the good city sidewalk never repeats itself from place to place, and in any one place is always replete with new improvisations."[2] Jacobs's vision is most achievable with small development and its ability to create a vibrant street life and support the art form that is a city.

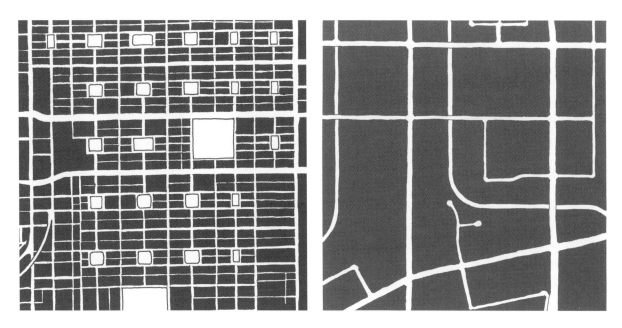

OPPOSITE: Goff D'Antonio Associates designed the Hotel Bella Grace, skillfully inserting a 50-room hotel into Charleston's historic blockscape while still introducing a more contemporary language. *(© paulcheney.com)* **ABOVE:** These two diagrams from Allan Jacobs's seminal book *Great Streets* show how street system choices inform a community's grain. *(Jacobs, Allan B., Great Streets, ©1993 Massachusetts Institute of Technology, by permission of The MIT Press)*

THE URBAN FABRIC AND GRANULARITY

Small development supports and enables finer *urban grain* or *granularity*. In his essay "Fine-Grained vs. Coarse-Grained Urbanism" for Strong Towns—a nonprofit organization that "challenges every American to fundamentally rethink how our cities are built"—founding member Andrew Price defines this concept in both physical and economic terms:

> The word "granular" is used to describe something that is made up of multiple elements. If the elements are small, we call it "fine-grained," and if the elements are large, we call it "coarse-grained." . . .
>
> I use "granularity" to talk about how the ownership of a city is divided, particularly in terms of the size of the lots that city blocks are divided into. There's a big difference between these two types of development and one will create a far better outcome for our cities. . . .
>
> We can also talk about the granularity of an economy; an economy is fine-grained if it is made up of many small businesses and coarse-grained if it is made up of a few large businesses. (Of course, most economies are somewhere in between.)[3]

Price notes that older urban areas in the United States tend to be fine-grained, whereas newer ones tend to be coarse-grained. Fine-grained urbanism is preferable, he writes, because it implies

- diverse ownership;
- a lower cost of entry, because in general it costs less to build a shop or a home on a small, narrow lot than to build, for instance, an entire apartment complex;
- more destinations within walking distance; and
- greater resistance to bad buildings because bad buildings can have less of an impact when they are limited in size.[4]

Liz Dunn, principal of Seattle-based developer Dunn & Hobbes, has spent a lot of time thinking about granularity both in her development work and as one of the driving forces behind the Research & Policy Lab (part of the National Trust for Historic Preservation). "There are many possible interpretations of the phrase *urban grain* or *granularity* that have to do with the scale and composition of cities. A lot of work has gone into analyzing the street grid—for example, the size of blocks within a grid. I'm personally most interested in blockscapes, and the elements that coexist within a block or set of blocks," she told *Atlantic* magazine.[5]

ABOVE: The built form of Savannah, Georgia, *(left)* compared with that of Irvine, California, *(right)* illustrates the character that results from street patterns illustrated on page 25. Savannah's finer-grained fabric encourages long-term adaptation and small infill, leading to more interesting and evolutionary outcomes. Irvine's superblock grain requires large singular developments that lack a sense of evolution and human scale.

Alumina Apartments

HOW GRAIN CREATES OPPORTUNITIES FOR ENTREPRENEURS TO LEVERAGE *SMALL* WHILE HELPING REBUILD NEIGHBORHOODS

IN 2015, ARCHITECT SAMUEL DAY BEGAN TO EXPLORE how he could create work beyond traditional clients. He embarked on developing a fourplex, because it was "the biggest thing that I could build without bringing in outside capital." It also represented a building type that Day could design for residents at a similar life stage as his own.

After sending letters to the owners of over a dozen vacant lots, he ended up purchasing a lot at the edge of a popular local commercial district near downtown Oklahoma City in 2016. Rezoning, research, and design of the project took place over the following year.

To encourage street life, each unit has a dedicated front door and porch facing the street. There is no interior common area. Units have a high total window area that ranges from 11 to 18 percent of each unit's floor area. Each apartment has different finishes, which allows experimentation with varied materials in the knowledge that any unsuccessful choices will be limited to just one unit.

Being owner, developer, and occupant allowed Day to approach the project incrementally, planning for future improvements and additions from the outset. By taking a long-term stake in the building, Day was able to approach the project more like an urban planning assignment, where modifications are anticipated from the beginning.

Reflecting on the experience, Day noted the project convinced him of the economics of small scale. By using residential contractors and doing some of the finish work himself, he was able to get building costs low enough so that units were affordable to couples making 100 percent of area median income—a rarity for new apartments in the area.

TOP: Architect Sam Day's four-unit apartment building fits neatly onto an existing lot while helping strengthen the blockscape surrounding Oklahoma City's Plaza District. **ABOVE:** Although small, the airy, simple design of the units makes them a comfortable option for missing middle housing. *(All images ©2020 Leonid Furmansky)*

It is this idea of blockscapes that creates the context for place. Blockscapes are to human living what habitat is to biologic ecosystems. As with ecosystems, the healthiest blockscapes are those with the highest level of diversity and granularity. Megablock developments do not foster diversity, nor do they allow for blurred edges between ecosystems where the most vitality occurs.

Victor Dover, a charter member of the Congress for the New Urbanism (CNU) and recognized as one of the most articulate proponents of the new urbanism movement, explains it another way: "There's a lot of leaves on each tree in case a few fall off. Nature doesn't look to one big leaf to do all the work. Similarly, great cities have texture because we let a lot of investors try a lot of ideas. And some get left behind, but others learn from what's going on around them."[6]

Dover's concept supports another idea inherent in the elegance of *small*: *urban fabric*. The beauty of fabric as a way to describe great urban systems is that fabric at its essence is a flexible network of interrelated, connected components, able to bend and twist as different stressors present themselves, and all the while adapting and still functioning as a whole. The many smaller elements that make up fabric each contribute its own character, but collectively they create the strength of the system. Where the urban fabric—the foundation of great places—is strong, it is flexible enough to allow new things consistent with that fabric to be inserted, adapted, and repurposed alongside the old.

This mix of old and new, and of different uses in the urban fabric, can contribute to an attribute sometimes called "messiness." As Christine McLaren noted in her Guggenheim blog:

> When New York Lab Team member Charles Montgomery and environmental psychologist Colin Ellard gathered data about people's emotional and physiological reactions to different forms of streetscape and urban design, . . . one of their surprising findings reflected, to a certain extent, the case for messiness.
>
> They found that people actually felt happier and more [engaged] standing in front of an older, more crowded, messier streetscape . . . than they did in front of the newer, simple, clean, blank facade of Whole Foods on Houston Street. What's more, . . . the contrast was even stronger in visitors to the neighborhood and city than it was with local residents.[7]

ABOVE: Streetscapes from New Orleans *(left)* and Charleston *(right)* show how the strength of the street fabric allows new, larger developments to fit into each block seamlessly. **OPPOSITE:** The Belt created a neighborhood brand to revitalize a block of downtown Detroit by infusing the sense of "messiness" and delight that comes from urban art. *(All images: ©2020 CRAFT Development)*

Grain, messiness, and vitality work together to create great places, all on a foundation of *small*.

Besides architects and urban designers, many other professions recognize the important role the built environment plays in the human condition. Social scientists speak of social equity and how the physical environment improves social connectivity and mental health. Economic development specialists look at how the built environment affects job creation and attraction, as well as economic resilience in times of rapid change. Environmental researchers measure how the physical environment can change behavior that in turn can increase mobility choices and reduce reliance on fossil fuel–based transportation. Health specialists look at how to increase the opportunities to walk rather than ride in order to reduce obesity, while designers look at how the built environment can increase the sense of personal delight and joy that comes from being part of a great place.

MEASURING URBAN CHARACTER

What was intuitively understood by Jane Jacobs and early urban designers can be quantified and studied to meet today's greater demand for data. Among the efforts to quantify what constitutes high-quality small design are the following:

- **The U.S. Green Building Council**—in the Neighborhood Pattern and Design category of its Leadership in Energy and Environmental Design for Neighborhood Development (LEED ND) rating system—codifies key design elements that create smaller, finer-grained street frontages. For example, LEED ND, through its credit system, drives planning and design to create smaller block sizes, mixed uses, more entrances to buildings, active edges along pedestrian areas, and reduced parking areas.
- **The Research & Policy Lab** combined maps and other data sources to prove the thesis that an older, smaller-scale building stock with greater size diversity creates more jobs and more resilient communities.
- **Strong Towns** uses Urban3's work to show in both quantitative and graphic form that municipalities receive a higher return on investment (ROI) for investing in denser, incremental forms of development in their core than they do for more conventional, large-scale sprawl development on the suburban edge. Because the financial health of a community is directly related to the taxable returns on those public investments, Urban3's ROI tool is intended to identify high-return investments on a consistent and continuous basis, enabling city officials to make better capital improvement decisions.

In his 2013 book *Happy City*, Charles Montgomery argues that by retrofitting cities for happiness, people can tackle the urgent challenges of the age. The happy city, the green city, and the low-carbon city are, in fact, the same place, he writes. Because the way cities are built has a powerful influence on mood and behavior, city planners and developers should pay more attention to the growing body of knowledge about happiness to create cities that make the people who live there happier. From the psychological and physical impact of a 90-minute commute to work by car to the physiological response to greenery along an urban sidewalk and the importance of casual relationships with neighbors, Montgomery walks readers through the ways in which people can live happily in their communities.

In 2014, the Research & Policy Lab released its breakout report *Older, Smaller, Better: Measuring How the Character of Buildings and Blocks Influences Urban Vitality.* It quantified and tabulated what Jacobs described from her firsthand accounts—demonstrating the statistical link between blocks of older, smaller, and mixed-age buildings and measures of vitality related to women and minority business ownership, intensity of cellphone activity, and walkability, to name a few.

The lab's research uses a metric called the Character Score, which measures the median age of buildings, drawn from county assessor records; the diversity of the age of buildings; and the size of the buildings and parcels. The key findings reinforce the idea that *small* matters (see sidebar).

As Ed McMahon, ULI senior resident fellow for sustainable development, noted of the Research & Policy Lab findings: "[S]maller, older buildings and blocks 'punch above their weight class' when one is considering the full spectrum of outcomes on the per-square-foot basis. Cities need older buildings as well as new ones, and neighborhoods with small-scale historic buildings can be economic and cultural powerhouses when given a chance to survive and evolve."[8]

SMALL IS MORE RESILIENT

ULI has adopted the definition of *resilience* from the National Academy of Sciences: "the ability to prepare and plan for, absorb, recover from, and more successfully adapt to adverse events." This definition is part of a statement that affirms that "the promotion of resilience will improve the economic competitiveness of the United States."[9]

Resilience can also be thought of as future-proofing. Although small businesses and building owners may find it harder to obtain capital than do their larger counterparts, these smaller ventures often are more capable—or committed to—adapting to economic changes more quickly. As proved by the market success of adaptively used buildings, much of the older building stock can be creatively repurposed because it was inherently flexible in its design, making it more resilient to market changes and the passage of time.

To the extent that more individual—that is, small-scale—resources are available in a neighborhood, it becomes more insulated from any external shock. Just as a neighborhood with a single big-box grocery store would suffer if that store went out of business, cities are equally vulnerable if they, as Detroit once did, rely on a single industry and a handful of employers to survive.

Beyond the building and at the block or neighborhood level, Price points out that fine-grained development made up of many small businesses is more resilient than coarse-grained development because if one business fails, it has less effect on the overall economy. "There is often a correlation between the environment that we physically see and interact with, and the underlying economics that built it,"[10] he writes.

This holds true during times of duress, such as the 2008 Great Recession. Economists at Yale University and the University of Bristol found that "in times of high unemployment, small businesses both retain and create more jobs than large firms do. During the recession of March 2008 to March 2009, for instance, the employment growth rate of large employers fell 1.65 percent more than the growth rate of small employers, compared with the previous year. In every other recession and recovery in the study's sample, large firms took years to recover relative to small firms."[11]

> ## "There is often a correlation between the environment that we physically see and interact with, and the underlying economics that built it."

Findings from *Older, Smaller, Better* and *The Atlas of ReUrbanism*

THE SEMINAL 2014 REPORT *Older, Smaller, Better: Measuring How the Character of Buildings and Blocks Influences Urban Vitality*, from the National Trust's Research & Policy Lab, provided hard data for what many urban designers and developers have come to know intuitively: that fine-grained development—old and new—is a key factor in the economic success of communities. Key findings from this research, as well as from the National Trust's *Atlas of ReUrbanism*, released two years later, include the following:

- Blocks of smaller and older buildings provide the distinctiveness and character that engender success. These types of buildings give cities a sense of identity and history, as well as authenticity—the most important competitive advantage they can have in today's economy.

- Young people love old buildings. In San Francisco, Seattle, and Washington, D.C., the median age of residents in areas with a mix of small, old, and new buildings is lower than that of residents in areas with larger, predominantly new buildings. These areas are also home to a significantly more diverse mix of residents from different age groups.

- Older, mixed-use neighborhoods are more walkable, according to Walk Score, which evaluates a place's walkability, and Transit Score, which evaluates how well a place is served by transit.

- The nightlife is liveliest on streets with a diverse range of building ages. In San Francisco and Washington, D.C., city blocks composed of mixed-vintage buildings show greater cellphone activity on Friday nights. In Seattle, areas with older, smaller buildings see greater cellphone use and have more businesses open at 10 p.m. on Fridays.

- Older neighborhoods are economic engines. Research shows that neighborhoods with a mix of older and newer buildings perform better in a number of social, economic, cultural, and environmental metrics than areas with only new buildings. New ideas and the new economy thrive in smaller and older buildings. America's most innovative companies are choosing to make their homes in older buildings because they are rich in character, endlessly adaptable, and often low cost.

- Older business districts provide affordable, flexible space for entrepreneurs from all backgrounds. The Atlas found that blocks with older, smaller, mixed-age buildings have 60 percent more women- and minority-owned businesses than do areas with larger, newer developments, and in many cities the number is twice as high.

- The creative economy thrives in older, mixed-use neighborhoods. In Seattle and Washington, D.C., older, smaller buildings house significantly greater concentrations of creative jobs per square foot of commercial space. Media production businesses, software publishers, and performing arts companies can be found in areas that have a smaller-scaled historic fabric.

- Older, smaller buildings provide space for a strong local economy; they have a significantly higher proportion of nonchain restaurants and retailers.

- Older commercial and mixed-use districts contain hidden density. Areas with a mix of smaller, older, and newer fabric tend to be denser than new-only neighborhoods, and they achieve that density at a human scale. Across the 50 cities studied in *Atlas*, researchers found that areas with a high Character Score have 46 percent more jobs in small businesses and 33 percent more jobs in new businesses than do areas with large, new buildings.

The way small neighborhoods are built also makes for more resilient social networks. In his 2011 book *Pocket Neighborhoods: Creating Small-Scale Community in a Large-Scale World*, Ross Chapin argues that *pocket neighborhoods*—defined as small groups of houses or apartments gathered around a shared open space—are primary building blocks for community resilience. Pocket neighborhoods offer the bonds of small-scale community within a large-scale world. Though pocket neighborhoods exist in all development forms—urban centers, urban neighborhoods, suburbs, small towns, and rural areas—the key idea is that a relatively small number of neighbors share and care for a common space together and through that process begin looking out for one another, thereby creating the element of a social network that is essential to resilience from stress events.[12]

Building *small* is a common strategy used after extreme weather events or other natural disasters. After the 2011 Christchurch, New Zealand, earthquake, which destroyed 10,000 homes and 1,100 commercial buildings, the task of reconstruction was daunting and still moving slowly eight years later. But shortly after the quake, it was entrepreneurial

splashes of color in a city dominated by scaffolding and building sites.

One response to the disaster was the Gap Filler project, created by University of Canterbury teacher Ryan Reynolds to fill vacant sites after the earthquake. The project is a creative urban-regeneration initiative that facilitates a wide range of temporary projects, events, installations, and amenities in the city. According to the Gap Filler website, these short-term and comparatively small-scale projects are far less risky than new permanent developments and consequently open up opportunities for experimentation—trying new ideas for uses, building forms, and land uses; pushing social boundaries; and adopting participatory processes to get people involved in creating their city.

MORE VALUE CREATION

Research shows that small development creates more value per acre than large-scale, big-box, and suburban-style development. Joe Minicozzi, principal of Urban3, an urban planning consulting firm based in Asheville, North Carolina, studies this phenomenon all over the country. He explains that developing walkable main streets generates short-term economic activity while raising the value of area buildings, consequently increasing tax revenue for the city or town.

As an example, in Minicozzi's hometown of Asheville, a Walmart, valued at $20 million, eats up 34 acres of

Developing walkable main streets generates short-term economic activity while raising the value of area buildings, consequently increasing tax revenue for the city or town.

activity and small and temporary development that pioneered regeneration of the city's devastated urban fabric and brought back life, as well as raised the question of how to build better. Fashion retailers squeezed into shipping containers; pop-up shops colonized cleared sites; and whimsical installations such as a "Dance-o-mat" public dance floor—put $2 in a converted washing machine to hear your music piped out over a large linoleum floor—replaced damaged dance studios and allowed social life to pick up once again. Street art and sculptures provide

land, yielding about $6,500 per acre in annual property taxes. Two-and-a-half miles away in downtown Asheville, a repurposed department store houses retail space, offices, and 19 condominiums, all on one-fifth of an acre. This project generates $634,000 in tax revenue per acre—nearly 100 times the property tax productivity per acre of the Walmart.[13] Add sales tax revenue into the equation and the downtown property is still worth more than six times as much per acre as the Walmart.

Minicozzi sums it up this way: "The lesson here is that fine-grained, incremental mixed-use development can be as potent (and more, when including property tax production) than the newest of the retail big-box sectors."

LESS CAPITAL, SHORTER TIME FRAME, LOWER RISK

From the developer's perspective, *small* requires less overall capital and can usually be built quicker, which lowers the risk profile. Because small-scale development is incremental—meaning it involves one building at a time—it can adapt and be phased much better than can a single 400,000-square-foot office building or 200-unit apartment complex that may break ground on just the wrong side of the real estate curve.

Like a learning machine, as markets change and an initial small project adapts, the next project, too, can adapt and refine its program to take advantage of how the market responded to the first building. It is a much smaller bet for investors, who may include local investors with local businesses and a vested interest in the success of the project beyond just ROI. Investing locally is a more resilient strategy against market downturns than committing to a large project with out-of-town investors and formula tenants whose first obligation is to shareholder value, not sustainability of the local economy.

LESS OPPOSITION

The root of much opposition to new development is the perception that the proposed projects are out of scale and character with the existing neighborhood and fear that they will change the fabric of a place. Big new developments provide a bull's-eye for expensive opposition. This sets in motion the high-risk-requires-high-return attitude of capital, forcing maximization of square footage and reliance on the same "usual suspects" to fill the prescribed retail or commercial square footage with lender-mandated "credit tenants." Once built, the projects often lose their luster after the opening events fade away and the next new thing gets built down the block.

Because of its incremental nature and greater ease of blending in, small development can draw less neighborhood ire. *Small* is more agile, more understandable, and hence more likely to gain neighborhood approval. It is also more capable of creating a positive trajectory of evolutionary, organic improvement over time, rather than the often-hoped-for big-bang effect associated with big projects. *Small* can have less negative impact on a neighborhood because it affects one piece of a block rather than the entire block, and as Price notes, one bad design will not destroy the entire blockscape.

Small development can be a catalyst or produce change that instills positive momentum that other developers, nonprofits, business entrepreneurs, and even neighboring residents can build upon. This is the basic strategy Midtown Detroit Inc. has used to lead the remarkable transformation of one of Detroit's most disinvested neighborhoods (see "Small Success Stories," Midtown Detroit Inc., in chapter 12 of this book).

Small helps slowly shift neighborhoods toward vitality rather than gentrifying them overnight. These attributes allow unique neighborhoods to continue to refine—not replace—their identity and business model. A successful small developer can return to the same neighborhood to build on that success, incrementally harvesting value from what he or she has created, while also expanding a neighborhood portfolio by leveraging the positive relationship built with the community. Developer Kevin Cavenaugh of Guerrilla Development in Portland, Oregon, calls this "gentlefication" (see "Keeping It *Small*: Guerrilla Development, Portland, Oregon," in chapter 12).

A HEALTHIER LOCAL ECONOMIC ECOSYSTEM

A convergence of best practices in urban regeneration and economic development have been aided by, or directly related to, the following:

- small historic buildings, often adaptively repurposed;
- walkable neighborhoods, which benefit from more interesting streetscapes that evolve from *small*;
- arts and culture (often incubated in small buildings); and
- locally owned shops and restaurants, which create a symbiotic relationship with *small* because of their character, intimacy, and nonformulaic approach to design.

Kimber Lanning, founder and executive director for Local First Arizona, is a recognized champion and expert on the value of locally owned businesses in creating stronger, more economically resilient communities. Speaking at the CEOs for Cities 2017 annual conference in Phoenix, Lanning noted, "Cities and towns across the U.S. are rethinking their economic development strategies and taking a good look at measuring the true costs of incentivizing

retail chains." She cites the work of firms such as Civic Economics, whose 2012 analysis of book retailers in the Salt Lake region found that locally owned businesses recirculated over 52 percent of the dollars spent in their stores back to the local economy, whereas national chains recirculate only 13.6 percent.[14] The reasons for this disparity include the reality that national chain stores rely on talent found in their headquarters cities rather than where the stores themselves are located. As Lanning explains, each chain store needs only one accountant, one graphic designer, and one marketing and public relations firm, and these jobs are often filled where the company's executives live and work. In comparison, a locally owned coffee shop or bookstore will likely employ the services of a local bookkeeper, advertising firm, and graphic designer, multiplying the benefits of local dollars spent in the community.

How does this relate to *small*? "Economic developers are focused on bringing in the big company with the big head count," Lanning says. "Instead, they should be focusing on incubators and startups, which grow jobs over time. And those businesses want to be in creative old buildings."

This recognition that repurposing smaller buildings is not only a more efficient use of resources but also a good economic development strategy is one of the main reasons Phoenix reinvented and redirected its Planning & Development Department to be more receptive, accommodating, and creative in helping

> **Repurposing smaller buildings is not only a more efficient use of resources, but also a good economic development strategy.**

ABOVE: Grill'd is an Australian quick-service restaurant that supports local issues by accompanying every order with tokens that patrons can place in one of three "local matters" jars to support the issue they are most attuned to. *(© 2017 CRAFT Development)*

Chasing Elephants or Building a Better Mousetrap?

EDWARD T. McMAHON

TODAY, THE WORLD IS CHANGING FASTER THAN EVER. Communities and regions are now in a global competition to attract and retain talented workers. Increasingly these workers are choosing where they want to live first, then figuring out their job situations later. Despite this, the traditional approach to economic development is focused on "elephant chasing." The few communities that are successful at attracting a major new business or industry—that is, the *one big thing*—typically depend on tax breaks and subsidies. This one-big-thing approach to economic development also pits one community against another. It means that taxpayers must subsidize big business, and often the business leaves or threatens to leave after the subsidies run out.

Experience shows that the one-big-thing approach to economic development rarely works. Today, successful cities and towns think small in a big way. They realize that successful economic development—more realistically—results from lots of smaller projects working synergistically together off a plan that makes sense. They focus on creating a great place and training a skilled workforce rather than putting all their eggs in one or two baskets.

This approach creates lasting assets that will pay dividends long into the future. It also helps existing businesses and creates diverse, durable local economies. In the old economy, companies were *cost* sensitive and market driven; in the new economy, companies are *value* sensitive and place driven. In the old economy, quality of life and character of a place did not really matter; today, businesses are increasingly seeking locations based on the *quality of place* rather than the *utility of location*.

ECONOMIC DEVELOPMENT: THEN AND NOW

20th-century model	21st-century model
Labor will follow jobs	Jobs will follow talent
Public-sector leadership	Public/private partnerships
One big "home run" employer	Lots of "singles," attracted through clustering and synergies
Cheap labor	Highly trained labor
Plentiful free parking	A high-quality public realm
Turnkey business and industrial parks	Innovation districts
Large, suburban office campuses	Fine-grained, regenerating urban neighborhoods

Adapted by Jim Heid from Edward T. McMahon, "A Proven Economic Development Strategy," *State of Main* (Chicago: National Main Street Center, 2019), p. 59.

small developers adaptively use much of the city's outdated building stock.[15] (See "Regulatory Change: City of Phoenix Office of Customer Advocacy" in chapter 12.)

Extrapolating from a Civic Economics study for Grand Rapids, Michigan,[16] nonprofit Arizona First demonstrated that if everyone in a city the size of Tucson shifted just 10 percent of their spending from national to locally owned businesses, an average of $132 million recirculating in the local economy, 1,600 new jobs, and $52 million in new local wages would be added. An average of an additional $30 of every $100 spent will stay in the local economy when money is spent with a local company rather than an out-of-town corporate entity.[17]

SMALL ATTRACTS THE TALENT THAT ATTRACTS DESIRABLE EMPLOYERS

Richard Florida's early work on the creative class and the concept that jobs chase talent—rather than employees going where the jobs are—turned economic development theory on its head. Since 2002, when he wrote *The Rise of the Creative Class*, the concept has played out, driving up the cost of living in the great

South Park in San Francisco, SoHo in New York City, Silicon Beach in Santa Monica, and H Street, N.E., in Washington, D.C., are places that evolved over time and are made up of a rich fabric of buildings of varied types, ages, and sizes. This is the basic construct that the Research & Policy Lab explains in its report *Older, Smaller, Better*—that these kinds of districts deliver a competitive advantage over those that were built all at once.

> *Is it better to invest dollars in attracting big employers, or to invest in creating places where talented people want to live, thereby attracting a workforce that employers will want to hire?*

cities around the globe. Talented people want to live in great places, and those people attract high incomes. This creates a direct and tangible link between the value of *small* and the long-term economic potential of communities. One debate among economic development directors today is whether it is better to invest big dollars in attracting big employers via tax credits and cash incentives, or to invest in creating places where talented people want to live, and thereby attract a workforce that employers will want to hire.

The kinds of places that knowledge workers prefer often are the product of small development.

Today, we live in a world where capital is footloose. Cellphones, the internet, and other technological advances make it possible to run a business almost anywhere in the world. The link between quality of place and the ability to attract and retain both businesses and talent is increasingly clear. As Mick Cornett, mayor of Oklahoma City, says, "Economic development is really the result of creating a city where people want to live."[18]

Successful communities are distinctive communities. If a community cannot differentiate itself from others, it has no competitive advantage. In the cities toured as part of the SSDF, small was clearly a critical component of each city's unique quality of place and hence its competitive economic advantage.

why *big* needs *small*

COMMUNITIES MADE UP SOLELY OF MEGABLOCK, insular, mixed-use buildings or created with a "district" approach may increase their property tax revenues and enjoy temporal economic vitality, but there is a good chance they will never develop a sense of character, place, and what may be considered a *soul*.

A developer cannot synthesize "quirky" or the patina of old, though many try to with a pastiche of architectural materials applied to larger buildings to make them look *small*. New development must be able to grow old gracefully—through adaptation,

augmentation, selective infill, and replacement. Allowing areas for small development to fit into big projects facilitates this process. Astra Zarina, architect and professor at the University of Washington, calls this *historical layering*—the richness that accrues to the built environment when the accretion of time is displayed on its surfaces. It provides a thread of connection to the past that comes from adaptation over time—rather than wholesale destruction and reconstruction.

Big development can benefit from embracing, encouraging, and helping sponsor small development. And when faced with a major redevelopment project on publicly owned lands, public officials might be wise to consider a series of small projects that are synergistically connected rather than seek out a single developer to take it all on.

By intentionally leaving gaps in a big development, developers and planners find that *small* can serve as an important and economically valuable yin to *big*'s yang, helping provide the texture needed to create a more interesting and authentice place. An argument can be made that city blocks and streets should be allowed to evolve over time. Though it is difficult to leave room for evolution in a legal setting—where approvals, infrastructure, and environmental review all require highly prescribed outcomes—leaving one or two opportunities for *small* to fill in, over time, can add the uniqueness and surprise that help enrich a block and bring new vitality and one small vignette of evolution to a megaproject after it is built.

Whether to be *big* or *small* should not be a binary question. Rather, the question should be how to encourage appropriate synergies and mutually supportive partnerships that permit *big* and *small* to be collaborators in creating great places.

As in other parts of the corporate world, an ideal future is one where large real estate companies help small projects gain access to new sources of capital, navigate long-term approval processes, and provide the operating infrastructure needed to get projects executed, help create better communities, access new ideas, and gain the benefit of innovation from the edge. Just as large companies buy small startups and keep them at their corporate edges to add dynamism to the staid corporate culture while

fostering innovation, big developments can gain by creating opportunities for small developers to bring their authenticity and magic to more institutional or conventional developments.

ABOVE: Chophouse Row repurposed an obsolete industrial shop *(top)* as an iconic small signature building *(below),* establishing the brand and intrinsic value for its much larger, less-iconic neighbor. *(Top: Liz Dunn; bottom: ©2015 Tim Dies)*

When Big Meets Small: Hayes Valley

SAN FRANCISCO'S HAYES VALLEY provides a clear study of *small/large* synergy. Following the 1989 Loma Prieta earthquake, the city was faced with demolishing the Central Freeway—a massive elevated freeway that fed into the Hayes Valley neighborhood from the I-80 freeway. When first built, the Central Freeway bifurcated this city neighborhood made up of fine-grained residential buildings and vibrant retail streets. From 60 years of dumping interstate traffic into the neighborhood, Hayes Valley had become an undesirable backwater of disinvestment, declining public safety, and marginal retail establishments.

After a contentious community process that spanned five years and three public referendums, the proposal to *not* rebuild the elevated freeway won out. Instead, an at-grade grand boulevard with side carriage streets won public approval. The resulting boulevard was meant to heal the neighborhood while demonstrating that vehicular movement can still be accommodated in high volumes, but not at the expense of a great neighborhood.

After the completion of Octavia Boulevard, a series of residual parcels remained along its edges, as a result of the replacement roadway's slimmer cross section.

The parcels adjoining the new boulevard were shallow in depth—in some cases less than 20 feet—and very small in area. This matrix of fragmented parcels made large-scale redevelopment by a single, well-capitalized developer untenable. The only option was smaller projects, ideally innovative in form and character, uniquely designed to reflect the finer grain of the existing neighborhood, and varied in use, while conforming to odd shapes and sizes of their former purpose. Their small size also meant lower acquisition and development costs, providing opportunities for entrepreneurial firms to pioneer new ideas.

In 2000, the state transferred 22 parcels to city ownership. Voters approved Proposition I permitting the city to sell the parcels for redevelopment, as long as 50 percent of the total new housing units were affordable.[a]

One of the first projects built was Envelope A+D's Proxy SF, which, according to Envelope founder and principal Douglas Burnham, was an effort to create "flexible urbanism"—an installation that would help establish a sense of place, that could then be captured in a more permanent development at a future date. One of the earliest examples of turning shipping containers into real estate, Envelope A+D crafted a model where local entrepreneurs could buy the container and fit it out for their business. Their location would be leased from Burnham, who had won the right to activate the site through the public request for proposal (RFP) process. This allowed the tenant/entrepreneur to have a lower monthly cost (through the ground lease) while building equity (through ownership of the storefront). Coming to market during the 2008 reces-

sion, this approach allowed Burnham to activate his site, create an early brand for the area, and land-bank the underlying value while the economic downturn corrected itself.

The energy and "cool factor" of Proxy SF rose quickly, giving Burnham's site and the whole neighborhood a sense of identity and future promise. When seeking its first brick-and-mortar location, Aether, a high-end extreme-weather-gear manufacturer, selected Proxy SF because of its rising recognition as being the center of gravity for this emerging, cutting-edge neighborhood. True to Burnham's business model, Envelope A+D was hired to design and develop the storefront from shipping containers, creating a three-story vertical showroom that still serves today as Aether's flagship.

As Proxy SF gained notoriety, other sites were bought by local developers seeking to develop finer-grained projects in the emerging neighborhood. Pocket Development's 300 Ivy brought an innovative mix of townhouses to the neighborhood, while the

---

OPPOSITE: Envelope A+D's Proxy SF was an experiment in temporary urbanism, helping catalyze the regeneration of San Francisco's Hayes Valley through *small*. **ABOVE:** *Left:* The removal of a freeway viaduct left the neighborhood with a patchwork of small parcels (shown in red) that the city's Redevelopment Agency made available to private and nonprofit developers. *Right:* Envelope A+D pioneered a small corner site using shipping-container retail for local entrepreneurs and emerging brands to activate the neighborhood while fostering incremental expansion over several of the remnant parcels. *(All images ©2020 Envelope A+D; Map: City of San Francisco Redevelopment Agency)*

city's Redevelopment Agency purchased several sites to create a range of affordable housing projects—rather than one large institutional building—each with its own unique design and character.

Of a total 22 parcels, only two sites possessed the size and proportions to attract an institutional-scaled project. Parcel P, a two-acre site, was put out for a developer RFP before the neighborhood's fortunes began to rise. The rights to develop were won by Build, an innovative San Francisco–based development company whose prior projects had included warehouse-to-residential conversions in the city's Dogpatch neighborhood.

Parcel P was steeply sloped and bounded on three sides by the existing neighborhood's signature Victorian townhouses. To address the neighborhood context, Build's "big meets small" solution was to craft a single project containing multiple buildings, but with each responding differently to the adjoining streetfront. Rather than simply creating the appearance of different buildings with different materials hung on the same frame, Build went further and proposed having multiple architects design separate structures, which would be tied together to form one cohesive block.

During the 2008 economic downturn, the site attracted the attention of AvalonBay Communities,

a national real estate investment trust (REIT) with a successful Bay Area portfolio of downtown and transit-proximate locations. Although Hayes Valley was still emerging as an up-and-coming neighborhood, AvalonBay was attracted to the energy and rising tide that had already been created. Build and AvalonBay formed a partnership in 2010, and AvalonBay embraced Build's context-sensitive, finer-grained approach. To do so, the partners hired three different local architects—PYATOK architecture + urban design, Jon Worden Architects, and Kennerly Architecture & Planning—and assigned one building to each, while requiring that they collaborate on a material palette and essential systems to ensure the buildings were efficiently integrated. According to the project's executive architect PYATOK's project summary, the final design drew upon both historic neighborhood patterns and contemporary design, with each of the four frontages including individual stoops or shared entries at an average interval of 25 feet. Midblock courtyard and open-air passages result in a permeable neighborhood that lives and feels like a traditional block, rather than a single institutional-scaled development.[b]

AvalonBay's project director, Joe Kirchofer, noted: "[U]sing three different architects on the same building was more complicated than a traditional building

OPPOSITE AND ABOVE: As the neighborhood evolved from these small interventions, AvalonBay, an established apartment REIT, purchased the one large parcel to create 189 apartments. Working with multiple architects led by PYATOK Architects, AvalonBay broke the building into four "smaller" structures to respond to the grain and context of the neighborhood and allow a differentiated response to the each blockscape. *(Above and opposite, bottom left: Steve Proehl; opposite, top and bottom right: ©2015 David Wakely)*

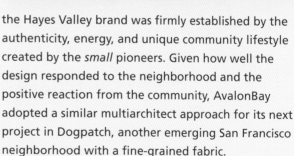

with a single point of contact for the design team. However, our team of architects organized themselves well and coordinated their work efficiently, and that was the key to unlocking the potential of the arrangement. Though it may have been more work, the building design was better for it, as each architect was able to truly realize their own unique vision in response to the variety of site and streetscape conditions at different parts of the site."

The resulting project—Avalon Hayes Valley—is a 182-unit, five-story, LEED Platinum residential community, comprising multiple buildings on a single connected podium. It came to market in 2015, at a time when the Hayes Valley brand was firmly established by the authenticity, energy, and unique community lifestyle created by the *small* pioneers. Given how well the design responded to the neighborhood and the positive reaction from the community, AvalonBay adopted a similar multiarchitect approach for its next project in Dogpatch, another emerging San Francisco neighborhood with a fine-grained fabric.

a. "Octavia Boulevard Project," San Francisco Office of Economic and Workforce Development, https://oewd.org/octavia-blvd-project.

b. "Avalon Hayes Valley," PYATOK, www.pyatok.com/work/project/9/AVALON-HAYES-VALLEY.

why *small* now?

THE RATIONALE FOR, AND BENEFITS OF, *SMALL* have been proven for centuries and will continue to be relevant. But after five decades of an industry shift toward increased mega-block development, this book's thesis is this: the next decade must be the decade of *small*, or cities and neighborhoods risk missing a once-in-several-generations chance to seize the opportunity created by a perfect storm. The conditions fueling the perfect storm in support of small development include the following:

- seismic demographic shifts;
- disruption of conventional economic development strategies; and
- a reaction to the digital age, expressed by a desire for the artisanal.

DEMOGRAPHIC SHIFTS

Seismic demographic shifts—the likes of which have not been seen since the 1980s— have created new markets of scale and power. These trends will continue. Growth of American households over the

---

ABOVE: Bevolo creates handcrafted gas lanterns from its retail/fabrication shop in the French Quarter of New Orleans. *(©2020 CRAFT Development)*

next decade (projected at 12.2 million from 2018 to 2028[19]) is occurring largely in two cohorts—millennials (those born between 1980 and 1999) and baby boomers (born between 1946 and 1964).

Older households want the independence and health benefits of being able to walk more frequently, and millennials—a generation that has grown up with less interest in the private automobile—prefer to live in places that provide a range of mobility options, including walkability.

Members of the millennial generation are less likely than their predecessors to buy their parents' home in the suburbs. Instead, they are looking for a more urbane lifestyle, even if not in an urban location. For their part, many baby boomers are seeking to downsize and find homes that require less maintenance in more vibrant and walkable locales, and perhaps discover new youthfulness through more "hip" surroundings.

Now, the millennials who fueled much of the urban renaissance have started their anticipated migration away from the urban core because of high costs, fatigue with urban living, and the need to find high-quality schools for their children. But they are not going to be willing to give up what brought them to the city in the first place—walkable urbanism, authenticity, and a sense of place.

These forces do not always mean that big cities will be the winners and small towns the losers; in fact, the opposite could be true. The 2013 survey *Americans' Views on Their Communities, Housing, and Transportation*, conducted for ULI by the Belden Russonello Strategists research firm, found that a majority of the respondents would prefer to live in a small town or rural setting over any other location.[20] What this means is that there is room in all kinds of locations—cities, suburbs, and small towns—for the small development that makes places great.

DISRUPTION OF CONVENTIONAL ECONOMIC DEVELOPMENT STRATEGIES

A disruption of conventional economic development strategies has been driven by the shift to a knowledge-based, entrepreneurial economy that first and foremost seeks to exist in great places. As noted, knowledge capital and entrepreneurship, which are creating the majority of jobs in the post–Great Recession economy, are looking for unique places to locate because of the synergies such places provide and the high-quality work environment they foster.

What this means is that there is room in all kinds of locations—cities, suburbs, and small towns—for small development to make great places, regardless of setting.

Before the Great Recession, the maxim "a rising tide lifts all boats" was evidenced by the reality that almost every city experienced economic growth regardless of its quality of place or level of commitment to innovation. But more than a decade after that recession, it has become clear that there are winners and losers in a disruptive and disrupted economy, and the winners appear to be those that have focused on creating great places.

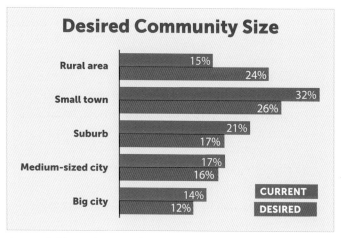

Desired Community Size

	Current	Desired
Rural area	15%	24%
Small town	32%	26%
Suburb	21%	17%
Medium-sized city	17%	16%
Big city	14%	12%

Source: Beldon and Russonello Strategies, *Americans' Views on Their Communities, Housing, and Transportation* (Washington, DC: Urban Land Institute, 2013).

DESIRE FOR ARTISANAL GOODS AND EXPERIENCES

One reaction to the ephemeral nature of the digital age has been the embrace and desire for the artisanal and handcrafted. Mass production is fine for paper towels and tires, but when it comes to food, restaurants, children's clothing, and cocktails, people look for distinctive experiences and products and want to know the person who created them. *Artisanal* and *small* go hand in hand because both have a unique story to tell, and they eschew both the perception and reality of mass produced and ubiquitous.

Whether traveling as tourists or visiting friends in a new city, people rarely remember the big shopping mall or the megablock development full of the same stores and restaurants found in any number of cities. People take photos for their travel blog or Facebook page in the one-of-a-kind places where the chef, craftsman, brewmaster, or farmer is working, engaged in his or her passion. It is in these settings that patrons experience the best of our century—learning something new, meeting interesting people passionate about what they do, and seeing and experiencing

art firsthand. They are not shopping for the lowest cost per unit; they are buying experience, memory, and inspiration, as well as a bite to eat.

What does this have to do with *small*? Everything. Rarely does that distinctive, bustling coffee shop, the cool steam-punk butcher, or the farm-to-table restaurant lease space in the charmless bottom floor of an uninspired podium apartment building. Melrose Market in Seattle, one of the first new-generation food halls, is located in a former auto dealership; Baltimore's Mount Vernon Marketplace is housed in what was once the main warehouse for the Hochschild Kohn's department store chain. Stanley Marketplace in Aurora, Colorado, is located in the former Stanley Aviation manufacturing plant. And the building that houses Pizitz Food Hall in Birmingham, Alabama, was a department store built in 1923.

Because *small* and artisanal go hand in hand, many of the best projects seen today involve adaptive use of existing buildings. The structures have a story to tell, as do the tenants. It is theater and art conspiring to create great places that are unique, memorable, and anchors of the local community's identity.

ABOVE: Artisan, handcrafted, and maker retail experiences fulfill consumer desire for more authenticity as mass market and internet shopping increasingly disconnect purchaser and provider. *(©2020 CRAFT Development)*

getting *small*

TO ATTRACT AND GAIN THE BENEFITS OF *SMALL*, regulators and citizens should focus less on prescribing every square foot of land through fear-driven master plans, and focus more on establishing optimistic frameworks that encourage evolution and experimentation. These frameworks should define what truly matters—a robust public realm that allows public life to thrive, while allowing for adaptation and evolution of the uses between.

Getting the framework right leads to development that is fine-grained and offers a street pattern that is human in scale; it creates economic and human diversity, as well an understandable urban structure. This approach is both inherently more humane and resilient than most current approaches.

Most important, the conversation, regulations, and collective effort should focus on how to encourage and facilitate the evolution of place by deliberately creating opportunities for small development to experiment, evolve, and ultimately succeed.

In the end, *big* and *small* should be viewed as related species of the same genus: *great communities*. Like any species, each has distinctive strengths and unique needs. But to thrive there must be a symbiotic balance between the two. The role of the real estate industry, civic leaders, and citizens is to foster and nurture this balance. To do this, new tools and techniques must be created to allow *small* to take root and thrive amid the growing monoculture of *big*.

FIVE WAYS TO BRING *SMALL* TO YOUR COMMUNITY

1   **Evolve, don't prescribe.** Focus on what matters in building great places—a vital and humane public realm, buildings that can endure and evolve, a timeless sense of design.

2   **Hack your codes.** Take a hard look at your local codes to figure out the real goal. Eliminate unnecessary costs and processing headaches through creative paths that fulfill your intent. Avoid blind subscription to the text.

3   **Right-size your fees.** Charge small projects smaller fees. It only makes sense.

4   **Ask for help.** Let the development community know you want *small*. Invite representatives to talk about the challenges they face working in your community and the opportunities they think you may be missing.

5   **Learn from others.** If you see something you like, find out how it got done. Talk to the city and the sponsor. People love to share what they learned in the spirit of helping others benefit from their hard-won lessons.

(Chapter 11 has more information on regulatory hurdles to *small* and how you can help overcome them in your community.)

Alumina Apartments, Oklahoma City. *(©2020 Leonid Furmansky)*

the
how
of *small*

the **toolkit**

getting
started

here are many compelling arguments for *why* small development is good for communities and good real estate. But the *how* of getting *small* done is anything but easy. Critical drivers of real estate—especially capital and regulations—are not set up to support or facilitate small development.

Regulatory requirements are often written to reduce the perceived impacts of large projects. But they get applied equally to small projects in a one-size-fits-all approach—adding burdensome time and costs to much lower-impact small projects, often rendering them financially infeasible. Capital, in contrast, is organized and oriented to efficiency, not always effectiveness. Everyone from underwriters to loan managers is eager to do large deals because the "fees per pound of effort" on a large deal are much greater

Critical drivers of real estate—especially capital and regulations—are not set up to support or facilitate small development.

than on small projects. In so many ways, succeeding at *small* is as much about knowing the necessary tools as it is about having the drive, personality, and tenacity to persevere against the odds. And a major objective of this book is to highlight these challenges, so these barriers can readily be removed or reduced, allowing *small* to fulfill its potential.

→ ## what does it take to develop *small*?

MANY PEOPLE WHO ARE NOT EXPERIENCED DEVELOPERS are drawn to developing *small*. They see the scale of the projects as not too daunting. They can see themselves crafting and owning a building or two that they have forged through tenacity, sweat, and personal equity. They feel more comfortable with the risk of *small*, because they assume they will be actively involved in the effort rather than simply investing passively in a big project.

In many ways, people who build or renovate their own home, add an accessory dwelling unit, or buy a lot and create a duplex are building *small*. And many of the small developers we have met (and profiled) started out this way. *Small* can also be just as appealing to seasoned developers who have worked at a range of scales and decided they prefer the challenges and rewards that small development offers. They prefer its character and ability to better reflect their own interests and values.

Most institutional developers eschew *small*—because the level of time and capital investment rarely produces a commensurate level of financial reward. But some experienced developers, entrepreneurial

developers, and unconventional professionals will choose this path. For them returns are measured holistically. This broader scorecard might include metrics such as positively catalyzing a neighborhood (see "Small Success Stories," Midtown Detroit, in chapter 12), partnering with colleagues to fill a missing gap in the local market (see Pivot Project, also in chapter 12), or making us rethink what is truly highest and best use (see Guerrilla Development, in chapter 12).

OPPOSITE: A breakout session of Small-Scale Development Forum 14 in Baltimore. *(©2019 Jim Heid)*

becoming a
small developer

"HOW DO I BECOME A SMALL DEVELOPER?" While there are courses you can take (for example, IncDev's developer boot camp[1] or ULI's Moving into the Role of Developer and Understanding the Real Estate Development Process), the first step is to be clear about your motivations, your goals, and your personal skill set.

If you are just getting started, there are some basics to think about and work through. Small real estate development is exciting because no two projects are alike. Unlike institutional real estate, which strives for efficiency by replicating the process and the product that may have been completed elsewhere, small development by its very nature cannot be relegated to a formula. It relies on a creative process that embraces the dynamics of its setting, curates the vision from its sponsor and associated stakeholders, and strives to tap hidden opportunities of the marketplace.

The process of *small* is not linear. It is iterative. A decision you made last month may be completely upended by a new regulation, a neighbor that just showed up for the first time at a hearing, a change in the market, or an unexpected cost overrun. You need to be able to adapt, regroup, and adjust quickly. This is where the ambiguity and sleepless nights emanate from.

For these reasons, not everyone can or should be a small developer. But some people *are* uniquely suited to small development. There are individuals that approach each project as its own distinctive endeavor, uniquely of its place. They approach their craft from a "site looking for an appropriate and transformative use" point of view rather than a "use looking for a site." They are about positively changing a place they are attached to, rather than trying to impose a use they have already used multiple times elsewhere.

Skills include the quiet tenacity needed to chase projects through the process and the ability to think

long term and holistically about what constitutes a "successful" project. And ultimately small developers find joy in creating great places, bringing new ideas to market, and nurturing their own success.

Successful small developers believe passionately in being part of a constructive solution in their communities, have the fortitude and resilience to endure the emotional roller coaster of change and risk that are inherent in *small*, and are comfortable thinking strategically and acting tactically, keeping the big vision while working in the trenches every day to bring a project to realization. To learn more about the stories and skills of successful small developers, see chapter 12, "Small Success Stories."

(©2016 CRAFT Development)

Understanding Development Risk

BEING A REAL ESTATE DEVELOPER ultimately requires the ability to be comfortable with and the ability to manage *risk*.

Five primary types of risk are associated with real estate development that will affect the success of a project. Understanding, planning for, and adapting to these risks is how developers create value. How you manage these risks affects your brand—and ultimately your ability to attract new projects and investors. These risks also have a significant role in the cost of capital—a key consideration in bringing a project vision to successful realization. The five kinds of risk are as follows:

→ **ENTITLEMENT RISK:** Can you get the project approved as envisioned? How much can actually be built on the site (i.e., you buy it thinking you can build 50 units, but because of neighborhood push back and discretionary approval concessions you can build only 30 units). This will ultimately affect the project yield, which could affect product pricing. The other part of entitlement risk is what public benefits might be asked of the developer to attain project approval. Where the number of units are reduced, but the "ask" for public benefits is high, you risk having a project that may not make financial sense—or has to sell at such a high price it no longer meets the market.

→ **DEVELOPMENT RISK:** Can the project get delivered as proposed, on time and on budget? This is where the track record of the developer matters most. If you are new to the game, lenders, investors, and even planning agencies may worry that you, as an inexperienced developer, will not be able to deliver on your promises. Partnering with an experienced and aligned development partner can provide valuable learning opportunities while making sure you succeed. The old adage says, "50 percent of a successful project is better than 100 percent of a project that goes nowhere."

→ **CONSTRUCTION RISK:** Will construction costs hold as budgeted? If the project is an adaptive use, will unknown construction challenges emerge once you start? Are you prepared for fire, theft, or some other externality that could change the construction outcome? Are there flaws in the design or construction that will come back to haunt you during the project's defect liability statute of limitations? Understanding these risks and obtaining the right partners—an experienced architect, contractor, or construction manager—helps reduce risk. Making sure you spend the money, and read the fine print for proper insurance policies (course of construction and defect liability), helps make sure the unexpected does not ruin you.

→ **FINANCING RISK:** This can take a variety of forms, from your ability to attract investment capital to your project, to your project's exposure to interest rate fluctuations. Even if you protect yourself by getting a fixed rate on a construction or mini-perm loan, keep in mind that most lenders require personal guarantees: a deficiency guarantee in case there is a shortfall in the ability to repay the loan and/or a completion guarantee that assures the project will get completed even if the loan is not enough to cover the work. These are not risks you can pass off easily through a construction contract or other instrument.

→ **MARKET RISK:** After all is said and done, will the market deliver the tenants or sales as predicted and at the price you assumed in your pro forma? Are there externalities that you could not foresee—such as rapid rise in interest rates that dampens for-sale demand or requires you to potentially reduce the price the finished product? Having flexibility in your plan (being able to rent residential units instead of selling them, or looking for "future-proofing" commercial space design to allow changing uses) provides some resilience while helping reduce this risk.

→ ask yourself the right questions

IF YOU DECIDE TO BECOME A SMALL DEVELOPER, start with a few key questions. Will this be a hobby or a career? Do you have the means to self-capitalize or do you need to raise funds? Does your family share your commitment to change and creative investment in the community, even if it may make for some difficult years?

Think about your strengths. Are you a great designer, are you financially detailed, do you have a lot of construction knowledge, or do you just want to run a business that will be housed in the real

If small development were a replicable process, more people would be doing it, and capital would be more plentiful.

estate you build? Assess what you are good at or willing to go to great lengths to learn, and note the gaps that will need to be filled by others. Fortunately, there are a lot of people with varied specialties, and the best developers are generalists, not specialists. They know what questions to ask, they are comfortable admitting what they do not know, and they are willing and able to find people who have the right answers. They act much like a conductor—calling on the right people, at the right time, to answer a

question, provide a technical report, or validate an idea or concept.

As you embark on a project, ask yourself if your vision is realistic. Be cautious of the "build it and they will come" attitude or "drinking too much of your own Kool-Aid." Test your thesis in multiple ways, and be prepared to hear the bad news. There may be a demand for your vision, but can it be executed at a price point that will coincide with the demand? This is a critical issue for developing *small*.

If small development were a singular, replicable process, many more people would be doing it, and capital would be more plentiful. So while each project process is unique, some key steps and milestones must be achieved to get to a successful outcome. The following toolkit is a compilation of lessons and tips from successful small developers, all organized in roughly the order one might follow to build *small*.

WANT TO BE A SMALL DEVELOPER?

Ask yourself these critical questions to help get started:

1 Will this be a hobby or my career?

2 What am I good at?

3 What am I NOT good at?

4 How can I fund my project?

5 How comfortable am I with risk and uncertainty?

small does not come easy

FROM INTERVIEWS WITH MORE THAN 100 SMALL DEVELOPERS and tours of more than 75 projects for this book, several common themes have emerged:

Small **takes a long time.** That hip coffee shop, indie bookstore, or interesting boutique you just visited did not happen overnight. Building *small* is not for the faint of heart and requires incredible levels of tenacity, patience, and optimism. If you are a linear thinker, not capable of pivoting direction on short notice, or uncomfortable with ambiguity and the frequent irrationality of regulations, small development may not be for you.

Things can turn bad quickly. Small projects have little margin for error. Because they take a long time, because there is no singular, efficient path, and because capital is hard to find, all of your compensation can evaporate in one fickle shift of the market. In one nine-unit residential infill project in San Francisco, for example, all of the developer's profit would be realized only when the last unit closed. And as the market moved toward the 2008 downturn, the two entrepre-

neurial developers endured an emotional roller coaster, as that last unit sat unsold, and they realized that years of sweat and personal risk might evaporate if it did not sell. If you are uncomfortable with uncertainty and the possibility you might lose a lot of your net worth, small development may not be for you.

ABOVE: Before *(bottom)* and after: Like numerous small developers, CRAFT Development started with a residential renovation— a 980-square-foot cottage from about 1876. *(©2018 CRAFT Development)*

Relationships matter. Even in large cities, the real estate development industry is a small ecosystem, and the small development industry is even smaller. All the actors who play a role in your first deal—lenders, investors, agency staff, designers, engineers, and even neighbors—will show up time and again throughout your career. Treating people professionally, valuing their contributions, paying them on time, and including them in the decision-making process helps build strong teams, long-term partners, and a credible personal brand. In other words, "what goes around comes around."

Relationships matter most when things go badly. How you deal with people during the bad times will be remembered and either strengthen or erode your personal brand as a developer. Your reputation will have a big impact in the next cycle, when new opportunities arise and you embark on a new project.

Regulators do not always share your vision—but it is not their fault. As the city of Phoenix learned (see "Small Success Stories," Phoenix Office of Customer Advocacy, in chapter

Relationships matter most when things go badly. How you deal with people during the bad times will be remembered and either strengthen or erode your personal brand as a developer.

12), many regulations, and more important, *agency cultures* are designed to accommodate large-scale projects. As more and more agencies move to cost-recovery models (where permit and planning fees need to fully cover the cost of staff that work

on the projects), small projects do not provide the level of fees needed to cover the requisite time and resources that small reviews require. And most agencies are not equipped, or motivated, to encourage smaller projects even though they may be more in tune with what local residents and officials prefer.

Capital wants *big*, not *small*. Most capital providers would rather place one $40 million loan than 40 $1 million loans. Although you can argue the latter is much better for diversification of risk, the total effort for underwriting, allocating, closing, and reporting 40 small loans is exponentially greater than would be required for one large loan.

You are not building projects; you are building a brand. Real estate developers often think of their career as a series of projects. But everything you do should be considered in terms of how it builds your brand. If your interest in *small* is not only to build wealth, but also to transform, create, and generate positive social impact, then your ability to realize that vision begins with securing great sites, partners, and tenants. The intellectual property you create is your creative problem-solving process, the relationships you build, and the reputation you earn. Your brand is not just a "signature design move" or being the "cool apartment developer," but a brand of being someone who listens to the community, thinks creatively and contextually, and can deliver projects that are uniquely additive to their neighborhood and breakthrough economic catalysts for the long term.

Small Lessons from Unexpected Events

EVERY CRISIS YIELDS IMPORTANT LESSONS if you take time to listen. As an example, the COVID-19 pandemic is no exception. My experience wading through it, coupled with conversations with many colleagues, yielded valuable lessons for anyone working in the small arena. Here are some enduring takeaways for the next time an unexpected crisis arises:

→ **YOU CAN ONLY CONTROL SO MUCH.** As entrepreneurs our lives are focused on forward movement, control, and action. When the world is rapidly changing around you, you can only control so much. There are times when nothing can be done, and it is time to just let go and take advantage of the unscheduled break the crisis created. Use the time to reach out to others or work on long-forgotten projects—rather than trying to single-handedly "will" the crisis to end.

→ **BE PROACTIVE.** Knowing what you can control and what you cannot is the first step. Then get in front of what you can control. My landlord was very appreciative that I called two days after shelter-in-place went into effect only to say, "I do not think I can pay full rent." I made a proposal (65 percent payments for the next 90 days, and 35 percent deferral to be determined), which the landlord accepted. Afterward, the landlord told me I was the only tenant to bring a solution. The other tenants emerged two months after the crisis started only to ask what the landlord could do for them. By being proactive, I built a good foundation for the future with a key component of my business.

→ **YOU ARE NOT ALONE.** Everyone is going through this. Misery might love company, but moral support during a tough time is an incredible gift that is far better. Pick up the phone, reach out to others, ask both how they are doing and what they are doing. There is a human connection that gets strengthened during difficult times and makes life that much better when things get positive again.

→ **STAY POSITIVE.** There is no doubt it is hard. It is much easier to go to that dark place of worry and sorrow. But being positive has an intoxicating effect on those around you. During a crisis, people are searching for others who can be positive and offer good news. Emails I sent to friends, business newsletters that offered candid but positive appraisals of our situation, were extremely well received. And the act of communicating helped me stay positive and reinforced that we would survive.

→ **PIVOT, ADAPT, AND EXPERIMENT.** Small businesses throughout the country demonstrated an uncanny ability to reinvent and repurpose ideas. Restaurants that had long lagged getting online did it overnight. Cities closed streets and allowed outdoor dining. Alcohol rules were relaxed; people tried new menus; fitness facilities brought their spin cycles and yoga classes into parking lots. Every day something new popped up and some new idea was tried. Some were a resounding success; others fizzled out. But the creativity and experimentation created a new level of energy and animation at a time communities needed it most.

→ **THE LONGER YOU WORK IN THIS BUSINESS, THE MORE YOU KNOW THERE WILL ALWAYS BE ANOTHER CRISIS, ANOTHER DOWNTURN.** Just when you think you have it figured out, something unexpected happens. The key to success in this business is not avoiding crises and downturns, but being prepared and capable of dealing with them. One of the lessons of this book is the importance of resilience, adaptability, and managing risk. And one of the key themes of this book is *small is a better way to build our communities because it is inherently more resilient, adaptable, and lower risk*.

site control and

project feasibility

WITH CONTRIBUTIONS FROM DAVID FARMER AND LORENZO PEREZ

cquiring your site intelligently requires a combination of math, intuition, and dispassionate objectivity. A project has so many unknowns that you can never "perfect the model" and use it to replicate the next project. But you can establish the basic assumptions that matter, test potential scenarios, and gain a working knowledge of the key factors that will ultimately influence the project's financial outcome. This process helps identify which "dials" you need to pay attention to and which deserve constant review to manage to a successful result. That result always starts with acquiring your site intelligently.

This section covers two of the earliest steps in the development process: site control and feasibility testing. The first is the industry term for getting control of your development site. The second comprises the analyses that help determine whether a project makes economic sense and what it will take to be successful.

taking site control

MOST NONDEVELOPERS ASSUME that developers just buy the site outright and thereby have control of it. But small developers typically have limited financial resources, and the process of envisioning, designing, gaining approval, and then constructing may take a while. This makes obtaining site control through an outright purchase difficult. And even if they could buy the site outright, taking on that level of cash outlay upfront can seriously hinder the project's ultimate return.

In addition, the process to secure a site is time consuming. There are initial inquiries. If the property is not for sale, making sure the owner knows you are interested and has a comfort level with you are key. Do not think tying up off-market properties is just about price. Or that price is a function of a rational process. Most legacy landowners have a lot of emotion tied up in their properties—they recall working there; they hear their parents still in the building. They remember family moments. And while dollars are critical, they also want to know you are creating something that could honor that legacy, add to the neighborhood, and make sure their history continues.

This is a rarely a rational process. If it is a great site, or great building, owners have probably heard decades of pitches and many brokers who offered unrealistic values for the property. In their minds owners have "already sold" the building or site and have "spent" the proceeds. If they are multiple heirs, they each want their share, which is generally a big, round number. In chasing deals with legacy landowners, the seller formula at valuation is pretty simple: there are four of us, and we each want $500,000. So the price is $2 million. Land residuals, comps, and complicated where-is, as-is appraisals rarely help win

the day. Persistent, personal communication and *building trust* does.

Your objective is to help them see your vision, help them understand how your idea is a win-win for everyone, earn their trust, and get them to sell the property at a price that will make your project work and ensure they feel they were appropriately compensated.

WHY THIS MATTERS

Site control is critical because there is inherent value created from your idea once you control the site. The chicken-and-egg dilemma for many small developers is how to get control of the site while still protecting the intellectual property of their idea. If you have a killer concept from another community that you feel is ripe for your neighborhood, it may be hard to raise funding on just an idea. If you have an idea, a financial feasibility model or pro forma, some market data (see chapter 8, "Assessing Market Potential"), *and* site control, you now have something of interest to prospective investors. But before you share all your ideas with prospective investors, you want to make sure you have the site locked up, so that someone else will not take your concept and beat you to the acquisition.

OPPOSITE: In partnership with the Urban Redevelopment Authority of Pittsburgh, Trek Development has worked for over a decade to revitalize the Garden Theater. *(©2016 CRAFT Development)*

SMALL TIPS FOR FINDING SITES

The ultimate objective is to secure a site where you can get a reasonable return on your investment of time, capital, creativity, and commitment. Many great projects have been doomed from the start—not because of the program, developer, or market—but because they overpaid for the land. It not just about price—there are multiple factors in what constitutes a reasonable price for the land. The biggest mistake a developer can make is to overpay for the real estate and overestimate demand (and hence revenue) and underestimate the difficulty in permitting. Smaller projects have less room for miscalculation in these

areas. When looking for potential projects, the developer must keep these mistakes in mind and work to avoid them.

Sources and leads for new deals or projects are generally found in these four ways:

- listings from brokers;
- pocket listings from agents and brokers;
- unlisted property of interest; and
- real estate already owned by you or your family.

Many small developers do not rely on buying sites that are already on the market. They are more inclined to find an off-market site—an interesting building with character, an underused plot of land in

---

ABOVE: Pivot Project's Sunshine Laundry building after acquisition and before renovation. *(©2017 Pivot Project)*

an emerging neighborhood, a family property held for generations that is now in the path of change. Here are some ways to identify such properties:

Approach other developers about remnants of land from their existing and future deals.
From time to time a developer must buy more land than is needed for the primary project or may have an odd parcel that will not work with the more formulaic or conventional product template. Letting a larger developer know the price, size and shape, zoning, and entitlements necessary for your project can lead to a win-win for both developers. Of course it will be essential to know that the other developer's project will complement yours and not be a negative either in terms of product or market potential.

Find suitable surplus public properties.
School districts, property yards, storage buildings, and parking lots are often owned by public agencies. The entity may be cash-strapped, or the former use may no longer be needed or helpful to the community. Although your inquiries may ultimately require you to compete for the land in an open RFP process, small enough sites may not command much competition. By doing your homework in advance, you can have a stronger leg up to win. If you can secure an exclusive negotiating agreement early and without an RFP, you may be able to structure a better land price or long-term ground lease in return for providing much-needed public benefits (open space, affordable housing, community meeting space) as part of your project, thereby reducing your upfront cash requirements.

Consider family or "legacy" real estate, which may be right for a development project.
The developer must be careful to go through the same analysis as if buying the land to determine the suitability for the intended project. The analysis should include the potential value of selling the property and looking elsewhere for a more suitable site. Land value is strongly dependent on what can be developed and demand for said development.

Before reaching out to a landowner, think carefully about your first-contact strategy. This is where your reputation (or brand) can help or hurt you. Are you known as someone who has integrity, can execute and close a deal, and will honor their interest? Or are you considered to be a fast-talking, shady character who tells a great story but rarely closes or always asks for a discount once at the closing table?

Expect the owner to research your company to understand whom they are dealing with. The developer's vision may or may not help convince the owner to sell. The developer usually needs to show

Many small developers do not rely on buying sites that are already on the market. They are more inclined to find an off-market site—a building with character, an underused plot of land in an emerging neighborhood, a generational property that is now in the path of change.

the owner how he or she arrived at the offering price and show the offer is fair. When no brokers are involved, the developer can make a case the offer is better than a slightly higher price because no commission is required.

The Best Deal I Ever Did

LORENZO PEREZ, PRINCIPAL, VENUE PROJECTS, PHOENIX, ARIZONA

ONE OF THE BEST-RETURNING DEALS I EVER DID was a lease purchase with the right to sublease and sell the property. I came up with it because a property became available when I had very little cash available and had heard about a similar deal that seemed like a model. I basically positioned myself as a property manager and partner to the sellers, with very limited cash outlay and a solid return on the back end. The moral of the story is "control without ownership." While this deal involved a rental home, a similar deal could be structured for a property for redevelopment.

THE DEAL

A couple was being relocated and needed to sell their property, an outdated townhouse that was located in an emerging area. They had already closed on their new house and needed to move immediately. They were therefore motivated sellers, trying to sell an overpriced and unattractive property in a challenging market. The solution was for me to lease their property with an option to buy it within a three-year period. They effectively "sold" their property at list price to me via the option strike price when the purchase option was exercised, and the sale was closed. Until then, they granted me the right to sublease the property, whereupon I agreed to pay rent that covered their mortgage payment and yielded them a positive cash flow. For all of this, they initially received a nonrefundable *option consideration deposit* equivalent to two months' rent.

I assumed all management responsibility but split the cost of a home warranty and any deductible during the holding period (this proved to be valuable because the HVAC went out during tenure, but only cost the $500 deductible to replace). I also had the right to improve the townhouse with value-add cosmetic upgrades at my cost.

If obtaining site control is about aligning interests of the seller and buyer, here is how this deal accomplished that:

OWNER/LESSOR

- → Received an upfront nonrefundable cash deposit, equal to twice the market rent.
- → Received a secure payment to cover their monthly mortgage.
- → Received an additional $350/month positive cash flow.
- → Received relief from day-to-day property management responsibilities.
- → Received a quick transaction at a time when they needed it.

VENUE (LESSEE)

- → Paid owner/lessor $1,700 nonrefundable option consideration deposit, 100 percent credited against future option purchase price.
- → Paid owner/lessor $800/month in rent; received $250/month option credit against future option purchase price if option executed (monthly equity gain). These credits were forfeited if Venue did not exercise the option.
- → Secured a three-year lease option with right to purchase at a preestablished price of $118,000. (Note at the time of lease initiation the townhouse was worth about $98,000 on the open market.)
- → Secured the right to sublease the property and keep 100 percent of any margin created between Venue's rent obligation and what it received in monthly rent.
- → Secured permission to make cosmetic improvements to the property at Venue's cost.

THE TRANSACTION

Once the lease purchase agreement was signed, it was recorded at the county recorder to place a cloud on title and protect the option position. A contract servicing agreement was established with a title company to manage the payments between the lessee, the seller/lessor, and the mortgage company. That assured the mortgage and property taxes were paid and provided the seller/lessor an accounting of the rents and mortgage payments.

During the first two months, $3,500 was invested in cosmetic improvements to address the property's outdated attributes. After completion, the townhouse was leased for two years at $1,250/month, plus a $1,500 security deposit. Upon extension of the lease, rent was increased to $1,400 per month. Toward the end of the lease purchase period, the property was marketed and sold to a buyer for $145,000.

To close the sale, a dual escrow was opened—one between the current owner/lessor and the lessee (Venue), and a second between the lessee and the new buyer. Closing dates were coordinated to be sequential on the same day, and as the new buyer and Venue closed the purchase, the proceeds were used by the escrow agent to pay off the current owner. Venue never took title or ownership of the property.

CONCLUSION

This is a solid way to get control of the property putting little money down and using the investment opportunity without ever directly owning or taking title to the property. This strategy was learned from a colleague who *only* invested this way, because of challenges he encountered in the late 1980s savings and loan crisis that made him never want to be on the hook for a mortgage again. He used to market to older landlords who wanted to start disposing of their holdings, and this process would save them the cost of a sales commission, preserving the passive income while taking on their management burdens. He used it for residential and commercial properties. He was in total control with very little to risk other than his low dollar investments. He often said, "Why own when you just need to control?"

This strategy may not work in a sellers' market where you will find sellers resistant to such ideas unless the property has problems to fix and they cannot sell it or it is unfinanceable. But it is a great strategy for distressed properties, motivated sellers, or people who inherit properties and want passive income without the headaches.

THE NUMBERS

OWNER/LESSOR

→ Received $350/month positive cash flow for 32 months, or $11,200.

→ Sold the house at the price the owner initially wanted: $118,000.

LESSEE/VENUE

→ Initial cash required for deal was $1,700.

→ Improvements of $3,500 were made on a credit card and paid off in the first nine months with surplus cash flow.

→ Recovered $1,500 of the $1,700 option consideration deposit from the tenant security deposit.

→ Received $450/month positive cash flow so recovered the rest of the cash investment in the first month and was on house money the remainder of the term ($450 × 32 months = $14,400 − $3,500 credit card = $10,900 net).

→ Also received $250/month in purchase option credits to offset against Venue's purchase price ($250 × 32 months = $8,000 in earned equity).

→ Property sold for $145,000, after purchasing the property for $108,300; for gain of $36,700 ($118,000 option price, less $1,700 option deposit and $8,000 in purchase option credits during term of lease).

Note—because of the deal structure, the owner was able to sell the property directly to a buyer who was a Realtor but who did not take a commission in exchange for discounting the price by the same amount as the commission split would have been. That allowed the buyer to avoid the income tax from the commission.

SMALL TIPS FOR GAINING SITE CONTROL

A small developer often lacks the cash to buy a site outright. It pays to think creatively to craft a purchase strategy that can benefit both the seller and the purchaser.

Option agreement. An option agreement provides the seller some immediate compensation and secures your option to buy the property at an agreed-upon price. This helps you minimize the upfront expenditure of funds while you are doing studies, testing the market, and raising funding, without risking having someone else take your idea and buy

> *A small developer often lacks the cash to buy a site outright. It pays to think creatively to craft a purchase strategy that can benefit both the seller and the purchaser.*

the property. Terms are typically based on a certain milestone (i.e., completion of due diligence, receipt of entitlements, and so on). Price at the milestone that can be "where-is-as-is" or, in some cases, the value of the property after you have created value by securing the approvals. In this scenario, you take the risk and bear the cost for securing the approvals, but you do not have the cost burden for acquiring the land until you know you can actually implement the project from a regulatory standpoint. Because you are not buying the land until you are certain your entitlements will be granted, the seller receives a higher price for the land than if it was sold as is. This is because the seller is sharing some risk with you in the entitlement process and therefore has earned more than if the property sold as is. (See a sample option agreement in the Resources section at the end of this book.)

Project participation. In some cases, the seller may agree to invest the land in the project. If the seller is aligned from a vision standpoint, and has both the capacity and the experience, this can be a great technique for small developers. It provides site control with little to no cost, while helping provide equity for the project. In this scenario the seller would contribute the land to a newly created, project-specific special-purpose entity (SPE) as part of the capital stack. Although this is typically an equity contribution, the deal terms and where they fall in the stack are part of the negotiations. One caution is to ensure the seller possesses the sophistication and long-term staying power to ride out the approval and development process. Sometimes legacy landowners—especially third- or fourth-generation family owners—get impatient waiting for their payments, are not comfortable with the risk involved in real estate development, and may have monetary gains as their sole motivation. This situation can be extremely difficult when a project hits a rough patch or needs to change course. (See sample LLC Executive Summary in chapter 6, "Protecting Yourself," for an example of a seller participation structure.)

Seller carry. In this case the seller may act as the bank, providing financing for the purchase of the property. Some sellers may prefer the long-term income and revenue stream this kind of agreement generates, reducing the immediate tax liability that could occur from a one-time sale. It also permits you to reduce the amount of upfront capital you require. Critical in this approach, however, will be ensuring that the landowners are willing to subordinate their debt to any construction financing or other commercial debt you may place on the property. If they remain in first position for all future payments, finding a lender to provide your other debt will be very hard—or very expensive.

testing project feasibility

REGARDLESS OF THE SOURCE, every deal must be evaluated for potential to return investment of time and money. As the developer, you need to research the specific market to understand construction costs, market lease and common area maintenance charges, actual sales prices (not listing prices), and existing supply/pipeline of competing projects. To accomplish these tasks, continuous research is required. Pricing and rates can change quickly such that information can soon become irrelevant. Armed with accurate and up-to-date information, the developer is ready to evaluate potential projects.

Most project feasibility starts with the "back-of-the-napkin" rough estimate because, more often than not, an idea for a project starts over a dinner conversation or over coffee with someone testing an idea. How much will the land cost? How much can I develop on the site? What kind of rents or sale prices can I expect? What will it cost to build? How long will it take, and how much money will I need to make it happen?

These are all inputs that can be quickly assembled to frame a project scenario and test the result. Although graduate-level courses will teach you about leverage and internal rates of return, most small projects result from a simpler capital structure and feasibility test that starts with "what if" and ends with a detailed pro forma.

WHY THIS MATTERS

The purpose of the initial feasibility effort is to assess whether your kernel of an idea has potential. It helps you confirm whether the price you are considering (or have negotiated) is appropriate for the contemplated project. More than anything, it helps you identify the metrics to watch, so you can constantly assess and reassess whether your ultimate project outcome will be a home run, cost you everything you own, or result in what developer and author Howard Kozloff calls a "volunteer" or break-even project.

SMALL TIPS FOR TESTING PROJECT FEASIBILITY

There are multiple ways and techniques for testing project feasibility. But at the initial stage, here are some tools that help.

Return on cost as the first test. Before running a complex pro forma or dynamic model of cash flows, costs of capital, and timing flows, a simple static (meaning not time-dependent) model can tell you if you have a project that could make sense. Total all your project costs: land cost, construction, fees, and sales or leasing commissions. Do not underestimate soft costs, approvals, design and engineering, permits, and your fee. Calculate total potential revenue—as an exit sale price or as a function of anticipated net operating income at

the value of the land after all (residual) costs are subtracted from the future development. This is the value the land can support, after costs of construction, development, required profit to attract needed capital, and your fees or upside to make the project worth undertaking. And in an ideal situation, the list price will be less than the RLV, giving the project an excellent foundation for future success. In cases where the asking or listing price is higher than the RLV, be cautious about compromising or paying more than the analysis indicated.

Sensitivity analysis to understand deal resilience. Sensitivity analysis is one way to manage risk and is an important tool for talking to investors. The basic premise is: "How much can exit prices fall, or project costs go up, before the equity receives *no* return?" The goal of this analysis is to understand the "sensitivity" of the project's success to factors that are beyond your control. So if development costs go up by 10 percent, and all your profit and a good bit of your equity are wiped out, the project may be too marginal to succeed. Conversely, if you find that even if project prices fall by 30 percent you can still pay the bank back and return all equity, you have pretty good latitude to weather market cycles.

> *Things never go exactly according to plan. The goal of a sensitivity analysis is to understand the implication of factors that are beyond your control. How much can prices fall, or project costs go up, before the equity receives* no *return?*

a conservative cap rate—and subtract costs from income. If your resulting gross return is at or in excess of 20 percent, you have the beginning of a project that could make sense.

Most small developers use 20 percent because it provides adequate margin for changing costs, price reductions, and unforeseen surprises. This does not mean it is your profit from the project—it is just an indication that the project has enough latitude or margin of error to weather the inevitable changes that will occur over the project's development.

Residual land value analysis. To confirm you are not overpaying for a site, a residual land value (RLV) analysis should be prepared and compared to listing/asking prices for land. An RLV is basically

CONCLUSION

Site acquisition must be approached with the same attention to detail as every other step in the development process. While there are no formulas for developing *small*, there are tools and guidelines to help you through the process. Passion, tenacity, and brute force are good attributes to start with, but success is achieved only with rigorous analysis and continued "fiddling with the dials," fine-tuning the costs, capital structure, program, revenue projections, and schedule to ensure your project does not sink you forever.

Sample Return on Cost Worksheet

Return on Cost Worksheet Sample

Project Facts:
Redevelopment of existing 3,000 sf commercial building

Horizontal and Vertical Development Costs:

Acquisition/Purchase Cost	$	350,000
Due Diligence/Entitlement Fees	$	10,000
Design Fees	$	17,500
Building Remodel Cost	$	225,000
Exterior Improvements	$	25,000
Permitting Fees	$	1,125
Subtotal	$	628,625

Present Lending Rate	4.5%		Annual Rate
Developer Equity %	25%		
Length of Construction/Lease-up	12		Months
Estimated Financing/Carry Cost	$	28,288	
A&D Closing Costs	$	18,859	
Developer Equity Required	$	168,943	
Amount to Finance	$	478,541	
Cost of Equity (Investor)	9%		Annual Rate
Total Cost to Complete Project	$	672,118	

Potential Net Revenue (as a lease-up):

Annual Operating Costs:			
Utilities	$	4,200	(assumes 12 months of power and 12 months of water/sewer costs)
Property Taxes	$	9,429	(assumes a millage tax rate of 1.5)
Maintenance/Repairs	$	6,286	(assumes 1% of project cost)
Reserves	$	3,143	(assumes 0.5% of project cost)
Annual Lease Rate of Office Areas	$	18,000	(assumes $18/sf of gross lease income for 1,000 sf)
Annual Lease Rate of Retail Areas	$	25,000	(assumes $25/sf of gross lease income for 1,000 sf)
Annual Lease Apartment Units	$	24,000	(assumes lease of two 500 sf apartments @ $1,000 each with utilities included in rent)
Net Operating Income	$	43,941	
Return on Cost	6.5%		

Potential Net Revenue (as a mixed-use condominium):

Office Area	$	250,000	(assumes $250/sf sale price for 1,000 sf)
Retail Area	$	300,000	(assumes $300/sf sale price for 1,000 sf)
Residential Units	$	300,000	(assumes two units sold for $150,000 each)
Gross Sale Revenue	$	850,000	
Real Estate Commissions	$	51,000	(assumes 6%)
Other Closing Costs	$	8,500	(assumes 1% of seller paid costs)
Net Revenue	$	790,500	
Return on Cost	17.6%		

Source: David Farmer.

what to build

SMALL USES THAT WORK

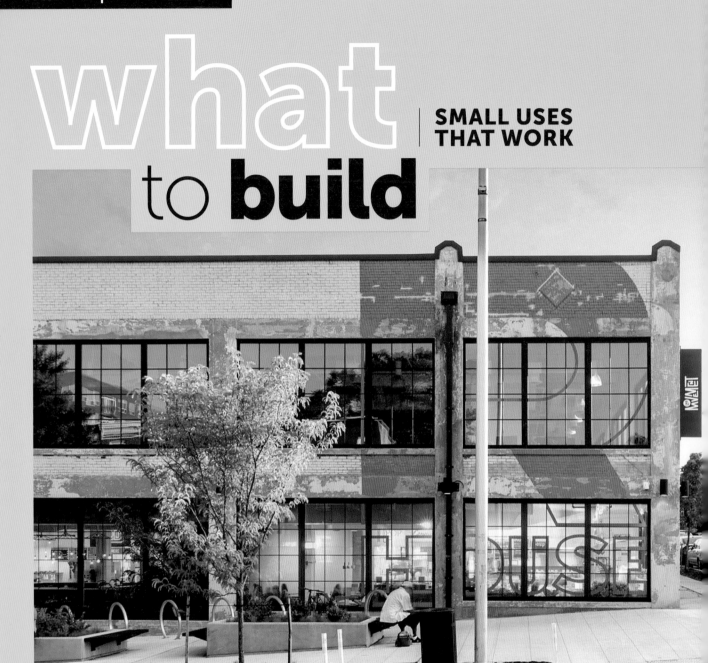

real estate is both an investment and a vessel in which great things happen. The attraction of adaptive use projects, and small developments, is their inherent ability to be reprogrammed or host a variety of other uses.

The allure and magic of small projects, when done correctly, is their flexibility and adaptability to be something else when the market warrants. Textile mill a century ago, artists' lofts today. Utilitarian warehouse 50 years ago, creative coworking space today. Iconic restaurant for power brokers in the 1950s, independent bookstore, garden shop, and restaurant today.

It could also mean planning today's new construction so that it may evolve into something else in future generations. The increased attention and desire for mixed use requires future-proofing designs so that a building can be repurposed if that great idea you had does not pan out or if market trends shift—an increasingly likely prospect given the hyper-evolution of niche markets.

Defining and detailing what you want to do with your space is called *programming*. It requires thinking about the use you want to place in the building and then gaining knowledge and expertise for how it operates. In conversations with numerous developers, designers, and even operators, there are many stories of a developer who had a great idea but failed miserably on the detailed design and execution, so that great idea was doomed to fail *operationally*.

Programming *small* is both art and science. Rather than just leasing the space, it is often called "curating tenants," meaning the synergy of users is critical to making the real estate achieve its potential both financially and in terms of creating a true place. In some of the most successful small projects, the developer actually partners with the tenant to ensure they operate consistently with the developer's vision, and so both parties share in the ultimate success if they get it right.

The following pages outline some of the emerging uses in small projects. They create the kinds of vibrant, interesting, and curated environments that make for a unique sense of place and establish a brand that over the long term can generate successful returns. This is not a complete list or an exhaustive compilation of everything you need to know, but rather a primer of uses to consider and the factors that often contribute to their success, based on lessons learned in our SSDF tours.

OPPOSITE: Seawall Development's R House combines a food hall, incubator offices, and a university extension and fitness facility into a 50,000-square-foot adaptive use of a former auto dealership. The mixed-use project has helped catalyze regeneration of Baltimore's Remington neighborhood. *(©2018 Steven Norris)* **ABOVE:** Good Weather is an artisan bike shop, café, and bar located in Dunn & Hobbes's Piston and Ring adaptive use project. *(©2017 Brandon Waterman)*

→ retail

When programming retail space, understanding the fine points is especially important. It is not enough to say "apartments above and retail below." Ground-floor retail is one of the most challenging real estate concepts to execute properly, and many neighborhood streets are littered with academically appropriate retail that makes no practical market sense. As such, it sits vacant for years, bringing down the value of the

residential units above, hollowing out the block, and creating a drag on the project's economics. As one broker noted, "sometimes $0.00 per square foot is just too much to pay," meaning the property was in such a poor location or so poorly designed, even with free rent a tenant would not be able to succeed.

POP-UP RETAIL

One way to overcome some of the difficulties of leasing appropriate retail uses is with pop-ups. Pop-ups are a way for the property owner and tenant to prove themselves to each other, and to the local market. A pop-up is a shop, a restaurant, a

collection of shops, or an event that opens quickly in a temporary location and is intended to operate for a short time. They work best in a location with high foot traffic, such as a city center, a mall, or a busy neighborhood commercial street.

Pop-ups may be used to launch a new product, generate awareness, or test a location. Or they may be used by marketers for seasonal items, like a Halloween costume shop or a Christmas market. They may operate for as little as a day or as long as several months. If successful, they may become permanent.

Popuphood is an Oakland, California–based business incubator with a creative approach to jump-starting new commercial activity that offers a model for cities struggling to help their beleaguered small business sector, battered by increasing rents. By negotiating short-term lease subsidies for local independent businesses, the group hopes to use temporary retail as a tool to permanently revitalize transitional urban areas.

Popuphood started in 2011, when cofounders Sarah Filley and Alfonso Dominguez worked out a deal to take over a 3,000-square-foot vacant space located across from Oakland's City Hall. With support from the city's redevelopment agency, five businesses received six months of free rent for a trial run of their businesses. Currently, Popuphood works with property developers to place aspiring businesses in the street levels of new buildings, giving three-month to five-year leases to micro entrepreneurs; the arrangement can also help anchor new residential developments.

OTHER TEMPORARY RETAIL SOLUTIONS

It is not just about profiting from every space; sometimes a space can be a catalyst for generating activity

for the overall project. Some landlords have leased vacant space on a month-to-month basis to artists or art galleries. Artists often need large, open, high-ceilinged spaces to produce large works, but not

It is not about profiting from every space. Sometimes a "loss leader" deal can be a catalyst for generating activity and greater income for the overall project.

much else in terms of fit-out. And when the artist or gallery holds opening events, they create a party atmosphere and draw foot traffic to the development, thus creating synergy for other tenants.

Peerspace.com offers another short-term way to use commercial space. Peerspace is an online clearinghouse for leasing space for events—meetings, parties, weddings, photo shoots, performances, or just about anything that requires a space for a few hours. The owner of the space lists it on Peerspace's website, and customers search by event and city to find appropriate space for their event. Peerspace handles the transaction and charges a percentage.

OPPOSITE: *Top:* Shinola's flagship store helped anchor the regeneration of Detroit's Midtown neighborhood. *Bottom:* A shelf of J. Stark custom bags in its maker/retail space on King Street in Charleston, South Carolina. **ABOVE:** Will, a Portland, Oregon–based artisan leather goods retailer, repurposed a former creamery in Detroit's Midtown neighborhood. *(All images ©2016 CRAFT Development)*

→ food-driven concepts

Food and beverage (F&B) is one of the mainstays of the small program of uses. As spending increases on eating out (millennials spend 20 percent more on F&B than prior generations, according to Tom Moriarty, managing principal at Retail Development Strategies LLC), unique artisan F&B options are sprouting to meeting their demands.

Although the F&B business is both fickle and difficult, branding or launching a project with a food anchor is a common technique. But this approach requires much more than designating a space and finding a tenant. Small F&B is a partnership—figuratively and literally—between tenant and landlord.

Over the years, as small developers have gotten creative with incorporating F&B into their real estate, a number of new and interesting models have

emerged that support local businesses, create new opportunities for entrepreneurs, and transform and brand whole neighborhoods. In some locations, developers have actually created a separate business entity with a rising chef to help brand and anchor the building, thus allowing the chef to start up a new business while allowing the developer access to and direct influence over the economics to ensure the rent will be paid.

RESTAURANTS AND PUBS

Given the "third place" function of many small projects, restaurants, pubs, and other traditional sit-down eateries are often ideal anchor uses for small projects. The best ones become favorite neighborhood gathering spots, generating traffic for the other tenants. Restaurants are also amenities that serve on-site or nearby office or residential space. (See case studies on Chophouse Row and The Newton in chapter 13 for examples.)

FOOD HALLS

Food halls are the millennial version of the food court. They generally curate food tenants around a theme or concept, with a mix of upstart and more established tenants who combine to create a unique place. The developer/operator may take on the operation, busing, and management of the common areas, but unlike at incubator kitchens, discussed below, the tenants are paying a base rent and a percentage of gross receipts. The food hall operator is usually not actively involved in their business or in training or coaching them along.

Pine Street Market is a food hall that is part of a successful adaptive use project housed in Portland, Oregon's historic Carriage & Baggage Building. The 10,000-square-foot food hall features nine different stalls providing a range of offerings from Korean street food classics to organic juices, smoothies,

OPPOSITE: St. James Cheese Company created a custom restaurant and retail operation in the New Orleans warehouse district. *(©2017 CRAFT Development)* **ABOVE:** *Top:* Edmund's Oast Exchange is Raven Cliff Company's new 2,700-square-foot retail shop with an extensive offering of craft beer and wine for sale. The building was timber framed by the chair of woodworking of the American College of the Building Arts, taking the concept of "craft" to another level. *(© paulcheney.com) Bottom:* Three Pacific Northwest firms—Alta Urban, Interurban Development, and Northwest Sustainable Properties—partnered to repurpose a 28,500-square–foot historic stable building as Portland's Pine Street Market, a ground-floor food hall with two floors of creative offices above. *(© Siteworks Design Build)*

and tonic shots. The food hall anchors a three-story mixed-use building with offices on the second and third floors. Built in 1886, the Carriage & Baggage Building was originally used as a livery and horse-drawn carriage storage facility until the early 1900s. Reopening in spring 2016, the developers retrofitted the massive Douglas fir timber-frame structure to modern seismic requirements and retained the original skylight in the roof. Pine Street Market has served as a catalyst for the transformation of Portland's Chinatown district.

Pacific Box and Crate, in North Charleston, South Carolina, contains a food hall and a brewery as part of a tech incubator and coworking complex. With six rotating vendors, the food hall serves both workers in the complex and residents in the rapidly transforming neighborhood. The food hall hosts a range of events and activities, such as cooking classes, guest chefs, and pop-up vendors. The complex also supports a Saturday farmers market.

INCUBATOR KITCHENS

Incubator kitchens are a mash-up of food hall, coworking, and business incubator. They combine a number of social, entrepreneurial, and placemaking ideas into a singular location. Rather than fast-food purveyors organized around a central seating court (as in the mall-style food courts), incubator kitchens provide aspiring chefs a permitted and ready-to-use kitchen for a low cost and without the headaches associated with operating table service and seating operations.

In a typical model, the developer will build out the kitchen facilities, operate the central seating, and provide the busing and plates and utensils. In many cases the developer/owner secures and retains the liquor license, letting the chefs provide food while the developer provides—and benefits from--the beverage service.

Rents are typically a percentage of the restaurateur's total gross receipts. This kind of arrangement not only ensures the restaurateur does not end up locked into a monthly rent that he or she might not be able to meet while establishing a client base, but also allows the developer to share in the upside of the restaurateur's success.

The social equity side of this model is that the developer will provide business training and operating tutorials for the tenant chefs. True to the incubator concept, the goal is for the chefs to stay on site for six to 12 months, establish a following, perfect their craft, gain operating experience, and then spin out to a location of their own. After establishing their following in a certain neighborhood, the logical extension of this concept would be for each chef to choose to stay in the same area, helping grow and increase the local economic multiplier effect of the initial kitchen. (See Smallman Galley, pages 74–75.)

R House in Baltimore, merges the idea of a food hall and an incubator kitchen by providing a central seating area with an owner-controlled bar surrounded by food vendors with longer-term leases. However, the developer has committed one stall to a rotating 30-day incubator concept where a new chef and food concept is rotated in every 30 days. This means there is always something new to try when returning patrons come back to R House, while giving local, aspiring chefs a chance to try their hand in a permanent location.

CULINARY "MAKER SPACE"

With the advent of everything "artisan"—from the evolution of boutique foods to ethnic specialties—an entire generation has grown up consuming "small batch" brands that are custom made by committed culinary specialists. But because they lack a health department–approved kitchen, many of them work long hours in the nonbusiness hours of existing

The Pop Up

The Pop Up is a kitchen with unlimited potential for chefs to test new recipes, meet new customers and join a new community. Every week or two, we'll host a new chef and their team in the Pop Up, who bring new menus and flavors into R. House.

Apply

THE POP UP

restaurant kitchens, preparing and packaging their goods for sale. This requires them to work late at night when the restaurants are not open and pack up their equipment and products each day. The alternative is trying to establish a dedicated kitchen to prep their foodstuffs—but because of byzantine health department regulations, this is a time-consuming and expensive process. The permitting and buildout can run $500,000 or more, an expense many startup food makers cannot sustain.

Watching this challenge play out with friends and business associates, developers Mott Smith and Brian Albert saw an opportunity to help both these chefs and food makers, while also creating a new economic development tool for vacant real estate in a transitioning corner of Los Angeles.

Amped Kitchens rents permit-ready kitchen spaces to growing food brands. What was once a 56,000-square-foot, trash-filled warehouse was converted into full-time production space for wholesale food producers by offering artisan food makers 54 licensed wholesale production spaces, each leased exclusively to one tenant. As a maker model, Amped Kitchens allows tenants to scale up faster through expedited approval processes for wholesaler's licenses, so what could take a year or

more can be done in a matter of weeks with just a two-page form.

On site is access to everything a growing food-making business needs: flexible cold, dry, and frozen storage; a demonstration kitchen; coworking space and more, and the site includes a fully staffed warehouse to assist with receiving and logistics. Total buildout was $18 million, and today kitchens are leased at a cost of between $2,000 and $9,000 a month, depending on the size of the space.

For makers who are interested in their craft and not interested in navigating the challenging world of real estate and health department approvals, this

Food halls are the millennial version of the food court. Incubator kitchens are a mash-up of food hall, coworking, and business incubator. And culinary maker space offers small-batch food producers space to grow their business.

means faster time to market. The developer will build to suit, providing customized space. The building has all required food production infrastructure—from hoods to grease interceptors to high-volume gas, water, and electricity. This reduces the barrier to entry for small food makers, while allowing the real estate developer to provide real added value.

OPPOSITE: R House dedicates one stall to a regularly rotating, enterprising chef as a 30-day incubator to help develop a following and test the market before investing in a more permanent location. *(© Seawall Development)* **ABOVE:** Amped Kitchens of Los Angeles provides startup boutique food producers precertified, dedicated kitchen space for individual users and shared infrastructure such as walk-in coolers and storage to help culinary makers scale up their business. *(© Wundr Studio)*

The Incubator Kitchen: Smallman Galley in Pittsburgh's Strip District

OPENED IN 2015, Smallman Galley was founded on the belief that talented chefs in Pittsburgh deserve a fair shot. The brainchild of two U.S. Navy lieutenants, Tyler Benson and Ben Mantica, the goal was to break down the barriers to entry in a notoriously restrictive and highly regulated industry. In traveling the world, they experienced grand food halls featuring the most innovative culinary talent other nations had to offer. To get the concept off the ground, Benson and Mantica partnered with building owners and mentors Michael and Nicholas Troiani, who, at the time, owned a successful Italian restaurant in Pittsburgh's outskirts.

Aside from being a real estate enterprise, Smallman is designed to accelerate the careers of undiscovered chefs by providing a forum to showcase their capabilities, hone their craft, develop business acumen, and build a following. In addition to the use of the facilities and mentoring, each chef is given a Zipcar to conduct day-to-day sourcing. The chefs supply their own cookware, such as knives, pots, pans, and oven-ware. They are given autonomy to run their businesses the way they desire. They set the menu, hire the staff, interact directly with customers, and build their following.

THE REAL ESTATE

The 6,000-square-foot space showcases four innovative restaurants, a full bar, a coffee and espresso bar, and

200 seats. The space also includes event space that provides rising chefs an opportunity to earn additional revenue through private events, while collaborating with Smallman's acclaimed bar program.

The building that houses Smallman wears remnants of its many previous lives as warehouses and nightclubs. Exposed brick walls, naked light bulbs, a copper-topped bar, and long, reclaimed-wood tables complete the look. The design of the restaurant is such that each chef works in an open micro kitchen where diners can watch the work. Rather than ordering at the table, diners go up to each stall, check out the menu, and even talk to the chef who is preparing the food.

EVOLUTION

The first cohort of four chefs resided at Smallman for 18 months, from September 2015 to March 2017. They were selected from a pool of 20 applicants—with three chosen by an expert panel and the fourth chosen by social media. Less focused on résumés or conventional ways of screening applicants, Smallman selects its chefs/tenants by looking at what the chefs have dreamed for themselves, their background, and their story.

THE FINANCES

Smallman Galley cost approximately $900,000 to open. The group obtained this funding through a $350,000 Bridgeway Capital loan, a $100,000 Southwestern Pennsylvania Commission loan, a $150,000 loan from the Urban Redevelopment Authority, and the remainder through private and owner equity. Other funding comes from private investors.

Smallman Galley collects 30 percent of gross revenue from each chef/restaurateur. Chefs use the remaining 70 percent for inventory, staff, and themselves. All marketing, advertising, equipment maintenance, space upkeep, and utility costs are covered by Smallman Galley.

GRADUATING FROM THE INCUBATOR

Within the final months of their stay, these chefs will be assisted in finding a permanent site, building partnerships, and obtaining financing. The Smallman Galley team has partnerships with real estate developers and financiers eager to fund new restaurants in Pittsburgh. Successful chefs may serve extended terms at the Galley while they are working on their independent brick-and-mortar locations. The eventual goal is to have each restaurant running on its own within six months of leaving Smallman.

OPPOSITE: Smallman Galley provides enterprising chefs a 300-square-foot incubator kitchen in which to prepare their food.
ABOVE: *Top:* Chefs and their respective menus are curated to provide a range of food options that rotate on a 12- to 18-month basis. *Bottom:* The development team manages the bar and public space, including busing and dishware, letting chefs focus on their food and learning their business, while liquor sales help support the sponsors' overall business model. *(All images ©2016 CRAFT Development)*

→ residential

If food is the sizzle for many small developments, residential is the steak. In most markets, residential demand always exists, especially for rental products that are affordable or unique in design or location. There is no need to describe the most common residential products here, but a few of the niche products that work well in small projects are worth discussion. Urban lofts, micro units, townhouses, cottage courts, and a variety of cohousing and co-living are products that have been successfully produced by small developers.

The location will largely determine what kind of residential development is appropriate. Urban lofts, co-living, and micro units are suitable for a dense, downtown location, whereas cottage courts can provide greater density on a suburban or rural infill site. A small cluster of townhouses could function well in many kinds of locales and over the full spectrum of prices. Cohousing, which describes a living style more than a product type, can be adapted to a variety of locations.

Target markets are also an important consideration. For example, while micro units may be desirable to single young renters who value location over space, downsizing seniors generally want more space for all the "stuff" they have collected over the years. Developers should do their homework before going ahead with a product type that may have thin market appeal.

MICRO UNITS

In increasingly price-challenged metro markets, a new breed of residential product has emerged that puts the small in *small*: micro units.

ULI's Multifamily Housing Council's 2014 publication *The Macro View on Micro Units*[2] describes micro units as "a small studio apartment, typically less than 350 square feet, with a fully functioning and accessibility compliant kitchen and bathroom."

The study found that micro units outperform conventional units in the marketplace because they achieve higher occupancy rates and garner significant rental-rate premiums on a per square foot basis, compared with conventional units. However, the stock of very small units is still limited, so it is difficult to discern whether the performance of these smaller units is driven by their relative scarcity or whether significant pent-up demand for micro units actually exists. In addition, their long-term operational, maintenance, and turn costs remain unknown.

For micro units to function well, they must be well designed to make the most of the small amount of space. Typically, they rely on built-ins, Murphy beds, drop-down or tuck-away surfaces like tables or desks, and multifunction items.

Most small-unit developers tout the importance of their community amenities—the shared spaces outside the apartments where residents can spread out or enjoy the company of friends.

Many city codes set a size minimum for residential units—typically in the 400- to 500-square-foot range. But some of the most expensive urban areas

Location will inform what kind of residential development is appropriate. Urban lofts, co-living, and micro units are more suitable for downtown locations, whereas cottage courts can provide greater density on a suburban or rural infill site.

have been writing new legislation to reduce or even eliminate minimum size. In San Francisco, the minimum size for apartments is now 150 square feet. In 2016 New York City eliminated minimum sizes with certain exceptions.

OPPOSITE: Lander Group has built a significant portfolio of rental apartments in Minneapolis by focusing on smaller, infill projects in emerging locations, with attention to great design and the public realm; 3535 Grand is a three-story 24-unit walkup apartment with surface parking in the rear. *(© Lander Group)* **ABOVE:** Critical to making smaller residential units work is offering some form of shared outdoor space. *(Left: © Real Property; right: © Panoramic Interests)*

MicroPAD and CITYSPACES

PANORAMIC INTERESTS, BERKELEY, CALIFORNIA

MICRO UNITS ARE ONE RESPONSE TO THE HIGH COST OF HOUSING. In certain locations, they can be a good fit as part of a small development. Panoramic Interests is a Bay Area developer that entered the micro-unit market in 2013, in response to the Bay Area's rapidly rising housing costs and limited land area. Panoramic's MicroPAD® product was created to provide the homeless with high-quality housing, quickly and economically. PAD stands for Prefabricated Affordable Dwelling, and it is a fast, effective, and permanent homeless housing solution. Each dwelling comes fully furnished with a private bathroom, kitchenette, armoire, desk, and bed.

The MicroPAD unit is 160 square feet (8 feet × 20 feet), with a nine-foot ceiling height and seven-foot window height. It exceeds California Seismic Code and includes noncombustible construction, a 24/7 filtered ventilation system, and engineered soundproofing; it uses a steel, unibody construction method.

In San Francisco, conventionally built supportive housing costs the city $400,000 per unit. This high price results from three factors: the city's extraordinarily high land values, cost associated with a complex approvals system, and the high cost of construction in the local market. MicroPAD buildings provide sup-

portive housing at close to half the cost. This savings is achieved by prefabricating units off site, which mitigates the city's high construction costs and limits the inefficiencies of on-site construction. MicroPAD buildings can be built on or in the airspaces above unused and underused city lots, significantly reducing land costs.

Building on learnings from its efforts with Micro-PAD, Panoramic expanded the concept to market-rate housing under the name CITYSPACES. Using a modular approach, units are stacked like Legos to make multistory buildings. Unit interiors are delivered move-in ready. Even with site work that includes elevators, facade construction, and other site-specific work, the CITYSPACES building system reduces development times by 40 to 50 percent and offers project cost savings of 30 to 40 percent over conventional development.

Panoramic's initial CITYSPACES project was 38 Harriet Street, featuring 23 295-square-foot micro apartments stacked in a four-story configuration. Units were prefabricated off site and then erected on site in four days. By using prefab, overall construction time was shortened from 12 to four months while improving quality of construction, inside and out. Because of the inherent strength of their modular steel bodies, the units did not require conventional building frames and instead were stacked in a matter of days. Once units were stacked,

the building was wrapped with the exterior treatment selected by the designer and developer.

Though two-thirds of overall construction was done on site, off-site fabrication of the units themselves allowed construction to proceed much faster and irrespective of weather, significantly reducing overall project costs. Unit construction also ran concurrent with, rather than sequential to, the one-to-two-year permitting process most developments in San Francisco now undergo.

OPPOSITE: 38 Harriet Street used modular construction techniques to insert 23 new residential units on a vacant lot in San Francisco's South of Market (SoMa) neighborhood. **ABOVE:** *Left:* Vacant site before construction. *Right:* Built-in cabinetry and strategic window placement help make each unit feel larger than its 295 square feet. *(All images © Panoramic Interests)*

OTHER SMALL MULTIFAMILY PRODUCTS

The demand for affordable housing of various types is enormous, especially in high-cost cities. In Portland, Oregon, Jolene's First Cousin is a rare type: a privately subsidized low-income housing development. The project consists of a two-story, 6,600-square-foot pair of buildings housing two one-bedroom units and 13 single room occupancy (SRO) units that are leased to a transitional housing service provider. The SRO units share a kitchen, bath facilities, living and dining room, and an outdoor courtyard. Three retail spaces occupy the street levels. The market-rate units and retail help subsidize the SRO units. Portland-based Guerrilla Development completed the project in 2019 at a cost of $2.2 million. The project was partially crowdfunded so that the local community could invest in the property, thus being directly involved in its success. Now that the project has been completed, Jolene's Second Cousin is in the works on a nearby lot. (Chapter 7 describes crowdfunding and other ways to finance small development. Chapter 12 includes a profile on Guerrilla Development.)

Oslo, a nine-unit apartment building in Washington, D.C., is positioned to appeal to recent college

local developer Ditto Residential and was completed in 2014. (See the Oslo case study in chapter 13 for more details.)

Adaptive use of old buildings adds texture to a community while providing much-needed housing. In Philadelphia, AF Bornot Dye Works is an adaptive use and restoration of three old factory buildings to 17 rental loft apartments with 13,200 square feet of retail space. Developed by MMPartners LLC, the $10.5 million project made use of more than $2 million in historic tax credits. The developer specializes in adaptive use and urban infill in the Philadelphia area. (See the case study in chapter 13 for more details.)

COTTAGE COURTS

In less-urban markets, new housing types that provide a higher-quality living experience, but with less space, are still needed. "Less home, more community" is what many homebuyers want, according to Adam Ducker of RCLCO, a real estate advisory firm. Many buyers are willing to trade smaller homes for better locations with nearby amenities. As highly desirable communities become increasingly challenging to afford, and development sites become ever more scarce, higher unit density is one way to make more efficient use of land while creating a more desirable option for households at different life stages.

Creative new concepts are emerging that provide higher-density living without being relegated to multifamily buildings. Cottage courts, triplexes, and manor homes are all product types that architect and planner Dan Parolek has come to call "missing middle housing." These are housing types that create rich, interesting, and varied choices throughout some of the most beloved inner-suburban and less-dense urban neighborhoods. Missing middle housing types are an ideal product for the small developer because they do not require complex urban engineering, they

> *As highly desirable communities become challenging to afford and new development sites become more scarce, higher density is one way to make efficient use of land while creating new options for households at different life stages.*

grads looking for affordability in another way—sharing. Rather than micro units, the apartments are large enough for three or four people to share. Units range in size from about 1,000 to 1,400 square feet and include three or four bedrooms, each with its own bath. The $4.8 million project was built by

can be site-built by a good general contractor, and they provide "exit optionality" of either selling the property or holding and renting it.

One example of this housing type is the cottage court, successfully implemented in more than eight locations by Seattle's Cottage Companies and Ross Chapin Architects. Communities developed by the Cottage Company have been recognized as models of national importance by using innovative land use codes and demonstrating new approaches to single-family housing and medium-density infill development—smart growth without sacrifice.

The developers seek sunny, level parcels with a minimum size of 35,000 square feet in close-in employment center locations with city sewer and water on the property. Successful projects have helped demonstrate "quality versus quantity" precepts—embracing green building technologies, energy efficiency, sustainable building practices—and through their intentional design, a genuine sense of community.

In direct contrast to the business-as-usual approach of street-fronting driveways and garages, homes in these communities face toward common areas with gardens and walkways. Each cottage has a nearby secure garage, with additional parking located on the perimeter of the garden court.

As with any kind of smaller homes, builders must pay attention to details, making sure to get the most out of every square foot of space. Quality is one of the major selling points in mid-range-density developments. The tenets of Sarah Susanka's seminal book *The Not So Big House: A Blueprint for the Way We Really Live*,[3] in which quality supersedes size, are crucial. "You just have to get really creative with the floor plans," Parolek says. "You have to have built-ins, a smaller kitchen, probably a shared dining/living room space. You can get quite a bit into 650 square feet if it's designed well."

As imaginable and loved as this product type is, many local codes and regulations do not let it occur. The Cottage Company website includes model ordinances that can be adapted by communities that are seeking to create such a solution.[4]

ABOVE: CRAFT Development's RiverHouse cottage court project deftly inserted 12 new detached dwelling units amid 14 heritage trees on an existing 1.2-acre single-family lot, creating a unique infill residential neighborhood that achieves a density of 10 units per acre, all using as-of-right zoning. (©2020 CRAFT Development, courtesy JZMK Partners)

→ coworking, maker space, and urban manufacturing

Shared office space, or "coworking" space, is an abstractly defined location where individuals from multiple businesses can engage in work. In many cases, members of a shared workspace will pay a monthly membership fee for regular access to the building and premium charges for accommodations such as meeting rooms or special equipment or services.

Coworking spaces are an attractive setting for startup businesses, entrepreneurs, and "gig workers" or "lone eagles" looking for an alternative to working from home or the coffee shop. Often these spaces are occupied by freelancers growing businesses and getting their name out and are not tied to any specific business or industry. The major benefits are that coworking spaces allow startups to stay lean and are an inexpensive avenue for community

and collaboration, as well as a lively and dynamic atmosphere that inspires productivity. Another benefit of coworking, according to the Global Workplace Alliance, is that within six months over 70 percent of members are engaged in business with another member. For freelancers and independent entrepreneurs looking for a low-cost way to expand their business, surrounding themselves with similar self-starters who have unique specialties or support-

ive business skills is a great way to create what the industry calls a "business ecosystem."

Coworking is an evolving business model for small and large developers, spawning national conferences and how-to seminars, a dedicated podcast series, and a range of vendors and suppliers dedicated to servicing the market. While the pandemic of 2020 brought short-term stress to the industry, it also accelerated the long-projected potential of remote working. As major companies learned their employees could work effectively and happily while off the corporate campus, the coworking phenomenom gained new potential for long-term success as a new kind of use.

The concept of shared workspace is not new. Regus, a Swiss-based company that provides office space worldwide, introduced its "Executive Office" concept in 2000, when entrepreneur Mark Dixon saw the need for office space that could be used while traveling. But the idea that the office space itself is less important than the *community* that is created by the tenants *is* new.

Because coworking spaces are highly individualized with their own personality, they can serve as a great tenant and anchor use for small developments if the floor plate and "bones" of the building are suitable. Coworking office spaces are often defined by their amenities, many of which could be provided as part of the tenant mix in a small project. Yoga studios, coffee shops, and daycare centers are a few of the tenants that can serve as amenities for office workers as well as serving the surrounding neighborhood.

In addition to well-known players WeWork and Regus, many smaller niche and regional companies have entered the coworking realm. Workbar, which operates in the Boston area; NextSpace, in California and Illinois; and Techspace, with about a dozen locations in major markets across the country, are just a few examples.

OPPOSITE: Jack White's Third Man Records cuts original vinyl records behind its retail store and performance stage in Detroit's Midtown neighborhood. **ABOVE:** *Left:* Ruckus is a maker, coworking, and food incubator space that forms part of the revitalization occurring in 500,000 square feet of former industrial space in Indianapolis's Circle City Industrial Complex. *Right:* CraftWork transformed an obsolete strip center bank into 4,500 square feet of high-end coworking space. *(All images © CRAFT Development)*

hospitality: boutique and microhotels

In the past, the formula for hospitality uses relied on specific program standards, brand standards, and securing a "flag," meaning a major brand such as Hilton or Marriott, to manage the hotel property. Conventional wisdom is that, because of the demands of staffing, reservation programs, F&B services, and housekeeping, making money by operating a hotel of fewer than 100 rooms is very difficult. But with the emergence of Airbnb and similar websites, the hospitality sector has expanded to include everything from a castle in Europe to someone's couch in a spare room. Today, anyone can operate a "hotel."

At the same time, travelers' habits and interests have changed, and now a large segment of the "free and independent traveler" market is seeking a more individualized experience. Adventure seekers and other travelers who eschew the big chain hotels have helped usher in the rise of small boutique hotels and microhotels, and this is good news for small real estate developers.

These smaller hotels and inns at every price level provide overnight accommodations as well as a curated experience in new and adaptive use construction. Leveraging booking programs and websites such as Airbnb or HomeAway, microhotels can convert a well-located small building into boutique lodging that can better serve niche markets. Services may be limited, but the design and appointments can be uniquely tailored, creating an intimate, one-of-a-kind guest experience.

In Healdsburg, California, Wheelman House was originally a Quonset-style building built in 1948, serving as the town's first coin-operated laundromat. Today, the remodeled property includes two

600-square-foot junior suites and one 450-square-foot suite; each has a private courtyard and can be locked off or combined. The half-barrel ceiling from the original building is now a cathedral vault-style interior arch, fitted with wooden panels. Each suite has its own private courtyard with a water feature, garden, and art. This is inspired recycling and repurposing of vernacular architecture, from corrugated metal to first-class luxe.

The property is under a multiyear contract with Inspirato, a private club for luxury travelers. Members pay initiation fees starting at $7,500, with a $3,000 annual fee. After that, it costs as little as $325 per night to rent a room or as much as $1,500 to rent all three rooms.

Located in Midtown, Detroit, and nestled within a vibrant residential community, the El Moore Lodge offers urban sustainable lodging. The lodge offers a wide range of accommodations from garden-level bunkrooms with twin bunk beds to rooftop urban cabins with private balconies and kitchenettes. The lodge combines a mix of historic and reclaimed features, such as the original hardwood floors, ash paneling, and reclaimed subway tile. Sustainable technologies like geothermal heating and cooling, photovoltaic solar panels, a super-insulated building envelope, and Energy Star appliances help meet the project's comfort and conservation goals.

In Chicago's West Loop neighborhood, a 1909 three-story brick building that had served as a publishing house was renovated in 2017 to become the 11-room Publishing House Bed and Breakfast. With its loftlike aesthetic and upscale comforts, it appeals to a market sector looking for something beyond the bland chain hotel.

These are just a few of the many ways creative developers are appealing to hospitality markets with small new construction or small rehab.

CONCLUSION

This is just a sampling of potential uses that make up small-scale developments. While the names may

appear similar to institutional projects on the surface, there is a big difference. The first is the developer's willingness to buck conventional wisdom and introduce new approaches, new offerings, and new combinations to fill a niche in the market. The second is to introduce previously unnoticed program elements (food halls, smaller living units, microhotels) that are not being served by institutional-grade, formulaic developments. The third is the role and commitment for creating social impact (incubator kitchens, prep kitchens, coworking). Finally, the most interesting and challenging part is the blurring of lines between operator and tenant. Whereas conventional real estate seeks a very discrete separation between tenant and landlord (and is often agnostic regarding the use as long as it pays its rent), *small* relies on carefully curating the tenant mix and many times must be both landlord and business partner to ensure that the goals of the project—financial, social, and place branding—are carefully nurtured and the project is run with creativity, attention to detail, and business acumen.

OPPOSITE: Piazza Hospitality development Harmon Guest House is a new 37-room boutique hotel to complement the company's two other properties lining Healdsburg's main street. *(©2020 David Baker Associates/Bruce Damonte)* **ABOVE:** Austin, Texas–based Bunkhouse Properties creatively redeveloped strip motels into hip and affordable boutique hospitality starting in Austin. *(©2014 CRAFT Development)*

protecting | LEGAL BASICS
yourself

OPERATING AGREEMENT OF

KENNEDY COURTS, LLC

A California limited liability company

...PRESENTED BY THIS AGREEMENT
...RITIES ACT OF 1933 NOR REGISTERE
...LAWS. SUCH SECURITIES MAY N
...

ARTICLE...
...TAL CONTRIBU...

...Member
...drawals of Capital Contribu...

ARTICLE 4
CAPITAL ACCOUNTS

...Account for Each Member
...r to Modify Capital Accounts to Comply with Tax Regulations
...intenance of Income (Drawing) Accounts

ARTICLE 5
...ANAGEMENT AND CONTROL OF BUSINESS INCLUDING MEETINGS

5.01 Management of Company
5.02 Other Activities of Members Permitted
5.03 Specific Powers and Limitations of Manager
5.04 Warranted Reliance by Members on Others
5.05 Limitations on Liability of Members Acting as Manag...
5.06 Deadlock
5.07 Annual Meeting of Members Not Required
5.08 Special Meetings of Members
5.09 Notices, Voting And Procedures at Meeting...

...ARTIC...
ALLOCATIONS OF NET PROFITS AND...

6.01 Allocation of Net Profits and Net L...
...2 Allocations of Net Profits and ...
...ions ...NT

action. The written consent must describe the action to be taken, be signe...
vote on the action, and delivered to Company for inclusion in the Compa...
determining Members entitled to take action without a meeting is the...
consent to that action.

(h) Telephonic Participation by Members at Meetings of Memb...
participate in any annual or special Members' meeting by, or throu...
communication by which all Members participating may simultaneous...
meeting. A Member so participating is deemed to be present in person at t...

ARTICLE 6
ALLOCATIONS OF NET PROFITS AND NET LOSSES A...

6.01. Allocations of Net Profits and Net Losses. The Company's n...

IN COLLABORATION WITH ANDREW FREY

Small developers often rely on friends and the internet for legal advice as a way to save money. However, the development process is fraught with significant legal implications, and the magnitude of those implications cannot be known without consulting with an experienced attorney. A good developer is by nature an optimist focused on the upside.

But optimism should be tempered with the much-repeated advice: "Watch the downside, and the upside will take care of itself."

WHY THIS MATTERS

Working effectively and efficiently with lawyers is an art and skill. Your ultimate goal should be

- to benefit most from their advice;
- to become more knowledgeable about potential downsides and complexities of the laws affecting real estate; and
- to develop a longstanding relationship with someone who will become trusted counsel as your portfolio and experience grows.

The first thing to remember is that a lawyer is a consultant. Lawyers provide advice that you may follow or not. They do something called "issue spotting," giving you details about each issue and potential estimates of the magnitude and probability of loss. The better ones give possible solutions. But their advice must be filtered through your business judgment, your (and your investors') willingness to take risks, as well as your local project context. Ultimately, once you have the information, the decisions are yours. Do not let a lawyer "run the deal."

SMALL TIPS

Do not play attorney. Do not try to draft the documents yourself and then ask your lawyer to proof them. Every lawyer has his or her own way of structuring documents, and it is faster for them to write anew than to edit your attempt at being a lawyer. But also do not abdicate your review. Do not assume "I'm paying my lawyer a lot of money, so they have me covered."

Take the time to read documents carefully, and get your lawyer to explain things you do not understand. If this is the first of many deals, you want to be developing an understanding of the necessary documents, the key issues you need to decide, the potential risks you are trying to avoid or manage, and, when things go wrong, how the document will either help you resolve a tough issue or could be improved in your next deal.

Try to get a fixed fee. If the lawyer really is an expert in something, he or she will know best how to budget and schedule their time. The best approach is to ask for an hourly rate with a "not to exceed." This way if the lawyer is efficient and you follow through quickly, you save money.

Review every bill. It should be a quick read; a good lawyer knows how to write succinct descriptions that match the number of hours. If you end up spending a lot of time on your bills, you need a new lawyer. And each bill is an opportunity to learn or reinforce lessons about the process and where you can be more efficient later.

ABOVE: Attorney and developer Andrew Frey *(left)* at SSDF 6 in Miami. *(© ULI)*

→ forming a special-purpose entity

In real estate development, it is typical to form a legal entity for each deal—referred to as a special-purpose entity, or SPE. The SPE will acquire land, open a bank account, take out a loan, enter agreements with consultants and contractors, apply for government approvals, and make other decisions. In the eyes of the law, a legal entity is considered a person for all intents and purposes. In fact, the word *corporation* comes from the Latin word *corpus*, meaning body.

SPEs include entities such as a limited liability company (LLC), limited liability partnership (LLP), or limited partnership (LP), and corporations. Today almost all real estate deals are done using an LLC. Laws about LPs, LLPs, LLCs, corporations, and other entities vary by state, but in general corporations require more formalities (and thus costs, and are not ideal for small deals), but the LLC provides the most flexible protection, with the least amount of ongoing management of meetings, minutes, and filings.

Assuming you and (most of) your investors and your project are in the same state, you should form your LLC in that state (rather than Delaware or an-

the articles of organization. LLCs are formed by a very simple document—referred to as articles of organization—that serves only as evidence that the LLC exists for a general purpose and has at least one officer and/or contact person. It typically does not set forth any substantive rights or obligations of the LLC or its investors.

START WITH AN EXECUTIVE SUMMARY

While you should never try to write your own agreements (unless you are an attorney), you can help simplify your attorney's efforts by drafting an executive summary to help ensure you have thought through the parties involved, purpose, activities, responsibilities, and key issues. Although this will not replace the legal document that needs to be signed, it creates a more digestible version of the complete legal document, making it easier for investors to understand their obligations and discuss threshold issues before legal

Taking time to think through and summarize the key decisions needed to draft your legal documents helps streamline your attorney's drafting process while providing your investors a more accessible document for understanding "the deal."

other location) where the laws will be most familiar to local business lawyers.

The process starts with naming the entity and confirming the name is not already in use. This requires only a simple online search with the secretary of state—and then securing the name by filing

minutiae take over. Taking the time to think through this in advance of engaging your attorney helps streamline the process, helps you determine some key decisions the lawyer will need to draft your documents, and provides your investors a more accessible document for understanding "the deal."

Sample Executive Summary

LLC STRUCTURE AND ROLES

Small Project LLC member structure and roles	Project sponsor: *Small Project LLC* (single-purpose entity for this project) Land seller: *Land Partners LLC* (land seller) Investors: (third-party equity investors as members in *Project Sponsor LLC*) Developer: *CRAFT LLC* (third-party developer with fee and promote)
Estimated project cost	Estimated project cost is $12 million as follows: • Land: $1.95 million • Hard costs: $7.85 million • Soft costs: $2.2 million
Proposed capital structure	60% construction financing at market rate 40% project equity at preferred rates of return Bank financing = $7.2 million Equity = $4.8 million contributed as follows: • Project sponsor $3.8 million • Land seller carried interest $1.0 million
Project sponsor equity contribution	*Small Project LLC* will fund required predevelopment activities including, but not limited to, design, environmental studies, surveys, and city fees not to exceed $500,000. In addition, *Small Project LLC* will fund the initial $500,000 payable to *Land Partners LLC* in accordance with the Terms of the Purchase and Sale Agreement.
Investor contributions	*Small Project LLC* will be responsible for securing third-party equity needed to complete the anticipated capital structure.
Land seller equity	*Land Partners LLC* will convey land title to *Small Project LLC* upon close of escrow and consistent with the executed Purchase and Sale Agreement. Equity contribution basis shall equal $1.45 million.
Preferred returns	All member equity contributions will accrue a preferred return from date of contribution, calculated as simple, 30-day monthly interest at 8%.
Allocation of cash flow and proceeds from project exit	Available cash flow from sales will be distributed as follows: • First dollars—repayment of construction loan and interest plus any outstanding consultant or management fees, and establishment of reasonable reserves fund • Second dollars—return of Land Seller carried interest • Third dollars—return of investor contributed equity • Fourth dollars—preferred return, paid *pari passu* to all members • Fifth dollars—remaining distributable funds shall be allocated equal to proportional member interests in *Small Project LLC* and 35% to Developer
Developer fee	Developer will be entitled to a fee equal to 5% of all hard and soft costs, not including land, payable as follows: • 10% upon discretionary project approvals • 20% at close of construction financing • 20% at completion of project structural components • 25% at certificate of occupancy • 25% at final sale and/or 90% lease-up of project

→ the operating agreement

The second step is drafting the agreement among investors. This agreement is usually called the operating agreement (OA) and would accompany entities such as an LLC, LLP, or LP. If the deal entity is a corporation, the document is called a shareholder agreement.

An OA is a private document and not on public record. It should be short and understandable but cover all the key elements necessary to develop and operate the entity and, more important, the real estate outcome. It should include things like how to take decisions and actions on behalf of the LLC and how financial returns are divided among investors.

For a legal entity to make a decision or take an action, the OA memorializes how decisions are delegated and to whom. Most minor or day-to-day decisions and actions defined in the OA will be delegated to the manager. The manager may be an individual or another entity (e.g., another LLC). It may be one of the investors or "members," or it may be a third party. If the OA is structured properly, the manager should not need any permission or approval from (other) investors to make minor or day-to-day decisions.

It is important to spell out what the manager is authorized to do without going to members for approval, such as buy and sell the asset, secure new equity or take on debt, hire consultants, or sign approval documents with the city. As a small developer, you may want to have as broad a control as possible, so as to not lose time and agility to make the decisions you need to make to keep forward momentum. This goal typically would lead you to form a member-managed entity, and the managing member will be you.

Other key elements of an OA include the following:

- **Distributions:** This is the "punchline" for investors. How will the project profits be distributed, in what order, to whom, and at what rate? For a small developer, the majority of the profit may be on the back end and very fragile. Ensure you have structured distributions to be properly compensated for your efforts.

- **Decision-making:** When an issue arises that the manager is not permitted to decide solely, how will decisions get made? Is it simply a majority vote, or do certain members have more weight?

- **Winding up:** After the project is over and sold or moved into long-term management, what will happen to the entity?

SMALL TIPS

Keep it accessible. The easier your document is to read and understand, the larger your pool of potential investors. It is possible to draft a competent OA in just 10 pages or so. Many business lawyers have a standard form OA and may offer a reduced fee to reuse it. That document will likely be 40 pages full of terms that do not apply to your deal, references to complex federal Treasury Regulations (that apply whether or not you mention them), and "boilerplate." However, if it saves money and remains easy enough to read, you may want to consider this option.

Organize your OA so a nonlawyer can understand. For example, a standard form OA typically starts with definitions, which are difficult to understand out of context and even harder to remember once you encounter them later in the document. A more accessible approach would be to put each definition in the section that most relates to the defined term. For example, put the definition of "Major Decision" in the section that lists major decisions. Keep your words short. Some concepts cannot be reduced to simple terms, such as "internal rate of return (IRR)," but many other terms can and should be kept simple to maintain ease of understanding and using the document.

Define decision-making and control. Give your investors as little control as possible. This is not out of disrespect to your investors. Typically, an OA delegates to one member the right (and duty) to act on its behalf in most respects, except for a short list of major decisions that require the approval of other members. These include the following:

- to buy and sell the property (although not individual units if that is the entity's business);
- to enter into a merger with another company;
- to bring in new members;
- to encumber the property or entity with additional debt;
- to place the entity into bankruptcy; and
- to wind down the entity.

Major decisions have two functions: to give some members an opportunity to contribute expertise and to ensure that the interests of the authorized member and other members are aligned. But for small deals, no other member is likely to know the deal better than you, and as such, you should keep majority control.

defining financial returns

Give your investors clear and healthy financial returns, but also give them confidence that you will optimize returns if you provide yourself an adequate bonus to do so. High-quality small development is not charity, and it is not just a noble pursuit. You are taking risks, putting in outsized efforts, and your investors should realize you need to be appropriately compensated. If they do not understand that, they are probably not going to be good investors.

Your OA will set forth how the LLC distributes financial returns to members. Such returns may be proceeds of a one-time "capital event" such as a refinancing or sale, or annual "net operating income" (revenue minus expenses) at the end of a year or other period of time.

The OA will outline how distributions are made—first being credited to investors' original investment, and then additional return or profit on that investment. It will outline when your profit is to be granted and whether everyone gets their dollars equally at the same time (pari passu) or whether investors get their profits first and you get yours after they have achieved a defined hurdle. The important point is to state when and how all members get their returns and in what order (i.e., the waterfall[5]). Distributions

> *The important point is to state when and how all members get their returns and in what order. This is the waterfall.*

will be one of the primary parts of the agreement that investors will look at. Make sure you understand and can explain it.

Get everyone aligned. Part of the goal of the OA in general, and the distribution section in particular, is to demonstrate to investors that, up to the preferred return, the manager or authorized member's interests are aligned with the interests of other members or investors because all are treated equally. And it will give investors confidence that the manager or authorized member will maximize returns because, above the preferred return, he or she has a financial incentive to do so. Thus issues of control, which can involve delay and uncertainty, should become marginal.

Keep your house in order. When your investors sign the OA is also a good time to collect from them other documents that will be required later in the development process. For example, for future tax returns, you will need the name, address, and social security number or employer identification number (EIN) of each investor, whether an individual or a legal entity.

For your construction lender's "know your customer" policies, you may need for each investor the preceding information plus one or two forms of photo ID and an "affidavit of beneficial ownership" or similar document. If an investor in your company is also a company, and that company in turn has investors, your construction lender may require the same information for certain of those investors, usually those with 25 percent or more interest, but potentially a significantly lower threshold.

Ask your likely construction lender about its policies, obtain its forms, and ask investors to sign and provide information at the time that they sign your operating agreement. Even if the lender's forms later change closer to the time of construction loan closing, and the lender requires revised forms to be signed, your investors will already be comfortable with the concept, which will speed their review and signature.

other development steps with legal implications

Other steps of the development process that are key parts of the legal construct include the following:

- **Entity formation:** This is usually a simple process accomplished on your state government website, but the harm of not doing it correctly can be significant. If, for example, you sign a contract for land in the name of an entity, that entity should be formed before you sign the contract. You can do it yourself at little cost and avoid the costs of your lawyer's paralegal. You can complete the online forms, pay the fee yourself, and receive the articles of incorporation from the secretary of state electronically. Keep the documents in a safe place because you will need them many times throughout the devel- opment process: for the IRS to obtain an EIN, which is a critical piece of all future banking and loan documents; for opening a bank account; and for obtaining loans. You should form this entity before taking any action in its name, such as signing consultant contracts, entering into a purchase agreement or lease, taking investor money, or opening a bank account.

- **Zoning due diligence and approvals:** Before closing on a land purchase, know what you can and cannot do on it, and understand the government approvals process. Some localities have very clear zoning and staff interpretations;

others not so much. After you close and design a project, you will need to apply for and process those approvals and permits, with different legal requirements for application and processing. A good planner or architect can assist with most of the process. However, the locality will have legal commitments, such as subdivision agreements or even development agreements, that may benefit from legal review and input.

- **Consultant and contractor agreements:** Most consultant agreements are short and simple, except the architect's agreement, which is long and complex but mostly standardized in a form published by the American Institute of Architects. Because this standard agreement is time- and court-tested, you should not try to modify it extensively. But because it is written by the profession's trade organization, it tends to favor the architect. A lawyer familiar with construction contracts may be worth consulting about where there is room for modification to protect you, especially if you are new to the development process.

- **Leasing and sale agreements:** You and a tenant or buyer may agree in concept about all significant economic terms, but it takes skill to put them in clear writing in a way that a judge would enforce and protect you.

- **Lender documents:** These documents will include your personal guarantee to repay the construction loan, so you should fully understand your obligations and the implications of your loan. Having your lawyer read through them to explain your potential exposure is helpful. But do not let the lawyer spend a lot of time redlining the document because in small deals there is usually little room to negotiate with the bank.

- **Complex matters:** Many situations require special legal considerations. For example, a hotel management company may want a document that says your building can be used as a hotel.

Before closing on a land purchase, know what you can and cannot do on the site, and understand the government approvals process. Some localities have clear zoning and staff interpretations; others not so much.

Such a document may involve legal requirements of federal handicap accessibility, state building code, county bed tax, and city zoning. You probably want that document to come from a law firm, even if it includes exhibits like sidewalk slope measurements by a civil engineer, room measurements by an architect, and the like.

financing
small

WITH CONTRIBUTIONS FROM HOWARD KOZLOFF

s small development has evolved, so has the need for new financing techniques. Much like the genre itself, *small* cannot adapt itself to the more conventional methods of larger development, but must reinvent the way in which it accesses, raises, and funds projects.

WHY THIS MATTERS

It has never been easy to raise money for real estate development, but it used to be a lot simpler. The kind of real estate that most people know—their own home—is how most laypeople think real estate gets financed. Apply a downpayment of 10 to 20 percent of the total cost, and get a loan for the rest. Fifty years ago, small development worked like that. A local developer, who knew the local banker from Rotary or the country club, could ask for an acquisition and development loan. The developer would put in his money along with some friends' money as a downpayment. In return they would receive a loan to acquire, design, and ultimately build the project. They could then refinance to a permanent loan, paying off the mortgage with rental income. The banker knew the developer, and they both knew the community in which they were investing and felt a responsibility to help it succeed. The chances they would get paid back were pretty good because of the personal relationships and the commitment of both to the communities in which they lived.

The savings and loan crisis of the 1980s and the more recent Great Recession of 2008 eroded this model. After those two events, the idea that personal relationships are critical to lending and that banks willingly invest in their community for public good have been seriously compromised as small local banks were bought by big national banks. Underwriting standards became increasingly rigorous, investment committees no longer know the towns where they are investing, and no "personal contract" exists between the local banker and developer to work things out should the market turn south.

Documentation, security, and lending terms have become more complex and onerous.

Helping small development achieve its potential requires understanding the fundamentals of raising capital and revising the reasons investors may invest—including thinking more broadly about how they measure return.

> *It has never been easy to raise money for real estate development, but it used to be a lot simpler.*

Armed with the power of new technology and enlightened by a new attitude that "more is not always more," small projects are finding new forms of capital and accessing new avenues that conventional real estate developers would not think to pursue. These new approaches include crowdfunding, impact investment, high-net-worth patron capital, and public/private partnerships, to name a few.

OPPOSITE AND ABOVE: Cathartes spent over a decade developing Portwalk in Portsmouth, New Hampshire, in four stages. Consisting of three hotels, 149 apartments, 21 condominiums, and 50,000 square feet of ground-floor retail, Portwalk replaced a superblock shopping mall once dubbed Portsmouth's ugliest building *(above)*. Cathartes's incremental development strategy helped repair the town fabric with a restored street grid while allowing the ultimate program to evolve as the market grew into the project. Creative private and public financing including cross collateralizing parcels with imputed release prices; regional lenders for some construction loans; HUD financing when construction financing dried up during the Great Recession; and high-net-worth "friends and family" equity contributed to the project's capital cocktail. *(Both images ©2019 Cathartes)*

→ capital 101

Real estate development is a risky endeavor. That is both the perception and the reality. The fundamental concept behind real estate capital is that investors believe the risk of not getting their money back is higher than if they made a similar investment in a guaranteed savings instrument.

The difficult question is: How much more risky? Or, given that risk, how much more do investors deserve to be paid back for taking on the risk of investing in your project? This fundamental concept is how debt and equity get "priced."

DEBT OR EQUITY?

Capital, or the financing of real estate projects, is made up of two primary categories:

- **Debt:** This is a loan secured by the asset itself and possibly the developer's personal assets: the personal guarantee or "PG" (why most developers sleep less well than people who do something else for a living).
- **Equity:** This is the investment to make up the gap between the debt you can secure and what the project costs. It is like the downpayment on a home. And if the market turns and the project fails, equity investors are the first to lose their money. This is why they command a higher level of return than a debt lender.

The combination of debt and equity makes up the project's *capital stack* (or "capital cocktail," as described below).

Although there are market expectations of what debt and equity should cost, there is no hard and fast formula. Each lender, and each investor, has different ways of pricing these, but common factors they look at—and you can control as the developer—are the project team and the project's political setting. The following describe the *what* and *why* of these factors, and what you should consider.

- **The local jurisdiction:** Is it difficult to work with? Does it provide clear guidance and fair approvals? Or does it have a track record of protracted approval processes and last-minute demands?
- **The market:** Is this a highly speculative project that has never been done before or one of many already performing well in the area? This is why small, innovative projects are hard to fund— without a long list of comparable projects, banks see risk, not opportunity.
- **The developer:** What is their level of experience? Do they have a proven track record? What is their operating style? What is their infrastructure to manage the funds rigorously and report with credibility?
- **The contractor:** Are they experienced and reliable? Do they deliver on time and on budget, or do they have a history of overruns and change orders? Do they do good-quality work and reduce the risk of callbacks and defect suits later on?

Although all the items on this list factor into the cost of capital, the local jurisdiction and associated community can have an outsized effect. Dealing with approvals in markets with high barriers to entry (see chapters 9 and 11 on approvals and regulations) can lead to high perceived risk and drive return requirements—the cost of capital—up to two or three times what might be required in a more predictable environment. This does not mean communities have to reduce their expectations for quality, but they need to establish consistent rules so the citizens' expectations and the developer's path to approval are clear. If communities truly want to see more high-quality, small developments providing innovative solutions and local benefits, simplifying and clarifying the rules and process for approvals is one way to reduce overall project costs and make *small* possible.

A Tale of Two Developments

THE MISSION, CHARACTER, SHAPE, AND TENANTING of projects is very much influenced by its capital source and structure. The following hypothetical illustration shares two approaches to the same project, highlighting the variables and ways thinking must change if capital is to play a constructive role in building *small* and creating long-term value for the community.

CONVENTIONAL APPROACH

An out-of-town developer enters your neighborhood and acquires a site to build at the highest and best use. He proposes 100 apartments over a parking garage with retail on the ground floor, similar to the kind of project he has done in 20 other cities. He funds it with out-of-town capital from insurance companies and syndicated debt from banks located in another state. He constructs it as cost-effectively as possible. He hires a brokerage firm that places a "for lease" sign in the storefronts, which sit vacant for months. Finally, a nail salon and second-tier coffee shop move into one-third of the space. The apartments, in contrast, lease up handsomely, and the developer sells the building to an out-of-town pension fund that is looking for a consistent return. The developer then moves on to the next project, in another town. This is a scenario that plays out every day across cities large and small.

SMALL APPROACH

A local, small developer acquires the site. He or she lives in the neighborhood and has a more intimate understanding of what the neighborhood needs and wants, and decides to repurpose the uninteresting but already existing building. He seeks out local chefs who want their own place but can afford only a limited amount of real estate. He selects each chef so the food offerings are unique but complementary. On one corner he builds some micro rental units—less than the 100 of the conventional approach but enough to cover costs. The goal is to hold on to the project long term because the developer wants to stay in the community and continue to curate and refine the project. To fund the project, he reaches out to the neighborhood, offering a stake in the project as equity investors. As residents invest, a local community bank sees the support and local interest and steps up to provide the debt piece. The residents become investors and, more important, ambassadors to make sure the project succeeds. Instead of faceless, no-name retail, the community now wants to see businesses that are an interesting and unique part of the community. And they want them to succeed because they have a financial stake in the project. And while the developer has built less program than allowed by right, it is more in scale with the neighborhood, costs less in total construction costs, and provides an equivalent rate of return. This is a scenario that is just emerging in cities and small towns where interesting neighborhoods and motivated developers are looking for new ways to practice the art of real estate development.

WHAT DOES THIS MEAN?

These two scenarios are very real stories that are taking place across the country today. But to realize the small approach, a number of things have had to happen. The developer has to eschew conventional wisdom that "highest and best use" always means more square footage. And funding has to come from alternative sources that support a different way of thinking about returns and investment. Is it just a dollar value, or is there value in qualitative factors like social placemaking and retaining the authenticity of a place? The neighborhood and community may support development that may be different than what the zoning codes mandate. In the small approach scenario, investment is being made in both the project *and* the community. And the return is both to the investor and to the neighborhood.

This kind of scenario works only if everyone is aligned and a vehicle exists to efficiently and seamlessly let locals participate in the capital stack—and remove the one-dimensional view that many institutional lenders or investors have about how and where they will place their money.

SMALL TIPS

Regardless of the capital source, any small developer should consider some basic guidelines in its approach to financing a project.

Think capital cocktail, not capital stack.
Given all the complexities in financing *small*, developers no longer talk about a capital stack, but use the term "capital cocktail." It is still equity and debt, but from a wider variety of sources, layered together in a unique way for each project. The capital cocktail means each project is unique—not only in its outcome, but also in its capital structure. It requires inordinate amounts of time to raise, manage, document, and report, meaning that a lot of time spent building *small* is actually spent financing *small*.

Do not be greedy on your first few deals. If your vision is to build a career and track record around great small projects, but you have none to show, you may have to sweeten the pot to attract capital and prove your thesis. Getting a deal done and proving you can execute, manage someone else's money, and

> *"Don't take it personally if someone tells you 'no.' It's a business deal, and they need to be comfortable with your project, and you want them to be comfortable investing with you."*

give them an appropriate risk-adjusted return is an investment in future deals. So while you do not want to give away your work, think about the extra juice you may have to provide as investment in your business, not as failed negotiation. Once you have proven your vision works and that you can execute projects *and* return their money, your share of the deal can be increased as you build your relationship together.

Know investor metrics and reference points.
What is considered *small* to one investor may not be *small* to you. Find out early what their floor for investment is and how it relates to your deal. Spending time

courting someone for $1 million, when their lowest investment is $10 million, is a waste of everyone's time.

Understand their time horizon. Do they want out in three years when you know the project will take five to seven to stabilize?

Know what their return benchmarks are and how they measure them: IRR? multiple of equity? return on costs? Their investment parameters will rarely change no matter how good your vision is. Ask and understand what they need to know before you make your pitch, and carefully evaluate whether your deal will fit into their parameters. You ultimately want to spend time with investors whose terms and metrics align with your anticipated project, and you need to be able to speak their language to get their attention.

Do not be discouraged by "No!". Raising money is hard, demoralizing, grueling, and time consuming. Liz Dunn, a successful small developer from Seattle, told an audience during the Indianapolis SSDF: "Don't take it personally if someone tells you 'no.' It's a business deal, and they need to be comfortable with your project, and you want to make sure they are comfortable investing with you. If they say 'no,' just move on to the next person on your list."

You will talk to a hundred people before you get your first investor. If you need constant validation, this may not be a good outlet for your skills. You have to be able to take "no" for answer and then move on. But do not take it personally—take a minute to find out why. Was it a bad pitch? Was the project a mismatch? Was the timing bad—although they liked the project? Every "no" is a learning opportunity. And after you close the deal, go back and let everyone who turned you down know what you did. People move around in the industry, and your point of contact for the initial rejection may move to another firm where your project would be a "yes." Keeping in touch with potential investors and letting them know you have succeeded will open doors later.

Hedge your bets. There are too many stories where great time and effort focused on a single investor only to have it blow up in the end. Although most developers want to get the "money thing" behind them as quickly as possible and get on with building projects, do not count on the money until it is in your hands. Work as many avenues as possible concurrently because you never know where things will land. Be professional; be transparent: "Just to let you know, I am also talking with Joe Johnson." But do not count on the close until it happens. Banks, lenders, and investors can all turn on a dime, and no matter how many times they have assured you it is "in the bag," there are too many variables outside their control. Always have a backup plan for financing.

package your pitch

Getting the flywheel of a single project going takes time and front-end capital. Many small developers will undertake this stage themselves, trading their time, or "sweat equity," for dollars saved. With the advent of desktop publishing, readily available market data, and great case studies online, a compelling package can be created without spending a lot of money. But this is not just about packaging. You need a thoughtful and succinct but complete pitch.

SMALL TIPS

You get just 30 seconds. Investors get hundreds of deals and may only pick a handful for another look. While you have labored over your pitch for weeks, the investor will probably skim it in 30 seconds and decide whether they want to learn more or not. Put the best part of your pitch in a one-page executive summary with easily read bullet points.

Location, location, location. Provide a good summary of the context, surrounding market depth, and why this is a great site for what you are proposing. Make it easy to grasp quickly.

Do not hide the downside. Investors want to know the principal has already considered a downside scenario. Although investors want to hear about how great it can be, they are equally or more interested in hearing what happens if it does not go as planned.

Returns matter, but mean different things. Some investors are IRR focused, whereas some high-net-worth, community-minded investors want a simple return (i.e., multiple versus IRR), and they are interested in both returns and impact. Make sure you tell this in a balanced way.

Quality is everything. Renderings, graphics, and pictures matter. With the availability of cost-effective desktop graphics, stock photography, and infographics, there is no reason to do a lousy pitch book. The quality of your presentation speaks to your attention to detail, quality of work as an individual, and ability to execute at a high level.

Be professional. While the suit-and-tie world of business has been disrupted in multiple ways, when asking for money, showing up in a hoodie and flip flops is probably not the best approach. Nor is relying on a Gmail account for your email address, or forwarding documents from a friend's office. People who are about to take a risk on you for the first time want to know you are organized, detail oriented, and professional. Buy a real domain and email address; use a real bookkeeping program; set up your legal documents correctly. While you might be bootstrapping your first deal, it should not look that way.

Sage Advice for Raising Capital

ERIN ROEDER, MANAGING DIRECTOR OF KAP GROUP, A STRATEGIC ADVISORY FIRM FOR REAL ESTATE PRIVATE EQUITY FIRMS SEEKING CAPITAL

HERE ARE FIVE THINGS TO REMEMBER when trying to raise capital for *small*:

→ **BE ALL IN.** Unless you are talking to family or age-old friends, be committed to your project before you approach potential investors. It is rarely effective to suggest you will pursue a project if others support it. You are the one who has to be all in.

→ **BE READY.** Develop a detailed, working financial model, including multiple scenarios, in advance of any meetings. Be prepared to show prospects how returns fluctuate under different sets of circumstances, including a worst-case scenario.

→ **BE COMPLETE.** Prepare marketing materials that are professional in both content and format, such as a well-designed deal brochure that includes the following content:

- **Executive summary:** Describe the investment thesis, deal parameters, your track record in the space, and the specific ask (commitments, term) in one to two pages.

- **Investment highlights:** Dive into greater detail about the opportunity (sourcing, acquisition pricing, market, demographic trends, lack of competitive product). What makes this attractive?

- **Business plan:** What exactly do you intend to build on the site? How will that product compare to existing inventory in the market? To whom do you intend to lease and at what pace and rents? Which comps inform your assumptions? Who will you engage as brokers, marketers, and so on, and what is their track record?

- **Financials:** Present target deal capitalization and pro formas, including upside and downside scenarios.

- **Leadership team:** Provide bios and qualitative or quantitative track record information about the team behind the project.

Courtesy of Peter Kohlsaat
© 1999 Los Angeles Times Syndicate

→ **ANTICIPATE RESISTANCE.** Every development deal involves risk. Consider the concerns that will be top of mind for potential investors in your project. Late-cycle valuations? Rising interest rates? Rich pipeline of competitive supply in the local market? Rather than downplay the risks, acknowledge them and explain the steps you are taking to mitigate them.

→ **CULTIVATE RELATIONSHIPS FOR THE LONG TERM.** Investors who are just getting to know you may well decline to commit to the first project you share with them, but may develop comfort with you over time and be strong prospects for future deals. Build trust and credibility by continuing to update them on your progress, the success of the deal they declined to come into, and your perspective on the market. They will be more inclined to consider a commitment when you come back with the next opportunity.

→ where's the money?

The capital cocktail that supports small development can be made up of many different funding sources. Some of the options and opportunities available to small developers include the following.

FRIENDS AND FAMILY

Ask most small developers how they got their initial project financed, and they will most likely say "friends and family." Friends and family are the gateway for most small developers to learn their craft and get going. While it is never comfortable to take money from friends—knowing they may lose it all—the overwhelming sense of responsibility to succeed and return funds to people you know can be a powerful motivation. Moreover, having a vote of confidence from people you trust and respect can also be motivating and help build your confidence to take the big leap and go do your first deal.

Although funding from friends and family can be "papered" with a simple promissory note (if it is debt), it is both good discipline and good practice to develop a solid template and cover all the bases. Be sure the basics are covered:

- How return is calculated and paid.
- What their involvement is in project design, construction, and operations.
- How often they will get reports.
- What the tax consequences might be.

Investing in a good template with a lawyer, so you have a replicable document to use time and again, is good discipline and a good way to ensure you do not poison important relationships that go beyond your deal. Because most developers are optimists (Why else would we do this?), the standard default of "it will work out fine, and if not we can sort it out" is a bad approach. The most stress occurs when things do not go as planned, and relationships are saved by having the rules of engagement clearly outlined in writing.

DEFERRED FEES

Another form of equity is to defer all or a portion of your development fee. But this leads to the ongoing dilemma most small developers face on a daily basis—how to keep the lights on while waiting for the "promote" (your return of capital and disproportionate share of the profits)? Unless you have another steady source of income, it can be very difficult to weather the trials and tribulations of developing *small* when all of your income for those efforts is held until the end of the project. Although many lenders like to see a developer commit his fees to a later payout (because they feel it ensures "skin in the game"), it becomes very difficult to stay focused on the project if you have to work another job to support yourself and your family.

Learning from other small developers, you will find a successful negotiating technique is to split the fee—investing some in the project while ensuring you have a reliable income stream. The best argument to your lender or investors is: "You don't want me having to work two jobs to stay alive—having a regular income from this project allows me to stay focused on getting this done, and done well."

GAP DEBT

If your primary lender is only willing to provide you a loan up to 40 percent loan-to-cost, and you are able to raise 30 to 40 percent in equity, the difference or "gap" might be filled by a more expensive loan that sits between the senior fund and equity. Subordinated, junior, or even mezzanine debt is an additional loan that sits behind your main loan but before your equity. This adds one more layer of cost and investors to the project, but it can be cheaper than equity.

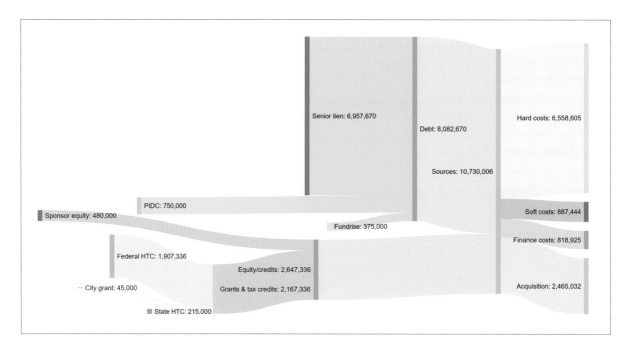

The diagram shows a Sankey flow with the following labeled values:

- Senior lien: 6,957,670
- Debt: 8,082,670
- Hard costs: 6,558,605
- Sources: 10,730,006
- PIDC: 750,000
- Sponsor equity: 480,000
- Fundrise: 375,000
- Soft costs: 887,444
- Finance costs: 818,925
- Federal HTC: 1,907,336
- Equity/credits: 2,647,336
- City grant: 45,000
- Grants & tax credits: 2,167,336
- Acquisition: 2,465,032
- State HTC: 215,000

CROWDFUNDING

Beginning in 2010 with the birth of FundRise, the concept of crowdfunding real estate has grown exponentially. Crowdfunding started with the egalitarian promise that "retail" investors could now participate in real estate investment without having to get into complicated partnerships or LLCs. Early-stage crowdfunding programs (FundRise, Realty Moguls, Crowdstreet) focused on the acquisition of income-producing assets, so what the income stream from an investment could be and how to underwrite the asset were clear.

While conceptually crowdfunding was envisioned as a means for local individuals to invest in helping shape development in their communities, the inability or unwillingness of crowdfunding platforms to take on ground-up funding reduced its promise. With the advent of the 2008 Jobs Act, a new crowdfunding vehicle was created that allowed nonaccredited investors to participate in real estate investment and in turn begin to support their local small developers with small investments, aggregated into a larger pool (see profile of Small Change in chapter 12). These platforms put out an offering to subscribers in specific projects with a target raise and time frame. They review the developer's proposal, underwrite the project's economics, and offer a return on investment from project revenue. The only requirements are that investors must be over 18 years of age and their maximum investment cannot exceed a ceiling that was indexed every year. In 2021 the rules were to change again, with the limit being tied to unaccredited investors' annual income and no limit for accredited investors.

HIGH-NET-WORTH AGGREGATION PLATFORMS (THE HEARTLAND MODEL)

Several projects described at SSDFs have received funding from what has been characterized as "patron capital," meaning high-net-worth individuals who would like to deploy some of their wealth to "do well but do good." Typically, they invest equity or debt in a single project, in which the "patron" wants to demonstrate belief and support, while supporting positive change in their community and achieving reasonable financial returns.

ABOVE: This diagram of the AF Bornot Dye Works project "capital cocktail" illustrates how small projects require a different way of thinking about capital structure and often require a creative approach to funding a complete project. (See Chapter 13 "Small Case Studies" for more information.) *(ULI)*

Heartland LLC of Seattle, Washington, formed a focused platform called Heartland Investment Opportunities in 2016, specifically designed to "provide a unique channel to connect informed, forward-looking capital partners to small-to-medium scale, best-in-class local real estate developers and operators."

Consistent with many of the concepts identified in chapter 2, "Why Build *Small*?," Heartland's investment thesis was built on three trends resulting from changing demographics and market demand:

- artisanal mixed-use projects that integrate exceptional tenant selection;
- projects that leverage creative adaptive use of existing building stock; and
- high-quality urban infill, for-sale or for-rent projects that take advantage of unique lot shapes and sizes in close-in Seattle neighborhoods.

Concurrently, Heartland evaluates potential developers for the following qualities:

- *Underwritable*—demonstrates a proven track record, financial strength, and business ethic;
- *Business model*—distinctive and leverages a unique brand and expertise;
- *Market need*—proposed project serves an identifiable market demand;
- *Income and profit potential*—product or market niche creates opportunity to invest in the local community and achieve attractive risk-adjusted returns; and
- *Scalable/repeatable*—product or market niche has potential for scalability and replication, creating the potential for long-term investment and relationship opportunities.

FREDDIE MAC SMALL BALANCE LOAN PROGRAM

Freddie Mac is one of the large quasi-governmental agencies that sit between the private capital markets and government policy. If the government wants to encourage apartment development, energy efficiency, transit use, or other activities, Freddie can do so by creating supportive financing vehicles that provide better terms than a commercial bank or private investor might.

Freddie Mac offers a series of programs to support small rental housing projects that might align with a need for "missing middle" housing—such as rental projects that are smaller in scale and form, that can be built into existing communities with less intrusion and disruption—and hopefully with faster approvals. The loans are called "small balance" because they are specifically targeted for project values between $1 million and $7.5 million. They are only for income-producing assets, so cannot be secured until a project is complete and stabilized. The terms are quite favorable, and the underwriting and speed of closing is meant to be much shorter than for traditional products.

LOCAL INITIATIVES SUPPORT CORPORATION

Founded in 1979 as "an intermediary that would connect hard-to-tap public and private resources with hard-to-reach communities struggling to revive," the Local Initiatives Support Corporation (LISC) has the following mission: "The premise was as simple then as it is now: government, foundations and for-profit companies have the capital; residents and local institutions understand the need; and LISC bridges the gap by offering the relationships and expertise to help community organizations attract the kinds of resources that allow them do their best work."

LISC receives funding from both the for-profit and nonprofit sectors, including banks, corporations, foundations, and government agencies. It distributes that funding through multiple channels, including loans, direct grants, or equity in projects. LISC funding can be used for housing and projects that create or help grow businesses and employment.

In 2018 alone, LISC invested a record $1.5 billion in American communities, in turn leveraging $4.4 billion in new projects, creating more than 20,000 new housing units and 4.2 million square feet of commercial and community space.

REDEVELOPMENT AGENCY FUNDS

Redevelopment agencies vary by state and city, but generally speaking they have funds set aside for specific neighborhoods designated as "blighted," as a way to encourage investment in those areas. Many such areas are prime locations for small projects. They are often older and gritty and hold the potential for incremental, organic kinds of improvement. And they often have great, fine-grained building stock that has lost its luster but not its promise.

Use of redevelopment agency funds will vary by jurisdiction, often with strings attached. They may trigger a prevailing wage requirement (i.e., the entire project must use union labor), or they may require certain features, such as below-market housing units, commercial space for nonprofit entities, and dedication of public open space or may trigger additional environmental approvals.

However, the funds can be extremely helpful in closing project financing gaps, sometimes offering the developer low- to no-cost predevelopment funding, or capital for off-site infrastructure improvements that the project may require but are not completely a result of the project.

GRANTS

Grants are often used by small developers because they provide additional gap financing and can serve a valuable role in the equity component of the capital stack. Grants can come in many forms and from many different sources. Many cities have "facade grant" programs to upgrade building fronts in disinvested neighborhoods. Other grants from utility companies exist to upgrade energy systems or create more water-conserving strategies for plumbing systems or low-impact approaches to stormwater management.

Certain foundations may offer grants if the proposed project is aligned with their mission, such as supporting the arts, helping the homeless, or providing places for community meetings or other special services. The grant process, however, can be long and arduous. What seems like a no-brainer to you (Why wouldn't they want to give me money for this great project?) may entail an unwritten and often difficult process. Be sure to take time to understand the mission and program objectives of the grant maker. Look at their board members to see if you

may know someone to sit down with and test how your project might match their goals. Review previous grants a foundation has awarded and even the applications, if available. Grant makers typically want to see something tangible and uniquely supported by their grant—not just to be part of a pool of funds. See if you can clearly attribute some element of your project to their grant. You may want to hire a grant writer if you think you have found a source that is particularly well aligned with your project and need some expert help to apply for the grant.

AMERICANS WITH DISABILITIES ACT TAX CREDIT

Because many small projects repurpose older buildings that were built before the Americans with Disabilities Act (ADA) was enacted in 1990, bringing the building to code often entails considerable costs. If the building is historic, or if the local jurisdiction is aligned with or supportive of your goals, these requirements often have some latitude for interpretation, but at a minimum, equal access must be provided and bathrooms, routes of travel, and amenities often have to meet established standards. To offset some of the expense, the federal government offers a tax credit for small businesses. The tax credit is limited to 50 percent of cost, up to $5,000 maximum credit, and can be captured annually, but the expenses incurred in one year cannot be carried over to a subsequent year.

HISTORIC TAX CREDITS

Historic tax credits have been a stalwart component of the capital stack for historic building renovation and, until recently, adaptive use. The federal tax code currently provides for a 20 percent tax credit for buildings designated as historic. Although valuable, this tax credit is very complicated to attain and creates limitations on building redevelopment and design.

Because it provides a *tax credit*, not actual funding, the developer must monetize the credit by finding an investor that is willing to "buy" the credit at a discount by providing equity for the project. This action requires a series of legal structures to be established, which can be complicated and costly. Richard Sidebottom, director of MacRostie Historic Advisors, noted during the 2018 SSDF in Charleston, South Carolina, that "historic tax credits may only be worth pursuing if the effort can generate at least $5 million in credits, meaning it must be applied to at least $25 million in total construction costs (20 percent credit)." He further advised bringing in an expert early in the project to ensure that design choices, floor plan modifications, and program concepts do not inadvertently compromise the project's ability to secure a tax credit.

OPPORTUNITY ZONES

One of the most promising innovations on the financing front is the advent of Opportunity Zones (OZs). A creation of the 2017 tax revisions, OZs provide a new channel for accessing equity for both projects and small businesses. The key is the project site or the business needs to be located in one of approximately 8,700 designated OZs. These are not the most blighted areas of a community, however, but intentionally those areas on the cusp of change, where the idea that new capital invested will help tip the scales and drive the area to a more robust and resilient economic future.

Key tips for small developers are to identify whether you have any designated OZ properties in your typical area of work (geographic) and if a qualified fund is aggregating money to invest in this area. Unlike some other vehicles, which require expensive and complicated formation, a small developer could create a focused fund for its own projects, but not without some effort. The value of an OZ is a much lower cost of capital because of the tax benefits given to investors, and the long-term-hold nature of the funds: the investors optimize their tax benefits after a 10-year hold.

OPPOSITE: Venue Projects used historic tax credits for part of its redevelopment of the historic Alhambra Hotel as student housing for Benedictine University in Mesa, Arizona. *(©2019 Andrew Pielage)* **ABOVE:** In repurposing a former retail bank space as coworking space, CRAFT Development was able to leverage the federal ADA tax credit to offset 50 percent of the cost of replacing the main entry and storefront for code-required access, while also gaining a more attractive presence on the street. *(©2020 CRAFT Development)*

NEW MARKETS TAX CREDITS

New Markets Tax Credits (NMTCs) work like historic tax credits, in that a third party buys the tax credit offered by a project owner, which in turn becomes part of the project's equity. But instead of renovating a historic building, NMTCs have to demonstrate that they will create jobs and new economic activity in an area designated as an Enterprise Zone. This determination is undertaken before the developer starts a project, to attract inward investment. Like historic tax credits, NMTCs are very complicated to secure and expensive to process. So their usefulness for a small project can be limited.

LOW-INCOME HOUSING TAX CREDITS

Low-Income Housing Tax Credits (LIHTCs) can be used for affordable rental housing investments. Like other tax credits, they are purchased by investors, or investor syndicates, in exchange for a federal tax credit equal to a percentage of the cost of developing the property. Applicants compete for approval through a state housing finance agency, which is allowed to determine which projects merit approval, with each state setting its own priorities. To be eligible, a project must meet at least one of the following criteria:

- At least 20 percent of units are for households at or below 50 percent of area median income (AMI).
- At least 40 percent of units are for those at or below 60 percent of AMI.
- The average household income of tenants shall not exceed 60 percent of AMI.

Low-income tenants cannot be charged more than 30 percent of the maximum eligible income. These requirements remain in effect for the first 15 years of operation and an additional 15 years if required by the local authority.

TAX INCREMENT FINANCING

Tax increment financing (TIF) is a way for a locality to use expected increases in property tax revenue that result from new development in a specified area (which is established as a special taxing district) for infrastructure or other public improvements or services in that area. The rules governing TIF districts vary by state.

COINVESTMENT WITH TENANTS

During many of the SSDFs, projects were profiled that relied on a unique combination of equity, some of which was raised from project tenants. In several instances a special tenant that helps brand the development, or provides essential synergy, also provides cash equity to the developer so everyone is aligned in their goal for a successful development. This approach of shared business interests provides multiple benefits:

- You, the landlord, have tenants who want to ensure you are successful, because your financial success in the development is also *their* success in building wealth by operating their business and owning a hard asset.
- All tenants in the building are aligned for the success of the development. In The Newton, in Phoenix (see case study in chapter 13), developer Lorenzo Perez shared how the individual tenants in the mixed-use project came together creatively to agree how to use each other's services to ensure each other's success. The bookstore would have the neighboring restaurant provide food for book-signing events, and the event space would tap into the bookstore's bar for meetings. Because each tenant had a vested interest in the total rent collected for the building through its ownership interest, all were more interested in making sure each tenant succeeded.

The converse of this strategy was also evident in other projects toured, where the developer invested in the tenant's business. In this case, the developer might provide working capital and business acumen to a rock star, startup restaurant that has little-to-no operating expertise. This helps ensure the building gets a unique brand and the tenant can be successful—and continue to pay rent. These deals are often structured as a percentage rent, where the tenant pays a base rent plus a percentage of the gross sales, once a minimum level of sales is achieved. In this way the developer has a vested interest in the success of the business, and the business owner has an aligned partner who is not focused solely on its rent check—instead looking at the entire ecosystem of success in the building and how that creates long-term value through a successful set of businesses that can pay more rent as their success grows.

COMMUNITY BANKS

Community banks have been around for a long time but are often overlooked in the world of national banks that have slick advertising campaigns, powerful mobile banking apps, and ATMs across the country.

But community banks are focused specifically on what their name implies—the community in which they are located. Because many of them actually hold their loans in their portfolio (portfolio lenders) and are invested and interested in the success of their local community, they can often see potential in new ideas or take a more aggressive view of a deal because it is good for the community.

At no time in recent history has the power of community banks as a friend of *small* been more evident than during the recent COVID-19 pandemic. As small businesses and small real estate developers scrambled while the pandemic unfolded during March and April 2020, it was community banks where small developers found the most accessible, flexible, and responsive lenders who were able to provide relief though forbearance and deferment. This agility and access is borne out in the numbers of Paycheck Protection Program loans that were disbursed in the first 60 days of the program. Of more than 500 billion provided, over 65 percent of them came from community banks, not their much larger brethren.

IMPACT INVESTING

Impact investing is investment made with the goal of generating a positive impact on a neighborhood or district while also creating a reasonable level of return to the investor. However, because the investor is thinking holistically and long term, success is measured across environmental and societal goals as well as financial return. In this calculus a more modest rate of return may be acceptable if the other goals are achieved as well.

Program-related investment—a type of lending or investment made by many nonprofits—is a form of impact investing. Based on a specific set of metrics and broad missions, a foundation or nonprofit may be willing to invest in a catalytic real estate project if it knows the principal will be repaid and a reasonable return (e.g., 3 to 5 percent) will be provided on that capital. Such an investor can be more flexible and patient than a lender or private investor and may be

> *In some instances, a unique tenant that helps brand the development or provide synergy also provides cash equity to the developer. This helps align everyone for a successful development.*

willing to provide the much-needed gap financing necessary between the equity raised and the debt originated with a commercial bank.

CONCLUSION

Funding a small development project requires time, effort, knowledge of all the varied sources, and lots of creativity. The preceding list of potential sources of investment, loans, and incentives is just a start. Developers of small projects will find others as they begin mixing the cocktail.

assessing **market**
potential

IN COLLABORATION WITH DAVID GREENSFELDER

**eizing unique opportunities** to create great places and to build upon existing community assets is core to the premise of building *small*. Despite its size, a small-scale project may provide incremental change or even be the catalyst for larger change in the area in which it is located. Because of its smaller scale, such a project is unlikely to create

a large-scale change immediately. In fact, many of the small-scale developers interviewed through the SSDFs lamented that while their project catalyzed significant value creation for the properties surrounding them, they were unable to assemble enough property initially to harvest the momentum they created. Market analysis and scenario planning for a proposed project's "what-ifs" should identify long-term opportunities that need to be considered when initiating a transformative project.

Small sponsors are more likely to be real estate entrepreneurs than deep-pocketed institutional developers. Successful execution demands a disciplined approach—knowing when your vision makes sense and when the vision may cross over into the "bleeding edge." The first step in testing a vision is market analysis.

Simply put, the vision is the hypothesis, and market research is one of the methods by which the hypothesis is tested. It is also a key part of the documentation banks and investors ask for to help them assess the project's likelihood of success. Given the enormous investment of personal capital, time, emotion, and money that most small-scale developers put into a project, knowing that you are working on the *right* project is of primary importance. In this case, "right" means a project that is viable in terms of attracting tenants, equity, and financing—and creating solid returns after it is up and open.

A technically correct market analysis will give you a better picture of whether to pursue a proposed project in the first place, and if so, how high a lift will be required to make it a success. A nuanced market analysis will help build the story that will attract capital and help you fine-tune your program. The good news is that small-scale developers can do a lot of market research and analysis themselves.

The best market research is forward-looking, assessing each situation as unique, and identifying which real estate, economic, and consumer trends apply. The best research also recognizes that real estate is demand driven and that while a "build it and they

> ### There is a fine line between vision and hallucination. Small *should innovate but not be the bleeding edge.*

will come" approach may work in select instances, it works only because underlying demand was truly there—it just may not have been recognized or properly quantified by less creative developers.

Understanding market potential relies on both art and science. Get to know the numbers, but instead of relying on sheer quantity of data, look for the *right* data on which to rely. Also rely on your own experience, but with an objective eye. Would you live or work or shop in the neighborhood where your proposed project is located? If the answer is yes, then identify the reasons why. Is it because the neighborhood or community has certain compelling attributes? a beautiful setting? walkability? compelling residential areas? Is a shopping district unlike every other shopping district, or does it offer needed services? If the answer is no, it is equally important to understand why. What is missing? What does not feel right? What would make it better? What would make you (or the targeted user) want to live, work, or play here? Remember, buildings create behaviors. What behaviors do you observe? What behaviors do you feel are missing? If you create buildings and by extension behaviors, will they add value to and unlock economic potential of the site and perhaps the neighborhood?

One way to frame market analysis is to think of it as a series of layers. Each layer adds an important

---

OPPOSITE: In an era when bookstores are becoming obsolete, Venue Projects anchored The Newton with Changing Hands, a beloved, local, independent bookstore. After gaining a deeper understanding of the community's attachment to the bookseller and its ongoing programming, Venue realized that what might have been considered a dying form of retail was actually a great market maker for Venue's mixed-use redevelopment. (© *Andrew Pielage*)

set of information to the original base analysis. Your objective evaluation about the area is your "base layer," which is the most fundamental understanding of your project's location: What uses are in the project's immediate area, who lives and works in the area, what are the traffic patterns, and so on?

This base layer articulates what the area's assets and failings are. More important, through the initial step you have identified questions that will direct you to seek relevant data to help answer those questions. Given the plethora of data available on the web and through services, developers can easily get lost collecting lots of data without really knowing why and mistakenly think they have done a meaningful analysis.

For example, many people start with demographic reports, which are readily available through census, local planning jurisdictions, and general plan documents. Again, remember that real estate is demand driven, not just numbers driven. Instead of just cataloging demographics, start by identifying market characteristics by answering the following questions:

- Who is the target market for the proposed project?
- Where do the project's customers come from (be they residential tenants or buyers, businesses leasing office space, or retailers and their patrons)?
- Is the project in a highly competitive or not particularly competitive environment?

- How much of total potential business do you or your tenants need to capture for the project or your tenants to be successful? Is this a realistic goal?

Retail is one of the most location sensitive of all property types, so it is a useful illustration of this approach. Potential sales for a retailer, the best way of quantifying market demand in a retail context, come from residents, daytime workers, visitors, traffic patterns, growth of any of these, and existing retailers. Which of these might apply to your situation? The answer will guide you about where to focus first. At its core, this analysis is about identifying who the customers are (demand), where they come from, and who you are competing with (supply) for the customer's attention and dollars.

The tools described in this chapter can easily be tailored to support other land use types typical of *small*: residential, office, hospitality, entertainment, and food and beverage uses. Thinking ahead to how consumer preferences are changing and last-mile requirements presents some interesting opportunities for small-scale developers to create value through adaptive use of class B or C retail space, or outdated warehouse and research and development facilities. This would require a very specialized analysis. And for mixed-use projects, a separate analysis would be conducted for each use component.

ABOVE: *Location* refers to geography and context. A desirable downtown location with storefront retail, street presence, wide sidewalks, diversity of uses, and historic assets gives buildings in this picture a sense of place. These attributes differentiate this district from nearby strip commercial areas, making it a more desirable place to own and operate commercial real estate. *(© David Greensfelder))*

location and improvements

It is common to intertwine location and improvements when talking about real estate. The holy grail is reached when the improvements harness the essential value of the location and create new synergy—hence greater value—than either could on their own.

A good market analysis will separate location and improvements each into its own analysis. If a given attribute of each element is "better than" competing properties, it makes your project more attractive to potential users and perhaps more valuable than alternatives. If your project is "equal to," then it is a wash, and if your project is "worse than" with respect to a given attribute, then it is less attractive and potentially less valuable. A project usually does not live or die on one attribute, although sometimes just one attribute that does not pass muster can be a reason to say no. It is important to evaluate your project holistically and objectively, taking all location and improvement attributes and their respective equal-to-or-better-than judgments into account.

Just as different apartment renters or office occupiers have distinct profiles, so do retailers and service providers. Your building's tenant and visitor behaviors will be influenced by your project's location and its design. As you examine the potential market for your project, think about the sense of place you will be creating, the project's larger location and context, and the sorts of improvements you plan to build. To what sorts of tenants do the location, neighborhood, customer base, and traffic patterns lend themselves? Are local planning sensibilities and design guidelines pushing you to build a utilitarian development, or more of a lifestyle, niche project? For what sorts of uses and behaviors are your improvements designed?

Will a potential shopper be more likely to purchase commodities like office supplies or to enjoy strolling through boutiques or eating a leisurely lunch? These questions speak to the essence of *small*. How can you assess which sort of project is appropriate and

> *It is important to evaluate your project holistically and objectively, taking all attributes and their respective equal-to-or-better-than judgments into account.*

the demand for that project? Both quantitative market research and a more nuanced, qualitative approach to assessing potential demand are needed.

ABOVE: *Improvements* refers to the building itself. Exterior improvements include a building's visibility, access, parking, and general presence, including storefront design, signage, and transparency that allows passersby to interact with the use inside. Interior improvements (seen here) include everything from interior clear height to flooring materials to buildout, such as a restroom and millwork. (© David Greensfelder)

→ procuring data

A wealth of data is available, much of it at no cost. The trick is knowing what kind of data is meaningful and then using it effectively.

DEMAND

Demographics are relatively easy to come by, and they are easy to over-rely on, misunderstand, or misuse. Whereas a specialized (and expensive) consultant used to be required to gather data, this information is now readily available at no or modest cost from a number of sources.

Often a locality will have a demographic profile on its website or available through its economic development office. Extensive raw demographic data are available by census tract from the U.S. Census Bureau's website, and consumer spending data are available from the Census Bureau's American Community Survey. These sources are more cumbersome to navigate, but they can provide extremely useful data not readily available elsewhere.

Third-party aggregators such as ESRI and Environics Analytics (formerly Claritas) provide more robust data sets in a variety of reports, the most basic of which will tell you residential population, daytime population, number and size of households, housing data, education, age and income distributions, commute times, and so on. Usually a long-form option is available that gives more detailed information and will give you a better idea of what your residential customer base looks like. Market potential reports that use proprietary algorithms are also able to give greater insight about both the supply and the demand sides of the market.

Although these reports typically require a subscription, often some can be procured free through your local economic development office, planning department, or a broker you have a connection with.

SUPPLY

Leasing brochures for existing retail projects are often available online through a brokerage website or a service such as LoopNet. Zillow can be a good source for housing data and trends. CoStar is expensive and requires a subscription, but it can give detailed information about existing and planned buildings. CoStar's rent and sales comparables are more or less reliable depending on the land use type, so that data should be used carefully. In many cases, the best information on the competition is gathered by getting to know the area yourself, talking to local brokers, business owners, residents, shoppers, and so on.

Retail Sales vs. Demand

Grocery stores	+ $90,634,418
Auto parts/accessories, tires	+ $32,527,371
Drinking places/alcoholic beverages	+ $7,690,023
Specialty food stores	+ $3,774,574
Special food services	+ $2,910,259
Beer, wine, liquor	−$8,851,566
Bldg materials, garden equip/supply	−$11,193,729
Miscellaneous retailers	−$18,717,402
Electronics/appliances	−$22,620,359
Restaurants/other eating places	−$64,329,673
Health/personal care stores	−$69,123,619
Furniture/home furnishings	−$72,730,878
Sporting goods, hobby/books/music	−$83,103,620
Nonstore retailers	−$104,789,270
General merchandise	−$154,207,149
Clothing/clothing accessories	−$239,265,007

Source: © Greensfelder Real Estate Strategy.

CHART: Retail supply and demand are often shown as the difference between actual sales and potential demand (often calculated from American Community Survey data). An area "pulls" when sales exceed local demand for a given area (positive numbers), and an area has "leakage" when demand exceeds local sales (negative numbers).

data gathering vs. data analysis

To make good use of these data sets, decide what geographic area you want to know about. The default is usually a one-, three-, and five-mile radius; however, this default is not always applicable. Daily-needs retailers rarely draw from a three- or five-mile radius. In a densely populated, urban area, the right radius might be just a half-mile. Often the trade area is not a radius at all, but a custom area that you will create (called a polygon) based on market knowledge about traffic patterns, barriers, and local habits. For example, a geographic impediment such as a freeway, river, nonpublic campus, or mountain might be a natural boundary from beyond which customers will not be drawn.

Market analysis is both art and science, requiring both data and intuition. For example, is there a large residential population but virtually no daytime population? This might indicate a commuter community with little lunchtime activity. So a restaurant serving lunch and dinner might not work well. You can also test assumptions about the dinner business by looking at age distributions and length of commute. If the data show lots of families with young kids, or a tendency toward long commutes, even the weekday dinner business may be challenging. A better fit might be a predominantly morning business serving coffee and to-go breakfast to residents heading out on their long commutes, or a family-friendly eatery with take-out options. An establishment relying heavily on lunch business is going to have a hard time in this hypothetical neighborhood. Spending time in the area will give more clues about what people do during the day and in the evening. Do you see families dining at casual eateries, couples splurging on high-end dinners, daytime activity frequenting boutiques? Are there businesses that are not drawing traffic? If so, why not?

Each retail use has its own specific customer profile, often described in terms of demographic attributes. Even one-off, bespoke concepts need to have a clear idea of who their customer base is. It is important to understand what key demographic characteristics overlap in a given location, and focus on the uses (tenants) that are compatible with those overlapping characteristics. For example, a luxury salon with spa services will need a significant daytime population of the appropriate age and income levels. The bottom line is to test your vision against the facts and see if your vision holds up, or if it needs to be adjusted.

Access to key data may require an expensive subscription, but some data may be procured for free through your local economic development office, planning department, or a broker with whom you have a connection.

→ other data

For years, market analysis relied on fairly common data sources to support project feasibility. Now, new insights are available with the advent of big data, access to more granular consumer values and patterns, and increased recognition of the important role qualitative factors play in shaping demand.

PSYCHOGRAPHICS

Psychographics are sexy, fun to look at, and interesting. Available from the same data providers, they divide the population into groups—or cohorts—with similar values by aggregating indicators such as credit card purchases, customer loyalty program data, magazine subscriptions, cellphone use, vehicle type driven, vacation and dining habits, and recreational interests.

A psychographic report will tell you which groups or "clusters" with similar overlapping demographic characteristics and behaviors show up most frequently in the area you are studying. It is important to take psychographic reports in context. They will often highlight only the three most frequently seen clusters, but these three clusters may account for a relatively small percentage of the overall population. Psychographics are one more method to confirm what you think you already know and to show another window into your market for your investor presentations. But given its very subjective nature, psychographics should not be your sole source of validation.

Other sources of data can provide useful information in evaluating your project:

SPENDING PATTERNS

Spending patterns are usually shown as under- or overspending as compared to a national or regional benchmark (regional being preferred). So, if a score of 100 shows spending in line with the benchmark, a score of less than 100 will indicate spending in a given category is less than the benchmark, and a score of more than 100 will indicate more spending in a category. These spending patterns often correlate strongly with income and education levels.

DAYTIME POPULATION REPORTS

Daytime population reports will show a breakdown of employment by sector. This breakdown will give you an idea about what sorts of goods and services might be appropriate for the area you are studying, but be careful about how you interpret the data. People tend to patronize daily-needs retailers closer to home than to work (ice cream doesn't travel well on a long commute). Think about daytime population as representing incremental demand but not primary demand. It might indicate a reason to build workforce housing if a housing-to-jobs ratio is out of balance, a breakfast-lunch food service venue, or an office supply outlet; however, it is not likely to indicate significant enough retail demand because that demand is driven more by real residential population, not daytime worker population. Similarly, a location near a university does not necessarily draw significant student clientele.

VISITOR INFORMATION

Visitor information can come in the form of tourism, convention traffic, or destination venues. Information on all of these visitor destinations can be found in a variety of places, including from the local convention and visitors bureau, lists in the local business journal, the economic development department of the cities in which the attraction is located, and STR, formerly Smith Travel Accommodations, Report (STAR Report) for hotel occupancy and room rates. As with demographic information, contextualize the data you receive. A large convention center that hosts 500,000 attendees annually may seem like an impressive source of demand. However, what really matters is the number of events, the frequency with which they occur, and the average group's attendance. If the venue hosts only 10 conventions annually and the facility is closed more than it is open, trying to capitalize on visitor count likely will not work because of the difficulty of surviving between meetings.

Similarly, concert and entertainment venues may boast impressive attendee numbers, but they are destination driven and tend to operate at a specific time of the day. This may or may not help support a business that needs customers all day long, seven days a week.

Finally, many locations and lifestyle communities where *small* is an important building block to both the community's economic base and its sense of authenticity are often the site of significant tourism. It is important to understand the volume of tourism and whether it is highly seasonal or year-round, and what goods and services could be purchased on or off site. A business that cannot point to a regular and sustainable customer base may not be a reliable long-term tenant or viable partner for your project and should prompt you to take a hard look at what is real.

MOBILITY OPTIONS AND PATTERNS

How people move is as important as demographic data. The power of generating sales from customers who consume "on their route" or who limit their retail consumption to what is conveniently located on their normal routes cannot be underestimated. The greater the density, the more pronounced localized consumption patterns become. For example, in traffic-burdened cities, a shopping trip may be much more of a commitment than in an easier to navigate small town or suburb. Density and transportation options will also provide information about how far people might go to consume a given good or service. Daily-needs commodities and casual dining may be purchased closer to where they are consumed and one's home, whereas customers may travel greater

distances for specialty entertainment venues, luxury goods, or destination dining.

Another factor to take into consideration is the "gravity direction" in a given area. The gravity direction is defined as the general direction from which residents and daytime workers enter a trade area and to which they travel to leave a trade area. Generally, the more frequently traveled route would be on the "gravity side" of the trade area. Examples would include routes to transit hubs, primary pedestrian routes to parks and residential centers, and in the more conventional sense, heavily traveled roadways such as arterials. Once the gravity side is identified, it becomes clearer which side of the street is the "going to work side" and which is the "going home side." Obtaining morning and evening peak-hour traffic counts from a municipality's public works or engineering department can validate your hunch. Some uses have a clear preference for one or the other side of the street that would allow their customers to have easier turning movements (i.e., right-in, right-out access). For example, a coffee shop would prefer the going-to-work side of the street, whereas a grocery store would be more convenient on the going-home side.

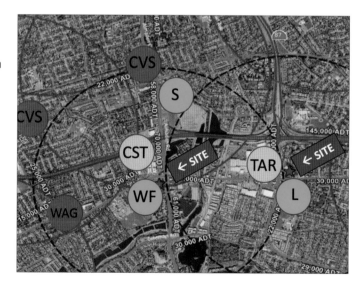

ABOVE: It is important to examine the site—and its potential market—contextually. This aerial photo shows existing retailers, sites being considered, traffic counts at various locations, and radius circles to add scale. A simple map only showing roads and land uses can lead to significantly different conclusions than one showing real buildings. In this case, the aerial highlights one area's much higher density, meaning more potential users. (© Greensfelder Real Estate Strategy)

COMPETITION

Regardless of land use type, understanding the competitive landscape is important. Real estate is developed because there is demand for a certain kind of space that is undersupplied (or projected to be undersupplied with reasonable certainty).

Although chain retailers are arguably the antithesis of *small*, their discipline and approach to proving market depth is a valuable instructor for the small developer. Because their focus is primarily on growth and sales, they do an excellent job of understanding from where their sales are generated and tend not to open stores in areas already served by "sister" stores from the same chain. Looking at the spacing of existing stores can offer a lot of good information. If you are building a space intended for a specialty grocery, look at where existing grocers are located and the types of grocers (mass market, specialty, discount, warehouse, etc.). Are multiple chains and independent operators in the immediate trade area already? Does a particular chain or type of grocer already have one or more stores in the area, or relatively close by in multiple directions along primary traffic corridors? Is the competitor in the gravity direction or perhaps intercepting traffic before it gets to your location? Is your site on the going-to-work or going-home side of the street it

experience and why they or their customers are there. Competitors will be surprisingly forthcoming, and the answers will be informative. A visit during nonpeak hours enables you to see how well and deeply a store is merchandised in anticipation of peak-hour shopping. As an example, for a grocery, look at perishables like meat and dairy leading up to a peak time. If they are stacked deeply in the cooler cases, you know the store is expecting a lot of business. During these slower periods, approach store management to ask how the store is performing and from where their customers come. Finally, look at how the store is being operated. A store with more checkout counters expects to do more business than a store with fewer. Are there a lot of out-of-stock empty spaces in the aisles? Ask delivery drivers what stores along their route get the biggest deliveries and how the store you are looking at stacks up against those. Look at operating hours; more hours mean a busier store.

PLACE AND ENVIRONMENT

"Place" and "environment" are key elements for most small developments. It is what distinguishes them, and what makes them a valuable asset to the community. Evaluating them is highly subjective and involves making a judgment about the "feel" of a particular location, and how your vision will fit or not fit in with the area's feel. Your evaluation can be supported by your "guerilla interviews" when mystery shopping a competitor.

One approach to evaluating place and environment is to look for an analogous project to your proposal that has been built in a location with similar location attributes. Evaluate what attributes about its specific location, environment, and improvements make it work well for its tenants and visitors. Then look at the specific location and environment for the project you plan to build. How well does your location hold up with respect to each attribute you identified when you evaluated the analog project? Will you be able to include the specific improvements

> *Chain retailers are arguably the antithesis of small, but their disciplined approach to proving market depth is a valuable instructor for the small developer.*

most desires? If the area is dense, are competitors close to each other, or conversely, if the area is not dense, how spread out are they?

Sizing up your competitors is important, so visit both during nonpeak and peak business hours for that particular business. Look at how busy the competitor is during these peak times; talk with employees, store managers, and customers about their

that made the other project work well? Is your project at a competitive advantage or disadvantage for including or not having these improvements?

Spending time both in the area of your site and in analogous areas is important. Get to know each. Talk to people. Window shop and talk to merchants. Ask friends and colleagues (both in and especially outside the real estate profession) for their unvarnished opinion about the area and what you are planning to build. Ask them if they would live, work, or shop at your project, and most important, *why*. At the end of the day, this is a qualitative analysis, so be careful to step back and look as objectively as possible at the overall situation.

IMPROVEMENT ATTRIBUTES

Evaluating the attributes associated with improvements is fairly straightforward because they represent functional requirements as well as the quality of design and construction. Desirable attributes differ, depending on the type of land use. Begin by listing the attributes to address as you evaluate competing properties.

The size and dimensions of the space can have far-ranging implications. Different kinds of retail require different footprints, just as apartments geared for different resident profiles will have different layouts and amenities. For shop space, an ideal depth is 60 feet with anything between 50 and 70 feet being workable. Under this range and the retailer's operations can be affected. If deeper, the retailer is likely paying for space "in the back" that it does not need. Space comes in three dimensions, and so do requirements. Clear height is particularly important. If there is not enough clear height, it will not be possible to distribute mechanical, electric, and plumbing (MEP) systems while still maintaining an 11- to 12-foot floor-to-ceiling plane for shop space. (Larger spaces require greater height.) For restaurants, it is important to have space for ventilation systems and refrigeration compressors or lines to remote compressors.

Aside from the practical, a space's volume has a direct relationship to its sense of place and environment. High ceilings can create either a dramatic space or one that feels awkward and poorly proportioned. They can also make sound transfer worse. Too-low ceilings can feel cramped and can make a space obsolete. Look carefully at life safety and ADA issues. Retrofitting to become compliant can be an expensive proposition, and upgrades are required at certain thresholds of improvement. So where one property may look less expensive and better suited to your needs at the outset, the cost of the retrofit may ultimately make it more expensive than a competing property that will not require the same level of intervention and expensive upgrades.

The exterior of the property is as important—or perhaps more so—than the interior. Blockscape, streetscape, and storefronts all add to the quality of the experience and functionality of a property—especially if an area is specialty and experience driven. Sidewalks should have ample width for desired outdoor displays, awnings, seating and dining areas, and storage for carts if they are used. Loading, service, and trash areas are often afterthoughts, but they are essential to smooth and efficient tenant operations—not to mention avoiding conflicts like outdoor seating that sits awkwardly near dumpsters on pickup day.

CONCLUSION

A systematic and objective evaluation of the market will help you understand if you should really undertake a proposed project in the first place. Beyond that initial go/no-go choice, the data gathered, analysis undertaken, and detailed assessment of features will better equip you to avoid mistakes that can be extremely costly. The most expensive project is one that gets built but does not meet the needs of its intended users. Doing your homework up front and understanding the depth and potential market for your project are critical elements of a disciplined approach to executing *small*.

winning

AGENCY AND NEIGHBORHOOD APPROVALS

small

WITH CONTRIBUTIONS BY JAY RENKENS

the ability to get a project approved—or "entitled"—may be one of the biggest value-add contributions a small developer can bring to a project. But having an understanding of your approval environment is critical for initiating the project approval process and is arguably a key requirement before even taking site control.

WHY THIS MATTERS

Project approvals and entitlements can be a high-value creation opportunity, if you possess the know-how, have good strategic skills, are politically savvy and incredibly patient, and possess the demeanor and emotional fortitude to run the approvals gauntlet. It is one of the earliest stages where a small developer's "sweat equity" can parlay into real equity if they are successful.

Development markets are often viewed in one of two ways: high barrier to entry and low barrier to entry.

High-barrier-to-entry markets are those where obtaining approvals can be very time consuming, require lots of documentation and public meetings, and can be highly politicized. These are often evidenced in coastal cities; small lifestyle, resort towns; neighborhoods adjoining institutions of higher education; or neighborhoods with high concentrations of wealth.

Low-barrier-to-entry markets open their arms to new development. They are typified by fewer regulations and may be more relaxed about what they demand from the developer. Approvals may be more about who you know or your reputation in the community. These can be found in rural communities; fast-growing emerging suburbs; and communities where there are few physical or geographic barriers to constrain growth and a strong ideology around private property rights.

Approvals in a high-barrier-to-entry location can be tortuous, but because of the high barrier, can create significant economic value for the developer. Because few people may have the resources, stomach, or time to undertake such a process, significant value can be created just by enduring and succeeding through the entitlement process. An approval in a

> *Too often developers from low-barrier-to-entry markets enter a high-barrier market thinking they can replicate their prior success as easily and quickly as they did in their low-barrier-to-market efforts. Several years and an extensive loss of capital later, they learn this distinction the hard way.*

low-barrier-to-entry location, in contrast, can move much faster and easier, but the added value may be less because most anyone could do it.

Too often developers from low-barrier-to-entry markets enter a high-barrier market thinking they can replicate their prior success as easily and quickly as they did in their low-barrier-to-market efforts. Several years and an extensive loss of capital later, they learn this distinction the hard way.

Understanding the approval process and setting early in your project due diligence will help you create a realistic schedule and front-end budget and know what skills you need to have on your team. Most important, it will help you form the best strategy for obtaining site control. For a small developer with limited resources, buying an expensive piece of land outright in a high-barrier-to-entry market can be a very challenging endeavor. Making the purchase contingent on obtaining the approvals can be a great way to create value, predominantly through sweat equity.

OPPOSITE: A community meeting and workshop to discuss potential options for development before submitting plans.
(© CRAFT Development)

→ understanding entitlements

Obtaining entitlements is not a single milestone or event. There are multiple episodes of approvals from concept to finished project. One reason obtaining entitlements creates so much value is because they remove a very significant level of uncertainty from the project. To investors and lenders, uncertainty equals risk. And if your project is risky, your funding will be very expensive, if you can get it at all. So approvals are critical to creating value through reduction of project risk, which in turn makes it more appealing to investors and lenders.

Approvals take on two predominant forms: discretionary and ministerial.

Discretionary approvals are just that. They are granted with discretion. That might happen after public officials feel community concerns have been addressed, after they feel the developer is providing enough public benefit to warrant them allowing the site to be developed within the approved policies of the governing documents, or after the project's proposed design has been deemed to be appropriate for the site. Appropriateness of a design is a highly

Ministerial approvals are much less fraught with uncertainty. They simply require that you demonstrate you have met the requirements—that is, the project is consistent with the building code—to be granted a permit. Ministerial approvals should be much more straightforward than discretionary approvals because the application is simply reviewed against an established set of written rules. However, there are still pitfalls, and anyone who has endured the building permit and inspection process knows that even working from the same codes, inspectors often still do some degree of interpretation. Ministerial approvals take time, patience, and most important, knowledge of what the codes really say and mean so you can counter a highly subjective interpretation correctly to get to the other side of the process.

> *This is why entitlement capital is so expensive: you may not receive an approval at all, or what does get approved may no longer be feasible.*

subjective decision, often made by commissioners who lack formal design training but are comfortable opining on designs they *like* versus those they *do not like*. Discretionary approvals typically occur at the front end of the project and are the most fraught with public involvement, political challenges, and even legal challenges. This is why initial project capital can be so expensive—it entails a high degree of risk that you may not get your discretionary approval at all; or if you do get it, the final approved project might be different from what you set out to do. After you have completed your discretionary approvals, you are often able to recapitalize the project with lower-cost capital.

Beyond the difficulty of just navigating the rules (what is really required, why there are often so many similar sounding requirements asking for different things), delays in the process from lack of staff capacity to review the application, or planning commissioner requests for more information add further expense and uncertainty. These may involve multiple submissions and consultant time, carrying cost of the site if you had to buy it outright, and the overhead of your operation. Worse than potential added costs is that delays can put your project on the wrong side of a market cycle, thereby affecting its financial feasibility or ultimate revenue potential.

laying the groundwork

The goal of a successful entitlement process is to facilitate the process and engage in a way that makes public officials and neighbors feel that their concerns have been heard and that you are responding to the larger community's desires. A well-designed, transparent and open approval process should streamline the outcome, engage potential new partners, and enlist project champions. A successful process does not mean that everyone gets everything they want, but it does mean those with a vested interest feel

they have had an opportunity to express concerns and desires, that you have taken them seriously and tried to accommodate them. And when you could not accommodate their wishes, you made the time and effort to explain why.

WHY THIS MATTERS

The greatest advantage the small developer has is being the face of the project. Unlike a corporate developer that may have an attorney do its approvals, or an institutional developer that has a range of entitlement experts in house, the small developer is usually the initiator, author, primary decision-maker, and main facilitator for the project. When concerned citizens want to talk to someone and get a straight answer, they are talking to the person in charge—not the appointed attorney or staff. Building trust, or at least an open relationship with those who want to have a say in the project, can go a long way to a successful outcome.

SMALL TIPS

Find champions. To leverage this important asset, the small developer should build the skills—and more important, the attitude—to think of neighbors as partners rather than as adversaries. This will require new levels of trust being forged, a transparent accounting of value and costs, and a dialogue about what the community wants and what the developer needs. It also requires finding champions within the

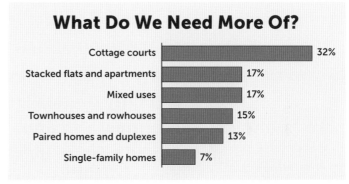

What Do We Need More Of?

Cottage courts	32%
Stacked flats and apartments	17%
Mixed uses	17%
Townhouses and rowhouses	15%
Paired homes and duplexes	13%
Single-family homes	7%

Source: Housing Our Community, a Healdsburg, California, community forum.

regulatory agencies who will confirm what the codes allow and help educate stakeholders on where they have the right to help shape the outcome and where you as developer have rights to do what you have proposed.

Learn what is important to the community. In many communities, multiple documents have accrued over the years to record community conversations about what they want, how they see themselves in the future, and what is important to their quality of life or reflects their values. These abstract visions and principles get translated into guiding goals and policies within comprehensive or general plans, master plans, vision plans, or specific plans. Whatever the document, it has one primary purpose—to record what the community and its leadership have said is important to them, and in

CHART: RiverHouse, an infill housing project, built on two years of community-sponsored workshops that had the community evaluate different housing types. Cottage court was the community's top preference by a wide margin, forming the cornerstone of CRAFT Development's strategy for accelerating planning approvals—despite the project's inconsistencies with existing zoning code. *(© CRAFT Development)*

many cases, what they prefer to happen on the site you have selected.

The first step in any successful approval process is to read and understand these documents and know whether your project will help deliver on these goals. Such documents can be one of your best allies in gaining an approval in a tough political setting. Your primary objective should be to seek and demonstrate a win-win for the community and the agencies responsible for administering the document's intent by explaining and showing how your proposal helps further the community's stated goals and policies.

If the idea of what you would like to do with a site is counter to what the community plans are suggest-

of each side protecting its downside, trying to anticipate what could go wrong, and if they cannot trust the other party, determining how they can best protect themselves.

Although building goodwill in and of itself will not preclude detailed technical documents and legal language, it will help as you navigate the process, allowing you to get to the core issues faster and to have an honest conversation about what the key concerns are.

Similarly, building trust with the community is critical, especially in contentious neighborhood and infill projects. While building trust will not (and should not) result in preferential treatment, it can provide more direct, open, and efficient communications and negotiations. As discussed previously, the benefit of being a small developer is that you are the face of the project, the person with the most intimate knowledge of the project details, and the person most at risk.

No matter how many documents encode policies, guidelines, and standards, the process of project entitlement is ultimately one of trust.

ing, you could be facing an uphill battle that will not end well. But if your vision and program are well aligned with the principles, make that explicit. Do not pitch your project in your language: pitch it in the language of the plans and policies that are already written. Approvals often have to rely on "findings"— meaning the approvals you are being granted are consistent with current policies and codes. If you do the work for staff by pointing out alignment from the beginning, they are more able to help usher your project through the process.

Build trust—a critical factor for success.

No matter how many documents encode policies, guidelines, and standards, the process of project entitlement is ultimately one of trust. Does the community trust you to do the right thing? Does the staff trust your judgment and trust that your interests are aligned with the responsibilities they have been charged to uphold? The prescriptive and detailed nature of many development documents is a function

For neighbors to know they are talking to the decision-maker, the individual responsible for the ideas and development, and not that person's attorney, planner, or public relations person, can go a long way toward building an honest and open relationship. Being willing to share your contact information from the start—cell and email—may seem like opening yourself to unwanted (and never-ending) feedback; but it often shows the community that you are open, accessible, and willing to listen. This can defuse initial misgivings about your intentions and avoid future frustrations. Although the community members may not agree with what you are doing, at least they know you are willing to listen to their concerns and perhaps be someone they can trust.

Building trust does not come from always saying yes. It may come from the candor and practical discussion that emerges when you say no. The best developers have the ability to say "no, we can't do that and this is why" without sounding condescending or alienating staff and the community.

The Plaza

Future Development Site

Proposed Project

Hotel Healdsburg

Foss St

Future Redevelopment Site

understand your context— existing and proposed

It is important to express your proposal in the context of its surroundings. Understand surrounding land uses, building forms, connectivity, and important community spaces. Know what is conforming and what is not so you do not propose a project element "because it matches our neighbor," only to be told that the adjoining precedent is nonconforming. That makes everyone look bad.

SMALL TIPS

Do your homework. Read up on projects that are in process or have been approved. Review previous correspondence and meeting minutes from planning commissions and council deliberations to better understand what issues are hot buttons for certain individuals who are reviewing your project, or what they have directed prior applicants to do. (Such records are always public unless there are issues under executive session.) This will afford you valuable insights into the locality's likely priorities and issues of greatest concern that you should be prepared to address.

Ask questions. You do not have to be an expert. Agency staff, community members, and neighbors are proud of what they can contribute to your project, and they will usually know things that you do not. Do not be afraid to ask questions. Many developers feel a need to appear knowledgeable and experienced so as to convey confidence and capability. Or they really do not want to hear what others think because they feel it will be impractical and inefficient. There is little room for the ego-driven and all-knowing in small development.

Successful small developers are knowledgeable about good practices, how to get things built, and what can and cannot work, but they are also willing to learn from others. It is not about just paying lip service, but genuinely asking thoughtful questions that will improve and ground your project in the community. By including input from many, your project earns the pride of those who can see their contributions realized—building more psychological ownership for a successful outcome while helping enhance your brand as a developer who listens and adds value to the neighborhood.

ABOVE: Figure ground and circulation mapping is one way to understand your project's context and emphasize how you plan to fit into— and add to—the existing community fabric. *(©2016 CRAFT Development)*

Become familiar with previous successful projects. Developers are generally proud of their accomplishments in the entitlement process—especially if they feel they created a successful win-win. Most are willing to share insights and what worked and what they might do differently. They can also provide great insight into the local approval landscape because they have seen it firsthand. Reach out to prior applicants and ask them for advice. In almost any community there are always projects that preceded your application—there is no sense in not taking advantage of their experience if they are willing to share.

Meet with city planning staff early. Meet with staff as early as possible to understand the process and its requirements and to get staff assessment of community and neighborhood concerns. Most

Meet with city staff early to understand their process and get an assessment of neighborhood concerns.

planning agencies require a pre-application meeting before you even apply for any kind of approval. Some communities even have a one-stop process where each department sends a representative to discuss a potential project and explain site constraints, city fees, and what will be required for approvals. Use these meetings early and effectively—potentially even before you close on the property. Come prepared with good questions, listen to what is shared, and take good notes. Send those notes back to the city's project representative to make sure they get into the file. A written record of all conversations and discussions is incredibly important because project approvals can drag out for years and staff—and policies—may change.

Know when an application is protected from future policy changes. Projects that take a long time to gain approval often risk changing

rules. As you start an application process, know at what point your project is secure from having the rules changed before it is approved. You do not want to spend a lot of time developing a design and detailed technical responses, only to find that the rules have changed just as you approach the finish line. Conversely, pay attention to matters before the council and planning commission that may have bearing on your project, and speak on your own behalf during public comment, or discuss with staff how a proposed code change may affect you, so you can be prepared.

Some communities rely on when an application is "deemed complete"—meaning your project application provides all the necessary reports and provides all the technical information required for the jurisdiction to effectively review the application—as the threshold by which your application is no longer subject to new code changes. Other thresholds might include simply having an application made and recorded, whereas higher-bar thresholds may not be until you have completed discretionary reviews. This may be an important place to obtain legal counsel to ensure you do not get caught sideways in a changing policy landscape.

Identify formal and informal stakeholders. Stakeholders can include neighbors, community advocacy groups, neighborhood associations, and others. Ask planning staff who the stakeholders are who may have the biggest concerns and that you should be engaging with. Review prior approval meeting minutes to see who may be a frequent opponent—or supporter—of new development, and what their common concerns are. If you are undertaking an infill project, survey your project's context and understand what neighborhood associations or business improvement districts adjoin or include your site. You will want to meet with their leadership, present your ideas, hear their concerns, and see if you can enlist their support.

If no formal association manages homes or development around your site, take time to meet with immediate neighbors, introduce yourself, and share your project concept. Be transparent in your process. As mentioned before—as a small developer, you are the face of the project and should be able to create a dialogue and sense of transparency that many corporate developers cannot. This does not mean everyone will love you or your project, but at least they should feel that you have been proactive and genuine with them about your intentions. The bodies that grant discretionary approvals often need political cover. Even if there is opposition to your project, if you have kept a good record of all efforts made to engage neighbors, demonstrate that you have been open and honest in your communications, and show that you have tried to find common ground, the ability to gain an approval can be greatly improved.

Create a clear vision for your project. Creating a genuine and memorable vision and set of values for your project helps create a shorthand way of expressing why it could be a good addition to the community. Once created, your vision can be used to pitch your project to a variety of audiences and even to discuss it with friends. Publish your vision and values often in conjunction with the project (even in marketing), and use it to frame every presentation and submission document. It shows consistency of thought and the higher purpose you always have in mind.

Identify and articulate project alignment with community goals. Articulate how your proposal aligns with and supports community goals, objectives, and policies. Take the time to review your project and write a response to every goal or policy that your project helps meet, and include it with your application. This will be important in the discretionary review process because it helps staff draft their report and ensures everything you have thought about in your design is represented in their findings. It also helps reinforce to the community that predecessor

documents have been written and approved to guide new development, and you are simply following those requirements.

Community benefits are often a requirement of the approval process—sometimes an outgrowth of discretionary approvals, sometimes a product of code requirements. Dedicating acreage for open space, paying a park impact fee, completing a section of public sidewalk, updating an obsolete building to meet new energy codes or ADA requirements: these are all mundane requirements that make up many planning and code requirements. Make sure you explain what you will be doing and take credit for how your project will improve the community at all levels.

Be humble, positive, and a good listener.
Being adversarial rarely works to your advantage. No matter how frustrating some conversations can get, keep your cool, be humble, and listen. Be honest and straightforward. If you know something they are asking for absolutely will not work, be upfront—

ABOVE: Not everyone will support your project. A neighbor's response to RiverHouse upon start of construction. *(©2021 CRAFT Development)*

"I hear what you are asking, but that's just not possible in this project, for this reason."

Spend time with people who are genuinely interested in what you have proposed. They may be willing to support your project if they feel they have been

community advocacy groups or even potential tenants or buyers—to speak on your behalf and tell why they want to see your project approved. Having a strong cohort of project supporters speak on your behalf—especially when they are people with a vested interest in the neighborhood or a successful outcome—goes a long way to balancing out voices of opposition.

Some opponents simply will never be convinced. Do not use valuable time and emotional energy trying to convert them—but do take time to listen to their concerns, potentially "agreeing to disagree" in the end.

Assume some opponents simply will never be convinced. Do not waste time and energy trying to convert them, but do take time to listen to their concerns. In the end, you may have to "agree to disagree" and move on. Time with

included and that they may have had some influence on the outcome. Ultimately you want people with a significant stake in your proposed project—immediate neighbors, the family that previously owned the land,

those who are interested in what you are doing and willing to provide support if you can accommodate some of their concerns, is the best use of your time and resources.

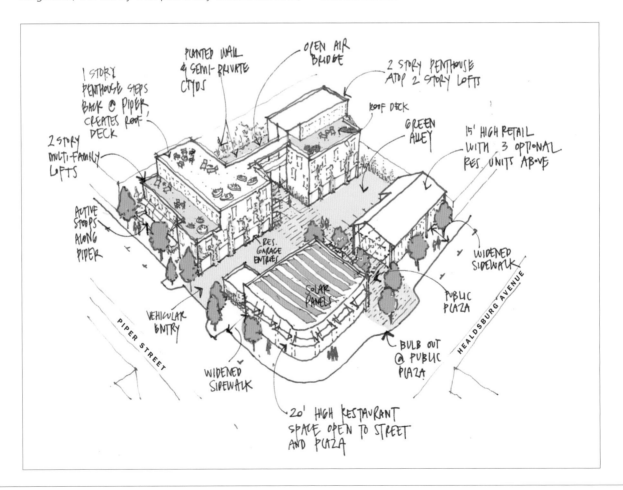

→

be proactive in your communications

Being proactive in your communication and public presence is key in the age of ubiquitous social media.

SMALL TIPS

Control your presence. Be sure to get control of project domains, Facebook pages, and Instagram sites early. Make sure that if someone googles your project, they get to the site that tells an accurate story—not one built to oppose your efforts.

- Use these sites to chronicle your efforts, share your vision and principles, enlist input, and share best practices using links to articles, other websites, and project examples from similar projects that have been successful.

- Post a running calendar of all your outreach efforts—upcoming public meetings, pop-ups and open houses, presentations to civic groups—and then a quick summary after each has been completed. This helps demonstrate you are being methodical in your efforts to engage the public and ideally are sharing what people are saying and how their input is helping shape the design.

- Start early gathering email addresses. Have a place on your website for people to sign up, get neighbors' addresses from public meetings and pop-ups, and gather contact information from anyone who expresses interest in the project. Send out regular communications on the project's process, what you are doing, and sharing when you need help. People appreciate being kept informed and hearing from the project sponsor directly. Consider offering *your* email address and cellphone contacts in an effort to further demonstrate transparency and accessibility. The downside potential of a persistent caller who wants to harass you is much lower than the upside of people knowing you are genuinely interested in hearing what they have to say. An added benefit is creating additional eyes and ears for your project—letting you know when something might be awry at the site or that something is being proposed that you may have missed that has a direct bearing on your proposal.

- Put links to plan documents on the website. Take the high road. Although they are public record and anyone can get them from the planning agency, make it easy for folks to find your documents in an effort to demonstrate transparency.

- Reach out to key movers and shakers with quick updates, emails, asks for support, or by presentations at upcoming hearings.

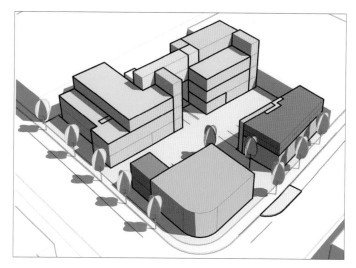

OPPOSITE AND ABOVE: Although computer-generated drawings provide great flexibility to accurately evaluate program, massing, and site organization for discussions with agency staff, they do not work well for conveying a project's vision. Hand-drawn renderings that retain an "in process" quality but still demonstrate accuracy help communicate your vision to the community without creating the feeling you have "already finished the design." *(© CRAFT Development and David Baker Associates)*

Regulatory Obstacles to *Small*

"THE PEGS ARE BIGGER THAN THE HOLE," is how Michael Lander, a developer and founder of the Minneapolis-based Lander Group, frames it. Lander believes the regulatory process is too siloed to work for small urban infill projects.

Getting the neighborhood's approval is often a challenge as well. For the Lander Group's West River Commons project in Minneapolis, Lander attended 45 public meetings, primarily with immediate neighbors who objected to the project—in spite of support from the city and the larger neighborhood organization. "The building is 60 stories tall in their mind," he says, noting people's inflated fear of how a proposed project will negatively affect their neighborhood. Although Lander believes that 45 meetings is excessive, some of the feedback from neighbors was not entirely negative, he concedes, and even helped improve the project's design. He strongly advises having a neighborhood champion for the project from the beginning.

"The city never reviewed a project like this before," explains architect Scott Harmon, one of three partners who developed the Mangum 506 project on the edge of downtown Durham, North Carolina. The city of Durham offers prime examples of the kinds of regulatory issues faced by developers in countless cities that encourage small infill development projects in principle, but that enforce codes that can create major hurdles. Although the municipality's comprehensive plan and zoning allowed the 21-unit project with four retail spaces, there were regulatory barriers. The city's solid waste department required a project of its size to include two Dumpsters. The transportation department would not let a Dumpster truck pull into the site and back out, but rather insisted it be able to drive through the site—something more easily accommodated in less dense suburban environments.

In addition, the major street fronting Mangum 506 is a one-way collector road that is part of the state highway system. Not only is no parking allowed on the street, which hampers the leasing of retail spaces, but the state highway department required a diagonal section to be removed from the building design so that vehicles on the cross street would have a better view of traffic on the one-way collector road—again, a rule that works better in a suburban context. The garbage issue was solved by a city compromise, but the developer did lose a 25-foot portion of the 506 Mangum building. However, the rule applies only to the first story of the structures, so no square footage was lost on the second and third floors.

Depending on circumstance, the neighborhood can be an ally rather than a deterrent. For instance, when Portland, Oregon–based Kemper Development proposed a 16-unit condominium building with 18,000 square feet of ground-floor retail space in the Hawthorne neighborhood of that city, the neighbors strongly supported it over an alternative proposal for a single-use McDonald's restaurant.

The rewards of developing small-size infill projects can be many, suggests Lander, who relates the story that when West River Commons was finished, a man approached him at the grand opening ceremony; Lander recognized him as one of the immediate neighbors who had been viscerally opposed to the project. The man shook Lander's hand and told him that his opposition was misplaced—instead, he loved the development and noted that it added to the character of the neighborhood.

Source: Excerpted from Sam Newberg, "Little Infill," *Urban Land*, March 1, 2010.

Get your graphics right. Communicate effectively in graphics and writing. Analyze every drawing, every chart, and every image you use. Make sure there are no hidden messages, unclear ideas, or complicated information that causes anxiety or adds to confusion. It is really hard to walk back from a graphic that sent the wrong message. As developers, we often read so much into the material we are presenting and miss some of the most obvious pitfalls. It helps to get fresh eyes on your presentation materials before you present in public to make sure your materials are conveying what you want them to say.

Engage face to face. Although social media should be part of the toolbox, community meetings are essential. "There is a magic that only happens when people get together face to face with neighbors and project leaders," says Dave Biggs, chief engagement officer at MetroQuest and an expert in public engagement.[6]

Use public meetings to get your message across and to hear the community's concerns and goals. (It is a good bet that those concerns will include traffic and parking.) You should go in already knowing most of the issues that will be brought up and be prepared to address all worries.

Public meetings do have pitfalls. They tend to attract people who have the strongest opinions—especially negative ones. Potential supporters can be intimidated by vocal naysayers. Angry groups may cause disruptions. Be ready for them. Often the most vocal critics represent a fairly small constituency.

Pop-up meetings are not substitutes for the more traditional public meetings that are advertised in advance, but they are another way to engage the local residents by meeting with them on their turf. It can be as simple as setting up a table on the project site. This can be very effective because you can have a real conversation about what is going on at the site and around the proposed project in real time—as opposed to recalling impressions that are not always accurate. Pop-ups also remove the formality of a

> *Pop-ups remove the formality of a public hearing, give neighbors the convenience to drop in when they can, and allow you, as project sponsor, to talk with them one-on-one.*

public hearing, give people the convenience to drop in when they can, and allow you to talk more in depth on a one-to-one basis—really understanding concerns, sharing your purpose and concepts in more detail, and being able to build a relationship.

ABOVE: Informal neighborhood "pop-ups" for RiverHouse made it easy for neighbors to drop in and discuss their concerns and to pose questions one-on-one with the developer. The informal nature of the setting (in this case the garage of the property to be redeveloped) was more successful in creating constructive conversations than the formal public hearing where Q&A is limited and dynamics can become contentious. *(© CRAFT Development)*

managing the design and construction process

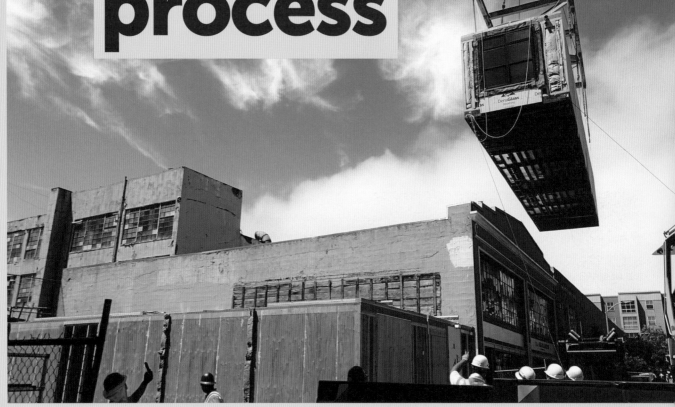

IN COLLABORATION WITH ALAN RAZAK

nvisioning a project is fun. Building it is hard—especially when you are breaking new ground, literally and figuratively. Although many of the forms, processes, documents, and protocols for the design and construction phase are fairly well institutionalized (much more so than front-end concept creation and financing), it is not a simple, rote process.

As a mentor of mine once said, "All the planning and conceptual work isn't worth a thing until it's built."

WHY THIS MATTERS

The challenge for developers of small projects is how to adapt complex construction processes that have evolved on big-budget projects to the scale and needs of smaller, lower-budget projects.

Although some of the standards embedded in the design and construction industry may seem like over-kill for smaller projects, understanding what their role is in reducing long-term risk and how they ensure a safe, habitable outcome that increases in value over time is important regardless of project size.

You will need to make several threshold design and construction decisions when entering this phase of a project:

- What will it take to get a construction permit and, more important, a certificate of occupancy? (This informs both the design documentation process and the construction timeline.)

- Where is your greatest risk and exposure, and what documents, insurance, and agreements do you need to protect yourself during construction and long after occupancy (or sale)?

- Who is best positioned to manage those risks? Do you have those skills or do you need to hire an experienced architect? Do you know enough about construction to act as your own owner/builder or should you pay a general contractor to manage all the trades and subcontractors, adding cost but greatly reducing construction risk?

How you answer these questions is the basis of how you—as a developer—add value to your project. And your answers should emanate from your own unique business model and play to your strengths while acknowledging you do not know what you do not know. Where inexperience looms large, seek out and retain the appropriate partners—either contractually or as part of your deal structure.

OPPOSITE: Panoramic Interests' 38 Harriet under construction. *(© Panoramic Interests)* **ABOVE:** CRAFT Development removed the rear 18-inch wall of a former bank vault to create a signature conference room. *(©2018 CRAFT Development)*

Is Building *Small* Different?

IN LARGER, MORE COMPLEX PROJECTS, very detailed and specific construction documents are required to control costs and make sure the project is designed as efficiently as possible. For example, space for corridors, mechanical rooms, and other nonleasable space must be minimized. Given the complexity of the systems and uses, the design team develops robust construction documents to avoid conflicts among the various disciplines, such as avoiding mechanical runs where electrical needs to go, and so on.

Small projects may require a somewhat different focus and approach. A high level of detail is expensive and may not serve the project as well as a more incremental process. Working to get construction drawings to a level of detail at which development costs can be established and permits received, but still allowing latitude to adjust elements in the field, is the holy grail of construction documents for a small project.

Also, only the best designers can really anticipate what small spaces will feel and look like in person. Framing and testing spatial relationships is almost always best done on site as new opportunities and ideas reveal themselves or new problems become evident.

Many small projects are adaptive use, which presents its own challenges. Reuse projects tend to evolve in their form and finishes as layers are removed during demolition, and new opportunities—and problems— are revealed. Too often, once demolition begins, it reveals a hidden column in a key space, or unexpected plumbing or electrical chases that cannot be moved. Or, on a more positive note, a covered-up window, interesting wall material, or some other appealing feature may be exposed that can make the building more distinctive and tell its story.

A well-thought-through design is always better than winging it, but this does not mean needlessly obsessing over every detail when producing drawings. A common mistake that developers make is to strive for a very exacting set of construction documents, under the assumption that it will eliminate cost surprises. And although it *is* important to cover all the bases, in too many instances, something changes part way through the project and all the money spent creating extremely tight drawings ends up being money not well spent.

It is important to draw the distinction between an appropriate level of detail and quality control: even though it is not necessary to draw every detail, what *is* drawn has to be right. This ideally means having the drawings checked by an independent reviewer for errors—especially for misses in coordination between disciplines—before they are put out for bid and construction. It *always* takes less time and money to correct errors on paper than in the field!

KEY TAKEAWAYS

→ Although you do not need to have every detail documented in your construction drawings, starting with a reliable data set of existing conditions is critical. Invest in good bases, including a site survey and "as-built" of the building/space. Do not cut corners on this phase—spend the money to do a thorough job of both, and document them well.

→ Anticipate that the design will change in the field. Establish construction layout based on relationships, not precise measurements—for example, set up symmetrical elements as "equal" about a centerline, rather than trying to prescribe the exact dimensions. Then confirm it in the field.

→ Create flexible infrastructure. Challenge your MEP and structural designers to create efficient, adaptable systems that will allow spaces and uses to be modified efficiently over time. Build in extra conduits, chases, and access to electrical panels, roof penetrations, and other ways to expand and revise your design over time. It is always cheaper to do while the walls are open and before you are occupied.

the team that builds small

Developing a property requires a wide variety of skill sets and an aligned team of experienced individuals. As a developer you possess some of these skills, but you need to assemble a team to fill in gaps or skills you do not have. Be honest about what you do not know, and assemble your team accordingly. While entrepreneurs in general—and entrepreneurial developers in particular—assume they can figure it out, pursuing the "rugged

individualist" approach on your first project is a recipe for failure. Do not cut corners to save dollars on design and construction—especially if it is your first project. Consider those costs part of your "tuition" and the price to help build your brand, to enhance your capacity and understanding, and to ensure your project succeeds. Conversely, keep a tight eye on work process and products, as consultants and subcontractors can sometimes get out of control wanting to do more than the owner can afford. It is important to hire team members who understand the developer's vision and budget and share your interest in creating great outcome cost-effectively. The key members, roles, and responsibilities of the design and construction process include the following:

The developer is like a movie producer whose job is to make the concept a reality. They oversee every aspect of the project, from selecting and securing the site to hiring and managing the team to seeing that the bills get paid to leasing and managing—or selling the project. The smaller the developer, the more likely these tasks will be handled directly rather than contracted out. Developers can ply their trade either as the project owner or working for the project owner. In the former, the developer may produce the project on spec (i.e., without tenants beforehand) or as a build-to-suit (to the specifications of an identified lessee or purchaser). In the latter, the developer produces a project to the specifications of the owner for a fee (*fee development* or *development management*). The key distinction between the owner/developer and the fee developer is *risk*: one takes it; the other typically does not.

The owner, as noted above, can be the developer, the end user, or a property owner who contracts with a developer to build the project. If the building is on spec, the owner/developer takes all the risk. If the developer is not also the owner, allocation of

---

ABOVE: Small infill projects are typically complex, and team workshops are the best way to get all consultants aligned quickly to achieve the desired outcome. *(©2018 CRAFT Development)*

risk between developer and owner depends on their agreement. In a build-to-suit project, the developer typically takes all or most of the risk, but in fee development the owner typically takes all or most of the risk. To be successful, the developer must satisfy the owner (if it is not the developer), financiers, government officials, and the market.

If the developer is working for an end user, the end user, working with the developer, determines all specifics for the building, from the design to the budget. If the project is a spec building, meaning no tenant or buyer has been identified, the developer needs to try to understand what is in demand in the market based on market studies (see chapter 8, "Assessing Market Potential").

The architect works for the developer and communicates between the developer and general contractor. Often, on small projects, the owner/developer is also the architect. "The architect" is a contractual term and includes not just the architectural firm, but all the consultants who work for the architect. The architectural firm will have its own insurance for errors and omissions. Subject to the usual difficulties of getting payment on an insurance claim, this coverage can help if the architect details something wrong or leaves out important construction information but provides no relief if you or the contractor makes a mistake.

The general contractor (GC) works for the developer to lead the construction process. The GC usually has its own employees, plus a pool of subcontractors who perform work beyond the capabilities of the GC's staff. Contractors usually bid on the job and complete it for a set price. The GC does not normally construct the project but manages those who do. Smaller GCs may self-perform some trades. The GC guarantees the project will be completed at a certain price, at a certain date. GCs have their own financing sources and insurers.

The construction manager (CM) is not the same as a GC. The term CM can be confusing because it is used to refer to two different kinds of consultants: (1) one who represents the owner (or developer) in managing a GC during construction, or (2) one who

manages the construction process like a GC but does not take a GC's risk for budget and schedule. In (1), the CM manages a GC; in (2) the CM acts like one. In both cases, the CM acts as an agent of the owner/developer whose scope of work is the building process and related financial management. A GC takes the risk for producing the project on time and on budget. If the owner/developer hires a CM but no GC, the owner/developer is taking budget and schedule risk. This professional works for a fixed fee, usually a set percentage of the project cost. Small projects are unlikely to warrant a CM *and* a GC, especially if you have a good working relationship with a GC.

Subcontractors are generally the people who perform the various tasks related to constructing the project. Besides the commonly thought of framing, roofing, electrical, plumbing, HVAC, and painting subcontractors, the increasing level of complexity of construction has created a whole list of specialist subcontractors who are critical to a successful project. These may include contractors who specialize in insulation/energy efficiency, waterproofing, glazing, cabinetry and millwork, concrete grinding and finishing, metalwork, and more. A project may use as many as 30 or 40 subcontractors, each with a specialty. They are the ones who physically build the project.

An owner might hire certain contractors directly. These might include specialties like audiovisual installers, furniture installers, and IT specialists. They may do their work while the subcontractors are still completing the building. They answer to the owner, whereas subcontractors answer to contractor; it is important that they do not get in each other's way.

The user/tenant is sometimes not known at the time of design and construction. In other cases, the project is built specifically for an end user (either a buyer or tenant). In that case the user becomes part of the team, giving specifics on design, quality, cost, and so on. When a project is built for a specific tenant, the timing of the tenant's need for the space may drive the construction schedule and therefore the contracting strategy.

→ design and permitting

The design process can be the most fun part of the small development process, and it is where many key decisions need to be made that will affect both the project cost and the ultimate outcomes. The design process should accomplish three main objectives:

- bring physical life to a proposed program that will support the intended real estate business model;
- generate documents necessary to successfully gain approvals and construction permits; and
- provide the information needed to secure accurate project pricing, construction bids, and ultimately construct the project as intended.

Whether you supply it from within your organization or engage a third party, it is important that you have construction expertise on board *during the design process*. You and the designers need real-time guidance from someone who has experience managing the construction process and working with the trades to provide expertise on cost, schedule, constructability, and construction logistics to ensure that design decisions are properly informed by these critical and potentially costly considerations.

The design process should be approached as an iterative (vs. linear) process that accretes increasing detail and results in a series of refinements to the original design concept. As design progresses, concepts and solutions get evaluated for constructability and code compliance, checked for cost (which should include both first cost and life-cycle cost). At times the evaluation will result in abandoning an idea and trying again. The final design documents should reflect the best balance of original intent, compliance with codes, and ability to construct and deliver on budget.

The American Institute of Architects outlines three basic stages of design documentation:

- **Schematic design (SD):** These are design intent drawings that may be drawn by the developer or an architect working with the developer to test the vision and create a quantifiable program that can be translated to income projections and construction costs. SDs are rough depictions of the project goals and requirements and start the formal design process. This process used to be done with a fat pencil and lots of paper but now is more likely to be done by computer-assisted design (CAD). While the broad adoption of CAD has accelerated the production process, provides the ability to quickly test alternatives, and allows for more accurate drawings to scale,

> *The design process should be approached as an iterative rather than a linear process that accrues increasing detail through a series of refinements to the original design concept.*

its downside is that work products often look more "resolved" than they actually are. Because the result looks like a well-thought-out design, or a technically sound detail, it may not receive the same scrutiny and study as a similar design sketched by hand. This can mislead uninitiated developers at best, or result in approval of incomplete or poorly conceived designs at worst.

- **Design development (DD):** This starts the construction document process and is the basis for all subconsultants to undertake their work. As CAD systems have accelerated the design process, the point at which design development stops and construction documents begin has become much less clear. However, DD drawings are helpful for early pricing of the overall project and discussing cost-saving measures with your contractor as details and constructability issues really come into visibility. In some construction procurement models, the completion of DDs coincides roughly with the first time contractually meaningful pricing is obtained from the contractor (e.g., in a fast-track timeline with a guaranteed maximum price).

- **Construction documents (CDs):** These constitute the documentation needed to secure building permits and construct the finished product. They also form the basis of legal protections that you will need should something go wrong in the end. These are usually best done by an architect or engineer. In many jurisdictions the package can be developed by a draftsperson, but an architect's or structural engineer's stamp is needed to secure a permit for any but the simplest projects. The construction drawings add detailed information to the DDs, creating a set of pictorial and narrative instructions the contractors need to build the project.

The basic elements necessary for a permit typically entail building code compliance and "life safety" issues. While closely interrelated, the evaluation and review of these two areas may fall to different governmental agencies. Compliance with the local building code (universally based on the International Building Code in the United States) may be adjudicated by the municipal building department and life safety by another agency, perhaps at the state level. ADA or accessibility, health code, and other requirements are either embedded in or overlaid on the basic building code and can vary by location. Increasingly, "green" design requirements are becoming mandatory, so certain calculations and requirements for energy use, material selection, water conservation, and enhanced on-site stormwater management must also be documented as part of the permit package. Each of these requirements can require different disciplines and consultants, which can get expensive.

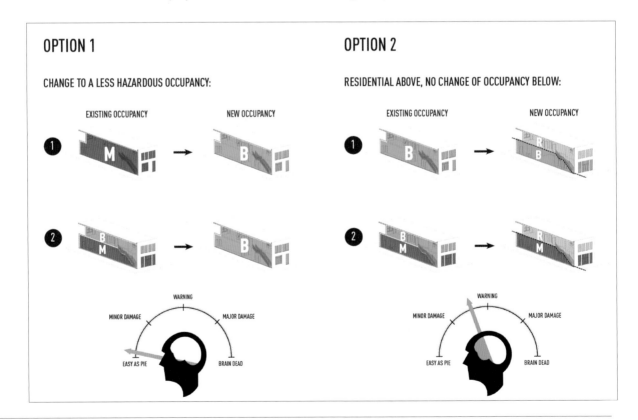

ABOVE: Eric Kronberg developed a graphic shorthand to help communicate "threshold" decisions for when program choices for small projects trigger extensive and expensive code requirements. (© *Kronberg Urbanists + Architects*)

from design to construction

The design process can be organized in several ways, which will affect engaging a contractor. The approach chosen can streamline design and construction processes, which can reduce upfront design costs, speed up the schedule, and enhance quality and constructability.

Design/bid/build is the conventional approach, wherein a full set of construction documents is completed and bid to several general contractors, most often to get a lump sum price. It is the most time-consuming process, and if you do not have contractor input during the design process, you risk spending a lot of time designing and detailing approaches that could be done more cost-effectively.

In *design assist,* a principal trade, such as mechanical systems, is contracted early and then participates as an essential member of the design team, working with the consulting designers. Note that this does not necessarily preclude bidding this trade upon completion of design.

With *design/build,* a trade (such as mechanical or fire protection) takes on even more design responsibility, essentially taking over the process based on a schematic design or criteria established by the architectural team. The contractor produces the detailed design and documentation, secures the permit, and builds to that design as part of a deferred submittal (meaning the drawings can be submitted at a date after the project permit has been issued, but before construction on that specific element can begin). Design/build can also extend to the entire general contractor relationship, where the owner simply engages a firm to turnkey design and build a project to meet the owner's specifications. Although design/build can potentially yield advantages in cost and schedule, a developer should be sure it has the capacity to monitor quality in this delivery method, since the architect now works for the contractor. For this reason, this method is most suited to simpler projects where the design criteria can be clearly stated before design begins.

Hybrid (construction manager at risk) is an approach entails simultaneously engaging the architect and a construction manager who will eventually morph into the general contractor. The architect and construction manager at risk work together as independent consultants to the owner in designing the project. Unlike design/build, in this method the architect and contractor remain independent of each other, each engaged directly by the owner. Later in the design process, the construction manager can move into the role of general contractor by engaging the trade contractors and guaranteeing a price and schedule to the owner. Because the contractor is already on board, this transition can occur much sooner, and you get the benefit of real-world pricing and constructability feedback as the design is evolving. You gain someone who intimately understands the details of the project and the design intent, ensuring your budget is more accurate and having fewer arguments about what you expected and what the contractor thought it was to build.

The design/build and hybrid methods can significantly accelerate the schedule by allowing early construction stages to get started while the design and procurement for later elements are being completed.

In addition, this method can actually provide more (and more transparent) price competition than the other methods described, because not only can you evaluate construction managers on the basis of their fee quotations at the beginning of the project, but

construction stages (e.g., demolition, excavation, site preparation, foundations) to get started while the design and procurement for later elements are being completed. This is also beneficial in adaptive use: having the demolition complete as construction drawings are underway often yields new opportunities to take advantage of hidden features or help avoid costly unknowns that cannot be seen. These methods also create better alignment of the team because the members work together from the beginning and are part of the decision-making process. With small, creative, and adaptive use projects, having all team members intellectually invested in the project from the start is essential to keeping on budget while achieving the design intent and desired outcome effectively.

> *Having the demolition complete as construction drawings get underway can provide opportunities to take advantage of hidden features that add character or help avoid costly unknowns that cannot be seen in advance.*

you also participate in the bidding process for each of the trades as they are procured when construction is ready to begin.

The design/build and hybrid methods can significantly accelerate the schedule by allowing early

ABOVE: Stripping out layers in older buildings always tends to reveal new design opportunities that add character and value to adaptive use projects. Demolition underway at Pivot Project's Sunshine Building. *(© Pivot Project)*

Small Lessons from the Trenches

THERE ARE MANY CONVENTIONS AND CONSTRUCTION PROCESS STANDARDS that are well developed after decades of evolution. But the challenges and tough lessons from working on smaller-scale projects bring key lessons that are worth emphasizing for those building *small*.

→ **INVEST IN GOOD BASE DRAWINGS.** Because many small projects are adaptive use of existing buildings, spending the money to get accurate base drawings of site conditions before construction begins is a good investment. Do not rely on drawings from permit files or from the broker to do your construction drawings. Hire someone to do a detailed as-built base drawing that accurately measures and locates all existing walls, structural members, openings, and so on. In the end this investment will save you money many times over.

→ **GOOD PLANS AND SPECS PAY FOR THEM-SELVES IN THE LONG RUN.** Architects and other designers should be involved during the construction phase to ensure quality and accuracy as work progresses and reveals conditions that might have been unknown at the start.

→ **INCLUDE A CONTINGENCY CONSISTENT WITH THE STAGE OF THE PROCESS.** The less you know for certain, the larger the contingency should be. This contingency is *not* the same as the contractor's contingency, which is the contractor's risk protection, not yours. When the pro forma is not working, do not convince yourself that "a 5 percent contingency should be plenty." Do the hard work of making the project work with a 10 percent contingency, and have money left over to spend at the end. Small projects have a smaller total budget, so 5 percent of a small budget will not go very far when the inevitable cost overrun emerges.

Guidance for contingency building is 15 to 20 percent at the very early concept/program stage, 10 to 15 percent at prebid, and 5 to 7.5 percent going into construction.

→ **PAY FOR AS-BUILT DRAWINGS UPON COM-PLETION.** If the project is being built to be held for the long term, it is important to have accurate documentation of the construction—not just to secure permits. Accurate as-built documents provide essential information for repair, replacement, maintenance, and as part of the basic marketing materials for the eventual sale of the property. It is worth the investment to have your architect or draftsperson update the final drawings to actual installed conditions, especially if a number of field changes were made during construction. The as-built information compiled during construction should be submitted in clear and complete form by the contractor so the architect can produce the as-built set. Spend the few extra dollars to have the drawings done in CAD. Contracts with both architect and contractor should provide for this service as part of the final scope.

→ **FIND OUT HOW MUCH WORK YOUR CON-TRACTOR SELF-PERFORMS.** Specialties like HVAC, plumbing, electrical, and sprinklers are normally bid out to subcontractors, but if you can find a contractor that does its own framing, concrete work, and demolition in house, you may save money on subcontactor markup. This is especially helpful in small projects, not only because it could save money, but also because it reduces the number of people that need to be coordinated, or who have their own overhead and profit to be covered by the project.

→ **PAY DIRECT FOR MATERIALS.** One way to save costs is to set up direct purchase accounts with all materials suppliers. Let the contractor order materials, but you pay directly, saving you the overhead and markup, in exchange for the contractor not having to manage billing you or making front-end payments. Be sure to ask for the "to the trade" discount, which can be significant. Be careful about ordering your own materials, however, because if something is wrong, it will be your problem, not the contractor's.

→ construction pricing

Just as there are different methods of procuring design and construction services, there are different types of contracts that set out the rules and understandings among the parties involved. With respect to pricing, the different forms of contracts for construction—and there are several—vary in two key respects:

- Who takes risk of budget, schedule, and quality?
- What is the basis of compensation (i.e., a fixed price or reimbursement of cost plus a fee)?

There are three basic types of construction pricing scenarios: lump sum, guaranteed maximum price, and cost plus.

Lump sum is the contract form most commonly used with a general contractor and is most appropriate when using the design/bid/build method of procurement.

Guaranteed maximum price (GMP) is the contract form most commonly used with a construction manager at risk. Pricing is based on the contractor's actual costs, with the GMP setting a cap on what the owner pays. It offers significantly more transparency into cost than does lump sum, along with protection of total price for the owner. However, this method of procurement and contracting generally requires a level of sophistication in both owner and contractor that may not be applicable to many small development projects, both because it is conceptually more complex and because it requires the owner to track construction costs much more closely than necessary (or possible) in a lump sum contract.

Cost plus (time and materials, or T&M) is an open-ended contract form most commonly used for limited scopes of work, where the work is difficult to define precisely or where schedule is the key driver. Pricing is based on the contractor's actual costs, whatever they end up totaling, plus a fee. It offers the same cost transparency as GMP but lacks any total price protection. An owner using this method must be able to monitor the contractor closely; clearly this works better when there is a high level of (warranted) trust between owner and construction manager. While a contract for "time and materials" might seem the best option because things can get done more efficiently and there are no change orders, T&M has huge risk implications because it puts absolutely *all* the risk on the owner/developer. There is a reason that general contractors almost always make trade contracts lump sum—they are pushing risk down to the subcontractors. T&M is justified if schedule is the primary driver, the owner knows how to manage, and/or the scope of work is so unclear that a lump sum (or a GMP) would leave too much money on the table. But an owner who builds everything T&M would not last very long.

CONTRACT PRICING MODELS

	Risk of budget, schedule, and quality	Basis of compensation
Lump sum	General contractor	Fixed price (not dependent on contractor's actual cost)
Guaranteed maximum price	Construction manager at risk	Actual cost of the work plus a fee, but with a guaranteed cap on total price no matter the cost to the contractor
Cost plus	Owner	Actual cost of the work plus a fee

Hire a Contractor or Act as Owner/Builder?

AS A SMALL DEVELOPER, you have a choice about whether to hire a company to oversee and take responsibility for managing the construction process or to do it yourself. The choice boils down to your own aptitudes, availability, and attitude toward risk. Some considerations follow.

IF YOU HIRE A CONTRACTOR

For a small developer, who may have little to no experience in construction, often the best process for getting from concept to finished project is to find an aligned contractor (whether general contractor or construction manager) to execute the construction phase. An experienced GC or CM can be invaluable. They understand the construction process; have experience in what might go wrong and how to prevent it; in tight markets they may have access to subs and materials that an inexperienced or new contractor may not have; and they bring the accounting, scheduling, and contracting know-how that can be very challenging for the small developer—especially if the developer has never done it before. Although you must not just turn things over to a contractor and stop paying attention, if you are careful, alert, and involved, you can benefit from a contractor's expertise and learn things along the way that will make you a better consumer of construction services and therefore a better developer.

General contractors and CMs at risk will also carry many of the required insurance policies. The developer should secure, or make sure the contractor has, an "all risk" or "course of construction" policy to cover work in progress. This covers the cost of replacing materials and construction underway should there be a fire or other damage to the project before the work is complete and occupied.

The contractor is responsible for gathering conditional and unconditional lien releases, which are your method of verifying that the GC is paying its subs. These should be submitted along with applications for payment each month. It is important to be rigorous about getting properly completed lien releases from everybody *before* making payment on an application. Lenders will insist on this protection, since a mechanic's lien can cloud title to a property in disruptive ways for the mortgage holder.

While the construction expertise and risk protection they afford can benefit the small developer, this benefit is not free. GCs and CMs at risk may add costs that sometimes cannot be sustained by smaller projects. These come in both the form of markups on costs and general conditions (which is the cost of personnel and infrastructure to manage the project in the field).

IF YOU ACT AS OWNER/BUILDER

If you have some experience in construction, another method is to work as an "owner/builder" (O/B). Many jurisdictions will permit building owners to act on their own behalf, overseeing the construction, coordinating the subs, and securing the inspections. However, sometimes this strategy requires that the owner warrant that it is not going to sell the building in the near future. It is essential to check with your local jurisdiction as to requirements for O/Bs.

An O/B takes on all responsibility a GC or CM at risk otherwise would, negotiating contracts and managing the subs, including making sure they are licensed and bonded, and writing clear and binding contracts for their work. Since no contractor is managing the overall process, the O/B will also be responsible for coordinating the work of all trade contractors. The O/B must also take responsibility for obtaining conditional and unconditional lien releases before paying the trade contractors. It is a common challenge in the building industry for mistakes to be continually pushed back and forth from one contractor to the other. A GC would normally shield the owner from these disputes, but the O/B must be prepared for a lot of finger-pointing and needs a strategy to confront conflicts head-on by regularly reviewing work progress and knowing what is happening when. It is important to keep good records of the work performed each day, who was on site, and how much they accomplished.

→ the construction process

Construction milestones include a "notice to proceed" to kick off construction, a temporary occupancy permit when you can begin to use the building, and a final occupancy permit when you are done with inspections and have approval to permanently occupy the building. The entire process ends when the final certificate of payment is issued, allowing the final check to be issued to the contractor.

The owner/developer determines when everything is ready for construction to start and keeps tabs on progress throughout by meeting with the architect and GC. These meetings are called owner-architect-contractor (OAC) meetings. If the contractor has been brought on board before the design process, OAC meetings start during the design phase. On small projects, where everyone (developer, architect, contractor) may be friends with professional relationships spanning many years, it is easy to lose rigor. Regardless of how well you know each other, implement and practice good process, including documenting changes, holding regular meetings with an agenda and minutes, and documenting requests for information and field changes.

Construction meetings, also known as OAC meetings, are typically run by the architect during design and by the GC during construction. Participants discuss progress, problems, and plans for the following weeks. Meeting every two weeks is recommended. Make sure someone is assigned to produce the meeting minutes, including key decisions made, changes made and why, and follow-up actions. Even when it does not appear there is anything to discuss, having a regular touch point—even for just 30 minutes—assures everyone stays in alignment and small issues do not fester into big problems.

ABOVE: Underground infiltration array under construction at RiverHouse. (© CRAFT Development)

CONTROLLING COSTS

Expectations relating to costs should be established at the start of the process. A realistic budget should be drawn up based on contractors' estimates. The developer should obtain estimates for as much as possible at the start: materials, labor, fees, permits, and so on. Allowances are useful budget line items when it is not possible to establish the cost of something, but enough information should be gathered to perform a commonsense evaluation and adjust as changes arise or more information is available. An effective design and estimating process uses continuous "value engineering," which is a term used by development professionals to mean a method of getting the most bang for your buck. While often thought of as the panicked effort to take money out of a project when it comes in over budget, it is not the same as cutting corners to save money. Instead, it is about ensuring quality while spending wisely, taking into consideration not just first cost but life-cycle cost as well.

Regardless of the method of procuring construction services, a competitive bidding process helps ensure fair and realistic costs. Bids should be used to create and maintain the budget. Bid documents are prepared by the architect. At least three bids should be solicited for each facet of the project. Subcontractors should be prequalified by the GC, then approved by the owner. For proper comparison, all bids should be for the same product quality and services. Costs should be written into the contract documents and then the contract reconciled against bills. Throughout the development process the developer should double-check and compare contracts to invoices to make sure everything is compliant.

Thinking to the future of your brand and company, take the time to really understand unit costs and track surprises. Accruing knowledge of what unit costs really are, how they are shifting over time, and what areas present the greatest potential for going over budget helps you build expertise and your value as a developer as your portfolio grows.

KEEPING ON SCHEDULE

As with costs, it is important to establish scheduling expectations and communicate with the team early. Major milestones should be identified, and weekly task targets should be set. The team should be kept on track with regular meetings and reporting—do not just call a meeting when there is a problem. Establish a regular meeting time and day and follow it. It can be a short meeting, but there are always things to go over and review, discuss, or troubleshoot, and without a meeting they may not rise to the surface. Besides keeping the project on track, use the meeting to issue specific weekly goals. This gives everyone involved a clear sense of the priorities—and a sense of accomplishment when they are met—while keeping everyone aligned to the vision.

GETTING THE QUALITY YOU WANT

Maintaining quality begins in the design phase. Careful plans and specifications pay for themselves in the long run. Architects and other designers need enough time to produce high-quality work. Architects should remain involved during construction to ensure that the development proceeds per their designs.

Bespoke (custom-built) projects require bespoke teams. With small projects—especially unique custom projects—it is important to build a sense of ownership and excitement among the team members. True craftspeople like to show what they can do and be part of something special. Select contractors and subs who are excited to be a part of what you are creating and do not consider it just another job or revenue stream. Their opinions and ideas should be considered to give them a sense of authorship in the end product.

Inspectors play a key role in quality assurance. It is important to hire the right inspectors—those with expertise in specific building systems—to provide third-party verification that the project is being built in accordance with the design. Municipal inspectors will review your project only for code compliance, which is not a very high bar. The architectural team is also not your inspector; their only duty is to generally (i.e., *not* exhaustively) review the project for compliance with the contract documents so that they can certify payment applications. To protect your interests, you need to hire special inspectors to scrutinize and test key building components during the construction

> *Value engineering is not the same as cutting corners to save money. It is about ensuring high quality while spending wisely, taking into consideration first cost and life-cycle cost as well.*

process: structural, envelope construction, and the major building systems. Because the inspectors work for you, they act on your behalf—not the architect, contractor, or municipality.

PAYMENTS

A schedule of payments extends throughout the entire construction period. The requisitions for payment are issued by the contractors, and payment is made by the GC or CM at risk. Payments are typically made monthly by the developer. Other contractors are paid per their individual contracts. Usually 10 percent is retained from each payment until the project is complete. This *retainage* is paid at the end to ensure that the job is completed and meets contract specifications. However, in some labor-constrained markets, a 10 percent retainage is a nonstarter for more qualified and in-demand subcontractors, so you may be required to reduce the percentage, provide for releasing early-work contractors, or even forgo retainage in some cases. Make a clear decision as to what the effect of requiring retainage may be on your pool of potential contractors.

COMPLETION AND OCCUPANCY

When the project has reached a stage of completion where it is suitable for occupancy, the contractor and architect will prepare a certificate of substantial completion. At this stage, small details may still need to be completed, so a list of these items—the "punch list"—is included with the certificate to indicate the parties' agreement as to what remains to be done before the project is fully complete. Upon substantial completion, the owner takes possession of—and responsibility for—the project.

Separate and distinct from the certificate of substantial completion, the local jurisdiction must issue a certificate of occupancy before the building can be legally occupied. The certificate of occupancy is the jurisdiction's indication that the project meets applicable code and is safe.

A number of things remain to be done after substantial completion before a project is finally complete. The process of completing these items is known as "close out" and includes the following:

- final testing and commissioning of building systems, if required;
- completion of punch list items;
- training of building operations staff;
- delivery of all operating and maintenance documentation;
- registrations and warranties for all equipment;
- as-built documentation; and
- final accounting for project pricing.

Because changes inevitably happen during construction, there will almost certainly be "out of scope changes," or changes that go beyond the contract and will need to be paid for. Changes will be added to the project accounting throughout the course of construction, altering the agreed contract sum. Reconciliation and full accounting for these change orders must be completed as part of close out. There may also be disputes and claims that have not been resolved, and the parties need to reach settlement on these items before the project is closed out.

Once all of the close-out items have been completed, the contractor will issue a final application for payment, which will include release of the retainage. The construction phase ends when the final payment is issued.

small in **your**
community

TIPS FOR REGULATORS AND CIVIC LEADERS

IN COLLABORATION WITH MARGARET O'NEAL

Working in communities around the country, we increasingly see interest in small-scale development. The question most often posed by civic leaders, and even community activists, is: "How do we attract developers and development that is more appropriate for our community—projects that are smaller, don't

ABOVE: Specialized Real Estate Group repurposed a former warehouse and industrial building as a new third place in downtown Fayetteville, Arkansas. *(© Timothy Hursley)*

look like they've been stamped out from someone else's template, and add to our economic vitality and sense of place?"

The answer is not simple. It takes a very different attitude by the agencies that regulate and oversee development, from what tends to be common practice and the perceived role of "regulation" in most cities. It requires updating and refining existing codes. It requires a culture of being willing to experiment and let projects evolve, rather than trying to prescribe the precise outcome 10 years hence. It requires understanding that long-term economic resilience comes from a combination of maintaining community identity, adapting to rapidly changing markets, and embracing change through more flexible permitting to ensure your economy stays vital and continues to thrive. More than anything, it requires working as a *partner* with developers to find creative solutions, not as a barrier whose role is to administer the codes verbatim.

These are not easy shifts, especially when highly detailed codes and regulations have been created to ensure they will meet the test of legal recourse. But the process of creating "litigation-proof" codes often eliminates the opportunity for interpretation, or the ability to break the rules when the proposed idea is a good one—and one that was not envisioned when the code was written. This dilemma is evident all too often. Just visit the most appealing and authentic places, vibrant main streets, or interesting neighborhoods in any town, and odds are they could never be built under today's codes and standards.

Recognizing the challenge that regulatory attitudes and tools have created for small development, both new construction and adaptive use/redevelopment that is desirable to so many communities, three organizations—the National Trust's Research and Policy Lab (RPL), the Project for Lean Urbanism, and the Project for Code Reform (under the Congress for the New Urbanism)—have focused their attention on how the public sector's role can better facilitate small-scale development as a path to more vibrant, economically diverse, and resilient places.

RPL has grouped the impediments into four categories: regulatory, technical, financial, and market. After evaluating the barriers to adaptive use in 11 cities and looking at successes and failures, the organization, in partnership with ULI, published *Untapped Potential: Strategies for Revitalization and Reuse.*[7]

The Project for Code Reform has developed a guide for communities to tackle those elements of their existing codes that create the biggest impediments to great places. Recognizing that code overhauls are expensive, long-term endeavors that require considerable governmental capacity, the Project for Code Reform's publication *Enabling Better Places: Users' Guide to Zoning Reform* provides a range of practical, low-hanging fruit and areas in existing code to focus on. The document provides four primary principles that set the stage for tackling reform and then offers communities a list of specific areas to refine in the near term, medium term, and long term. It is available as a download.[8]

The Project for Lean Urbanism has done more than identify the issues. Armed with a grant from the Knight and Kresge foundations, in 2015 it began a three-year program to research, analyze, and then pilot ways of "Making Small Possible" (see sidebar).

Of greatest importance to advancing the development of *small* is the idea that regulations—and the signal they send to the market—are the one area where communities can directly influence the outcome. Through local leadership—either elected or grassroots activism—changes to key regulations that often form the unintended barrier to *small* are the simplest way to fulfill a community's desire and support of *small*, in pursuit of more fine-grained and economically resilient development.

This chapter identifies three areas that encompass the majority of regulatory barriers faced by small developers: zoning and development standards; parking; and building codes.

Making Small Possible

BRIAN FALK, DIRECTOR, CENTER FOR APPLIED TRANSECT STUDIES AND THE PROJECT FOR LEAN URBANISM

A PROGRAM OF THE NONPROFIT Center for Applied Transect Studies, with funding from the Knight Foundation and the Kresge Foundation, the Project for Lean Urbanism was created by a group of new urbanists searching for ways to overcome the difficulties of small-scale development. Investigation quickly showed that such projects bore disproportionate burdens at nearly every stage in the development process. The Project for Lean Urbanism was created to raise awareness of the value of small-scale development, identify the problems it faces, conduct pilot projects, and provide tools for "Making Small Possible," the project's slogan.

One of its tools is called the Pink Zone—an area where the red tape is "lightened." The Project for Lean Urbanism has created a free *Pink Zone Manual* and provides technical assistance to cities that want help with the process. The creation of a Pink Zone has three phases: assessment, workshop, and implementation. First, an assessment tool called the Lean Scan identifies obstacles to small-scale development, assets that can be used, and potential locations for the Pink Zone. Obstacles are often found in zoning codes—maximum densities, minimum lot sizes, maximum lot coverage, minimum setbacks, open-space requirements, minimum parking requirements, and prohibition of mixed

uses. Underused assets often include not only empty buildings and lots, but also people, businesses, and organizations. A location for a Pink Zone might be a neighborhood that needs revitalization, or one where redevelopment is already happening and small-scale development is seen as a way to moderate the pace of growth and allow residents to participate in it.

The Lean Scan is used to identify the issues as well as the people who can address them in the next phase, then a workshop is conducted to create new protocols for the Pink Zone. For example, planning officials and staff are often asked to address issues found in the zoning code. The solution might require only a text

ABOVE: Participants in Pink Zone workshops create new protocols to address issues such as those found in zoning codes, permitting procedures, and financing. *(© Gianni Longo)*

change, or it might need the creation of an overlay district with multiple changes to enable small-scale development. A Lean Code Tool has been created to guide changes to local zoning codes. Procedural changes might also be made to streamline the permitting process. Preapproved building plans might be provided to make it easier, faster, and cheaper for novice developers to construct the kinds of buildings needed in the Pink Zone, and parcels might be preapproved for development when those building plans are used. Elected officials might be asked to adopt the International Existing Building Code to encourage renovation by reducing obstacles in the building code. Community lenders might agree to create programs targeted to the Pink Zone, enabling small-scale development while also satisfying their requirements for the Community Reinvestment Act.

Other goals of the workshop are to set the exact boundaries of the Pink Zone and to identify small-scale developers and entrepreneurs for new projects. The area is typically small enough for the projects to have an effect and for the city to be willing to experiment with new ways of doing things. The projects should be ready to start soon to take advantage of and evaluate the new protocols.

In some cases, conditions in an area are such that it is not likely to attract development investment, even after making those changes. Owners may have the desire to develop their properties, but the market will not support their specific plans. The most common response is to leave the property fallow and wait for the market to change. But the choice is not all or nothing. In the meantime, owners can use their properties in other ways. With the ultimate goal of permanent buildings, they can start as modestly as tents and tables, or trailers or containers. Or a one-story building might be justified while a three-story is not. With the goal of a retail store, they can start with a simple market, or with the goal of a restaurant, they can start with food trucks. These "Meantime Uses," as the Project for Lean Urbanism calls them, allow property owners and entrepreneurs not only to act rather than wait, to take small steps rather than no steps, and to

CONTENTS

make land useful, but also to improve market conditions by activating properties and demonstrating the viability of development and business opportunities.

Along the way, they also learn about the market and the industry, and how to operate within them. Meantime Uses have even more potential when coordinated among multiple properties, such as along a neighborhood main street. The coordination could be as simple as hosting events at the same time, or more involved, such as shared branding and marketing, curation of vendors, or managing operations, each benefitting from the work of the other to bring customers and attention to the area.

When the same requirements are placed on all projects regardless of scale, they create a disproportionate burden for the small projects. Communities that recognize the value of small-scale economic development and want to level the playing field can look to the Project for Lean Urbanism for tools to make it possible.

From outdated zoning codes to burdensome parking requirements to conflicting building and fire codes, the challenges and complexity of codes are daunting.

ABOVE: Rather than overhaul a zoning code, the Lean Code Tool offers strategies for faster, targeted repairs. www.leanurbanism.org

zoning and development standards

Zoning is typically developed with the big picture—and the big development project—in mind. Too often codes and zoning are written to guide large projects and direct the outcome to be compatible with the existing community, or its long-term vision. Conversely, zoning is rarely tested for how it will enable small projects to thrive or be accomplished. A finer-grained look at zoning may be useful for promoting *small*. For example, when enacting new codes and design standards, a simple test would be to look at beloved buildings or streets in your town and ask: "Could these be built today if this code was implemented?"

For small developers, the ability to secure a project approval is generally seen as the highest-risk aspect of real estate development. As a result, the cost of capital for predevelopment—or "preapproval processes"—is the most expensive part of the development process. It is not uncommon for preapproval equity to cost three to four times as much as what capital might cost for actual construction. And if approvals take a long time, that high-cost capital adds significant cost to the project by creating a heavy front-end expenditure that has to be borne through the entire life cycle of the project. If communities truly want smaller scale, fine-grained development, a clearer and more right-sized approval process can greatly improve the attractiveness for high-quality developers to enter the market. By making approvals for good projects (ones that demonstrate consistency with community vision) faster, the heavy burden of front-end approvals can be greatly reduced and allow more dollars to be higher-quality development, directed to community benefits, or even lower prices.

REGULATIONS AND PROCESS

To understand this process, it is important to understand the tools and regulations that small developers—and the community in which they work—must

ABOVE: A critical component of any regulatory change is ensuring that uses that meet today's market are allowed in buildings that served a different purpose during another era. Warehouses turned into residential townhouses in Portland, Oregon's Pearl District. (© 2017 CRAFT Development)

respond to, to obtain approvals. Although the details of each community's regulatory tools and processes are attuned to the community personality and state land use laws, there are generally four major tools:

- general or comprehensive plans;
- zoning and land use codes;
- design guidelines; and
- building codes and subdivision standards.

COMMON ZONING CHALLENGES FACED BY *SMALL*

The vast majority of zoning codes were written decades ago to encourage low-density, single-use development that separated and buffered perceived "conflicting uses" while accommodating—or some would argue, prioritizing—the growing number of cars. This is at odds with the vision of *small* and its promotion of authentic, human-scaled development that supports local economies. Some municipalities have begun to overhaul outdated zoning codes in favor of zoning that supports higher densities, walkable mixed-use neighborhoods, and public transportation alternatives. Many cities are unable to take on a complete code rewrite but instead are adopting new zoning districts and updating development standards to be more in line with smaller-scale development.

In 2017, the city of Baltimore's zoning code, "Transform Baltimore," was put into effect. The new code promotes opportunities for walkable, mixed-use redevelopment while preserving neighborhood character. The code lays out a set of predictable rules for business owners and developers and presents information in easy-to-read tables.

In 2010, the city of Denver adopted form-based code for nearly all property within the city. At the same time, the city created the Division of Development Services, which is outside the planning department and is tasked with streamlining the approval process. The form-based code was adopted because the city believed the more traditional zoning was outdated and had become a barrier to sustainable growth. The new code encourages mixed-use, compact development, pedestrian-friendly streets, and shared parking.

The following are common zoning and development standards that hinder small developers.

- **Use limitations:** Most of the original zoning codes segregated urban neighborhoods by land use with all of the residential uses in one area, the commercial uses in another, industrial uses in another, and so on. Furthermore, most residents had to drive to get from one area of use to another. For developers working in this environment, converting an older structure to an alternative use not supported by the underlying zoning or mixing uses within a single building is difficult and time consuming. Often, developers must apply for a variance, which can be an uncertain process and requires detailed "findings" that demonstrate why the project would be compromised by not being granted the variance. If a really good use or design solution requires a variance to proceed—and that variance is discretionary, requiring hearings and heavy documentation—the cost of pursuing the variance may not be warranted, and the project will never get started.

- **Rezoning:** In other circumstances, the developer can apply to rezone the property, which is also a discretionary approval. Rezoning a single parcel is often difficult without support from general plan policies and can add months of delay to a project—increasing both costs and uncertainty. Some of the more positively disruptive and interesting mixed uses that have evolved over the last decade (food trucks, pop-up retail, cohousing) do not fit neatly into existing categories. Allowing them to happen requires creativity on the part of the regulating agency in how it interprets existing codes, or collaboration with the developer to get to a shared understanding on how the existing codes might be interpreted.

- **Incompatible development standards:** Many contemporary development standards are written under an assumption that development will be working on a "clean slate" or empty parcel. *Small* is often about repurposing existing structures for new uses. Requirements written for new development (setbacks, parking requirements, minimum unit size, life safety, or open-space requirements) can be difficult, if not impossible, to achieve with an existing structure. In many cases, today's development standards makes adaptive use financially or functionally infeasible, leading to demolition of the structure and replacement with something new, more expensive, and potentially far less interesting.

- **Nonconforming properties:** Nonconforming structures and uses may have been built before current zoning standards and now no longer comply. Nonconforming uses are often allowed to continue, as long as the current use remains in operation. But a change in use or major renovation would trigger bringing the structure into compliance. Although bringing all community structures in line with current codes is a well-meaning policy objective, the economic

OPPOSITE: The city of Paso Robles, California, created an aggressive incentive effort to help use arts as a catalyzing tool to bring new energy to small retail spaces in downtown. *(© CRAFT Development)* **ABOVE:** Tecela's 761–771 NW First Street in Miami's Little Havana neighborhood comprises four contemporary "brownstones" (multifamily townhouses), each with four apartments and zero parking. Before starting development, developer Andrew Frey led a four-year effort to change city zoning to allow developments of up to 10,000 square feet with no required parking if located near transit. *(© Michael Stavaridis)*

reality of these requirements discourages reinvestment in the property. This leads to a long, slow downward spiral of blocks and neighborhoods as landlords refuse to reinvest and the cost of redeveloping the property cannot be rationalized because of compressed property values.

- **Zoning mismatch:** When blocks or parcels are "upzoned," it allows new construction that is much larger than what currently exists ("highest and best use," in conventional wisdom), and existing small buildings become vulnerable to disinvestment and demolition. If the zoning code allows an eight-story office building on a site more suited to a two-story ground-floor retail and residential walkup, the latter is not viewed as the highest and best use of the site. However, as Kevin Cavenaugh of Guerilla Development notes, it may be the highest and best use for the neighborhood. The two-story walkup may contribute more to the economic and social diversity of the community, but it would be unlikely to be pursued because it is not "maxing out" the site.
- **Process complexity:** Zoning codes gain complexity with each new overlay, revised standard, and additional definition. As a result, zoning approval in many cities has become highly transactional, requiring time-consuming one-off solutions for each project. Small developers often have less capacity—time, money, and carrying costs—to navigate these complex requirements.

ZONING THAT WORKS FOR *SMALL*

Given the significant role zoning plays in defining what is possible and how difficult an approval process can be, the following new techniques and tools have emerged to remove some of the inherent impediments to *small*:

Explore form-based codes. Some cities are experimenting with or adopting "form-based" zoning codes. Form-based codes focus on the physical character of buildings and how they relate to streets and public spaces, rather than solely on land use. This kind of zoning is reminiscent of how great neighborhoods and blocks live today, with well-designed, older buildings that frame the public realm or create the streetscape, but over their life span have been able to accommodate and adapt to varied uses as the market demanded. Because land use is less strictly segregated in form-based codes, they often align better with valued older buildings as well as older and smaller blocks. Examples of cities that have adopted form-based codes include Denver, Miami, and Buffalo.

Reduce the cost nonconformance. If a community goal is to preserve interesting, existing building stock and encourage reinvestment in properties constructed before current zoning codes, special consideration needs to be given to removing the arbitrary nature of nonconformance standards. Increasing the length of time by which nonconforming uses can remain in place (amortization period) is also an important tool, by encouraging investment in businesses or the buildings that are worthy of keeping.

Create new zone districts. As mentioned above, many planners are thinking about the creation of new zone districts and overlay districts that allow a greater mix of uses and reduce the need for variances and changes in use, or as described in the Project for Lean Urbanism's Pink Zones, are removing red tape and increasing innovation in targeted areas. These districts should align open space, setbacks, and minimum lot sizes to reflect valued historic patterns.

Remove barriers. Removing key barriers that prevent change of use in existing vacant and under-used buildings is important. Cities should consider establishing provisions within the zoning code for appropriate and compatible "sister uses" that can ease transition to a new use by creating more certainty and reducing red tape.

→ parking

Ask any experienced architect or urban designer what really influences the form, footprint, and character of buildings, especially small infill buildings, and you will always get the same answer: parking.

While mobility, and with it parking, is undergoing significant disruption, most zoning codes and community policies are still slavishly responding to a post–World War II culture of the single-occupant, privately owned vehicle and the perceived need for close-by parking. The century-long expectation, and hence behavior, is that parking should be plentiful, free (or at least cheap), and easy to find. And so public policy has encoded this in standards for decades, requiring new projects to "self-park" their anticipated demand, ensuring there would be no need to share spaces or use land resources more efficiently. This has led to an excessive amount of the built environment being unbuilt, but paved over. A 2018 study by Eric Scharnhorst of the Research Institute for Housing America used satellite images and other information to examine, in five cities, the amount of land taken up by parking. Using number of parking spaces per household as one of its measures, the study found that New York City, which is very dense and efficient in its land use, has 0.6 parking spaces per household, whereas Jackson, Wyoming, has a whopping 27 spaces per household.[9]

COMMON PARKING BARRIERS FACED BY *SMALL*

The vast majority of zoning codes include minimum requirements for off-street parking for most development projects outside downtown areas, adding construction and land costs that small reuse or new construction projects cannot bear. In addition, abundant parking—often in excess of local codes or emerging trends—is still viewed by lenders as necessary to secure project financing.

The burden of parking requirements is one of the most oft-cited challenges for small and large developers alike. According to Kronberg Wall Architects, the average parking space costs $16,167 to construct, when land and pavement are included. Underground parking is rarely feasible for small projects—both because of the high costs of construction (often three to five times the cost of a surface lot) and the few spaces required for a small project, which combined with drive aisles make parking very inefficient.

Compounding this challenge is that parking standards written for uses of another time (when everyone working in an office had a car and a private office) often do not reflect current trends (coworking, where people may drop in for an hour or two, and given more central location, will use alternative transportation). As a consequence small sites have to be aggregated and parking done in large blocks to make economic sense—leading to bigger projects and vast amounts of parking that destroy the blockscape

---

ABOVE: Camp and The LAB in Costa Mesa, California, converted obsolete industrial properties into the "anti-mall," starting with thinking about parking lots as part of the place-based retail experience. (© *CRAFT Development*)

Payment in Lieu of Parking

STEFFEN TUROFF, PRINCIPAL AND DIRECTOR OF PLANNING STUDIES/PACIFIC REGION, WALKER CONSULTANTS

AS SOME CITIES BEGIN TO ADDRESS PARKING HOLISTICALLY, the creation of parking districts allows conveniently located and efficiently shared "phantom" spaces to be created in a larger pool, which facilitates a "park once" strategy. Charging a per space "payment in lieu" to help fund the creation and maintenance of these spaces allows a small developer to use its full site, while supporting a broader parking strategy that benefits the entire district.

A frequent finding in many downtown parking analyses is that the supply of private parking in a commercial district is both the largest number of parking spaces and least utilized. Requiring parking nearly always translates into effectively requiring *reserved* parking. An oversupply of empty private parking spaces is one of many unintended, negative consequences of cities' minimum parking requirements, another being additional cost of building and additional asphalt or concrete space taking over valuable downtown land.

Making required parking available to the public can be onerous or impractical. Instead, offering developers the opportunity to pay in lieu of constructing required parking spaces reduces or eliminates this oversupply of underused parking spaces, allowing a commercial district to accommodate more productive development with fewer parking spaces. Payment in lieu of required parking reduces the amount of land devoted to rarely or never-used parking spaces while making it easier and less expensive to build or redevelop desirable land uses.

Thoughtful planning practices are leading to the phasing out of minimum parking requirements in many downtowns, from Buffalo to San Diego. One irony, however, is that a minimum parking requirement on the books, in some form, is necessary to implement the fee. Otherwise, there is no unit by which to calculate how much fee to pay. This need not be a bad thing. Public parking is expensive for a city to provide—both to build, and to operate and maintain. Requiring a one-time payment from developers, even if just a fraction of the full cost of building a parking space, can provide much-needed funding.

The cost of such fees depends on multiple factors and should depend on the uses planned for the fees, surface spaces, structured spaces, parking enhancements, or substitutes (such as sidewalks to remote lots or bicycle lanes or parking). Although it is intuitive that the fee equal the cost to build a space, setting fees that high is often not productive; there is little point in charging fees that would match what a developer would pay to build its own parking, particularly if the goal is to encourage shared parking, contributions to public parking funds, and less overbuilding of parking. Further, in most small cities, rarely if ever will a critical mass of fees sufficient to build a parking structure be paid in a reasonable amount of time.

Fees can reasonably represent a fraction of actual costs based on policy priorities or when multiple land uses share parking and each contributes to the cost of providing spaces. If parking generates revenue, it can be reasonable to subtract the revenue per space from the cost to build when calculating the parking in lieu fee charged.

Construction is not the only cost cities must pay to provide public parking. The cost to operate and maintain spaces—an unpleasant discovery when the cost of deferred maintenance adds up—can total millions of dollars. Many cities fail to budget and find themselves strapped to pay these costs; for example, $200 to $250 per space annually for maintenance costs is a reasonable expectation. The cost to operate parking is additional and varies based on multiple factors, including the extent to which access controls are in place. For this reason, an ongoing fee to help cities cover the costs of providing public parking, in addition to, or in place of a one-time upfront fee, is a reasonable fee to charge a developer in lieu of requiring parking, which may cost the developer even more.

that *small* seeks to create and the community says it wants.

Two of the most common parking barriers faced by *small* are high parking minimums and inflexible parking requirements.

- **High parking minimums:** Many zoning codes include formulas requiring a minimum amount of parking based on the zoned use. Many of these formulas are outdated and do not represent the realities of the market, public transportation alternatives, the walkability of neighborhoods, current rates of car ownership, and rising popularity of ride-sharing and ride-hailing apps. Minimums are typically by use and do not reflect the benefits of mixed use and changing demands throughout the day. Residential units require more parking at night, whereas office may need it only during the day, meaning one space could potentially meet both needs.

- **Inflexible parking requirements:** Many cities use one-size-fits-all parking requirements, which eliminate the opportunity for context-sensitive development. Parking demands will differ between neighborhoods or commercial corridors, depending on context, availability, and quality of transit infrastructure, and proximity to residential areas.

CREATIVE PARKING SOLUTIONS

Following are some of the ways a locality might more creatively customize parking requirements to local conditions.

Right-size parking requirements near transit. Seeking diversity, density, and accessibility, many cities are now focusing on multimodal transit, enhanced bike and pedestrian infrastructure, and car-sharing services. Accordingly, many planners are seeking to reduce or eliminate parking requirements for projects in proximity to transit nodes or in dense, walkable neighborhoods. As an example, the general standard of 1.5 spaces per residential unit in some

jurisdictions may be reduced to 0.75 to 0.5 per unit when readily accessible, frequent, and high-quality transit is nearby. In Minneapolis, residential projects with 50 or fewer units, located outside of downtown, can be built with no parking facilities as long as the site is no more than a quarter-mile from transit operating with 15-minute frequencies. This helps reduce development costs, and the savings translate to lower rents or sales prices.

In 2017, Buffalo, New York, became the first major city to completely eliminate parking requirements as part of the city's Buffalo Green Code. City officials found that excessive parking requirements caused a number of problems, including making historic preservation more difficult, and destroying the urban character of older neighborhoods because buildings often had to be torn down to provide more parking.

Following Buffalo, Hartford, Connecticut, also eliminated its parking minimums in an effort to spur development while making the city more pedestrian-friendly. By no longer mandating a specific number of spaces, the city is allowing the developer to determine how much parking the market demands.

ABOVE: Parking stackers are one way to accommodate more cars in less space. Given the higher ceiling height required to stack cars, forward-looking developers are considering how that space might be adaptively used in an era when parking is no longer needed. (© CRAFT Development)

In 2015, Miami adopted a new ordinance that eliminated all parking requirements for projects of less than 10,000 square feet that were located within one-half mile of a transit station or a quarter mile from a bus line, but not closer than 500 feet from single-family or duplex zoning.

Allow shared and off-site parking. Multiple properties on the same block may have differing peak parking needs and should be allowed to share use of a single parking facility located within a reasonable distance. In Austin, Texas, both on-site and off-site parking may be shared between different properties, subject to approval of a shared parking plan.

According to Costa Mesa, California, city code, The Harper, an event and banquet center, would require 86 parking spaces. However, the planning commission is allowing the center to have just 15 spaces on site and to take advantage of shared parking nearby.

Depending on the density and walkability of a neighborhood, the distance to off-site parking may be extended to provide more flexibility.

Consider restored parking spaces. Many small sites are fronted or surrounded by full curb cuts (think gas stations, garages, etc.). As small projects restore the public realm and associated sidewalks and curbs and gutters, on-street parking spaces are restored to the city's reservoir. Regulators should allow these spaces to be counted toward partial fulfillment of a required parking count.

Develop parking maximums. Changing a minimum parking requirement to a maximum parking requirement allows parking to be created in areas where the market values it. Parking maximums prevent overparking and devote more space to people and businesses. While eliminating parking minimums is increasingly common, parking maximums are less widely used. Since 1989, Zurich has mandated maximums to protect the city's urban character from being degraded by having too much parking. In 2004, as part of an overall transportation policy, London established parking maximums throughout its entire metropolitan area. More recently, in 2017, Mexico City joined the club, in an effort to make housing more affordable and reduce traffic and air pollution. In certain high-density neighborhoods in Chicago, parking maximums of 1.1 to 2.0 spaces per residential unit are mandated. Similarly, San Francisco mandates no more than 1.0 space per unit in high-density areas.

Manage parking at a district level. Like other critical resources (water, sewer) parking should be viewed as infrastructure and managed in a district sense to optimize value and effective use of resources. Parking districts incorporate many of the discussed techniques and treat parking as a resource that can be shared among varied users.

Create a parking clearinghouse. Phoenix's parking district strategy matches surplus spaces with underparked areas and then facilitates leasing of those spaces. This allows the city to approve projects without their having to provide additional permanent parking on site.

Provide exemptions for older buildings. Many cities provide exemptions from parking requirements for affordable housing projects. This incentive should also be applied to older buildings. The city of Baltimore waives parking requirements for structures more than 50 years old or properties that have received historic tax credits. The city of St. Petersburg, Florida, has an overlay for historic buildings that waives parking requirements.

Unbundle parking. Separating the cost of parking from the development itself can allow market demand for parking to be met while decreasing the price of housing for those who do not require parking. Cambrian Rise, a multifamily project in Burlington, Vermont, unbundled parking from its leasing agreements and promotes all of the ways you can get around without owning a vehicle in its marketing materials.

→ building codes

Building codes are state laws governing the design, construction, alteration, and maintenance of structures. They specify the minimum requirements to adequately safeguard the health, safety, and welfare of building occupants. The United States does not have a national building code or energy code; instead, states or local governments can choose to adopt one of the national model codes, a modified version of the model code, or their own state-specific code.

COMMON CODE BARRIERS FACED BY *SMALL*

Navigating a complex codes regime (see sidebar, "Developer's Viewpoint on Codes") can be a barrier for developers of any size or skill level, but it is particularly challenging to small developers. A list of common challenges follows.

- **Process complexity:** The various building, energy, and accessibility codes are often managed by different municipal departments, which can make plan approval time consuming, confusing, and expensive.
- **Conflicting codes:** Code requirements may conflict with historic preservation standards, especially those triggered by historic tax credit programs. Furthermore, conflicting terms or provisions may prevail between existing codes, such as the energy code and the fire code.

- **Opaque, arbitrary, or inconsistent approval process:** In many municipalities, permit approval depends on the judgment of code officials who may lack expertise in building reuse projects. In addition, a developer may be able to meet code on one project, but not another, depending on interpretation and the willingness of the code official to allow alternative solutions.
- **Upgrades triggered by change of use:** Changing the use of an existing structure (such as converting a class B office building to residential use) triggers a "change of use" and can lead to all kinds of code upgrade requirements, which may make the project no longer feasible. While many of these may be driven by life safety issues learned through the years, some have become overlapping or outdated and yet are still required to complete the project.

ABOVE: Transforming, underused but character-contributing buildings is a desired outcome for many communities. But too often costly and burdensome land use codes, parking requirements, and code-mandated upgrades make demolition and new construction the only economically viable option. All the benefits of adaptive use need to be considered as part of a holistic review and approval process. *(Right: Liz Dunn; left: ©2013 Jeff Beck)*

SOME SOLUTIONS

Some forward-thinking localities have addressed the problem of codes that do not work. A few ideas follow:

Write new code for rehab and reuse. Facing the codes barrier head-on, many municipalities are adopting building and energy codes specifically for reuse projects. The International Code Council has created a new code to specifically address reuse of existing structures, including their alteration, repair, addition, or change in occupancy. Localities should start there. The city of Los Angeles's Adaptive Reuse Ordinance is one example of code designed for reuse. It provides flexibility in life safety and fire measures through the approval and permitting process.

Create flexibility in the existing code. In many instances, code officials can provide flexibility in meeting code, if given the correct guidance. Code officials who are encouraged to be open to acceptable alternative solutions to code compliance when it comes to existing buildings have the power to alleviate undue financial burden on small developers.

Allow outcome-based or performance-based compliance. Many states and municipalities are experimenting with "outcome-based" compliance, which allows a project sponsor to comply by verifying actual energy use against the predicted baseline of the applicable code.

Provide coordinated technical assistance. Provide a central place where developers can get help navigating complex regulatory processes, including guidance on addressing complex code challenges through examples and case studies. As a component of Phoenix's Adaptive Reuse Program, the city's Office of Consumer Advocacy provides development assistance and dedicated case managers for customers new to the land development and building permit processes.

Identify thresholds and code hacks. A number of organizations working in the small space have focused on identifying "thresholds" of the building code. These are the minor but important trip points where a project moves from one code interpretation to a higher, much more expensive upgrade. Understanding the thresholds by which a code interpretation changes is critical and determines the language and terms one might use in their applications. "Hacks," in contrast, are techniques to work around the code—while still staying consistent with the law—by being careful in how certain elements are designed or described.

For example, some health regulations require a mop sink to be included in certain building space. This can be an expensive add in terms of plumbing changes and consumption of limited floor space. However, if a kitchen sink is rephrased as a utility sink, it can be interpreted under the code as fulfilling the mop sink requirement. Another example is the plumbing code requirement of the inclusion of drinking fountains in some

> *"Hacks" are techniques to work around the code—meeting intent without the unnecessary cost of meeting the letter—by being careful how certain elements are designed or described.*

with the desired intent of the code using a flexible, holistic approach to meeting code requirements in order to preserve the fabric of particular buildings. For example, Seattle's Outcome-Based Energy Code allows departures from prescriptive code paths and instead regulates whole-building energy consumption

uses of certain sizes. To fulfill ADA requirements the drinking fountain must be fully accessible, which adds further costs. However, if the mentioned kitchen sink contains a "water fill station," it will meet the intent and purpose of the drinking fountain, thereby saving construction dollars and floor space.

Developer's Viewpoint on Codes

FOR ELECTED OFFICIALS AND CITIZENS who want to see more small development in their community, a better understanding of the labyrinth of codes and their requirements as seen from the developer's perspective is helpful. The regulatory and approval framework for small projects has multiple layers of reviews and reviewers, inspectors and inspections. For a small project that is innovating, pioneering, or adaptively using an existing building, navigating this complex process can be a daunting task and is often a deal killer.

→ **BUILDING CODE:** The building code is the set of rules that define the standards for constructed works. Through their plans, developers must demonstrate that their projects conform to the code to obtain a building permit. The main purpose of building codes is to protect public health, safety, and general welfare as they relate to the construction and occupancy of buildings and structures.

→ **ENERGY CODE:** Energy codes and standards set minimum efficiency requirements for new and renovated buildings, ensuring reductions in energy use and emissions over the life of the building. Energy codes are a subset of building codes, which establish baseline requirements and govern building construction. But for adaptive use of existing buildings, energy codes often dictate such a high level of upgrade that renovation may be economically impractical.

→ **FIRE AND LIFE SAFETY CODE:** The fire and life safety code sets out standards to minimize danger from the effects of fire, including smoke, heat, and toxic gases. Retrofitting older buildings to add fire sprinklers is rarely easy. It is often an expensive undertaking that requires not only creative ways to provide for the sprinklers themselves, but also to update structural components for the additional loading of the charged pipes and upgrading of primary building water meters and connection to city mains to have proper flow.

→ **AMERICANS WITH DISABILITIES ACT:** The ADA is a federal civil rights law passed in 1990 that prohibits discrimination against people with disabilities in employment, transportation, public accommodation, communications, and governmental activities. Like the other codes, fulfilling accessibility requirements can be highly impractical or economically infeasible. Common economic challenges include addressing building entry upgrades, floor-level access, and kitchen and bathroom accommodations. Creative interpretations can be made by building departments to facilitate more economical solutions, but as ADA is enforced through civil legal action, a developer is always at risk if a creative interpretation or solution is made—even if approved by the building department.

Although little latitude exists to alter or deviate from these codes, city leadership can provide tax or other financial assistance to projects to help offset these important upgrades but reduce their effect on the project's feasibility. For example, the federal government provides both a tax credit and tax deduction for ADA upgrades. Some cities provide tax abatements or grants or low-cost/no-cost loans to help support code-required upgrades.

→ making *small* happen

Simple changes often lead to unintended consequences in some other area. So, although a few keystrokes can be made early on to facilitate the development of *small*, in the end a comprehensive, holistic review is needed to realign what are often competing regulations. There may also be a need to change cultures and attitudes. Small-scale development is a valuable tool for revitalization of existing communities and improving the form and texture of existing neighborhoods, and planning and building staff need to embrace and help realize its vision.

An example of a locality that made this kind of change is the city of Phoenix (see Phoenix Office of Customer Advocacy in chapter 12). City officials not only made major changes to their codes but also to the culture of their staff. As a cost recovery–driven department, the hidden incentive was to embrace large, formulaic, new-build projects because fees were high and level of review effort was low. Conversely, small, adaptive use projects paid little in fees and required extra effort to interpret codes, work with developers and tenants to find creative solutions, and review projects multiple times during construction. Not until the leadership of the city and the department made clear how important small-scale and adaptive use was to the city's long-term economic development vision did things begin to change.

If cities are interested in advancing the small agenda, they should consider two primary strategies: streamlining the process, and adopting a comprehensive adaptive use program.

STREAMLINE THE DEVELOPMENT PROCESS FOR *SMALL* AND CHANGE THE CULTURE OF GOVERNMENT

During ULI's 2016 Small-Scale Development Forum in Pittsburgh, Tom Murphy, ULI's senior fellow for public policy and former mayor of Pittsburgh, was asked what levers public officials have to support to facilitate creative small development. Murphy replied, "Regulatory relief and innovative approaches to regulation interpretation are two of the most powerful levers already in governments control." He added, "Governments thinking entrepreneurially, investing in tomorrow, and pursuing unlikely partnerships are crucial for supporting *small*."

As described previously, permitting and plan review for small projects can be unpredictable. Unexpected delays can add substantial cost from loan servicing, overhead of the team, and loss of projected near-term revenue. The complexity and uncertainty of reuse projects make them particularly susceptible to extended delays and large cost overruns in the construction process. Adding further delays and uncertainty at the front end only further hampers this form of development.

Conversely, streamlining the building permitting and approval process by aligning city departments is a critical part of streamlining the process and saving city staff as well as developers time.

An alternative approach is to create a new department or a centralized office with dedicated staff to help walk small developers through the process. Creating a multi-departmental team who will become familiar with small development and adaptive use can serve as a one-stop shop to provide efficient review of proposed projects, answer questions, and troubleshoot with developers.

Such a department should be in charge of providing coordinated technical assistance to small developers with a focus on identifying cost savings available for small projects as well as other financial incentives and city grant programs. Given that many developers and practitioners have found success in creatively overcoming complex code problems, cities should create and promote a database of proven solutions to challenges that may be encountered in reuse projects.

> *A multi-departmental team familiar with small development and adaptive use can serve as a one-stop shop to provide efficient review of proposed projects, answer questions, and troubleshoot issues with developers.*

Hiring staff whose job it is to support and facilitate small development will ultimately change the culture of government and is no small task. Cities may find it worthwhile to look beyond their boundaries to pull in the right person for a job; recruiting leaders from outside can make a clear difference. By reducing uncertainty, granting flexibility, and

OPPOSITE: Portland, Oregon, has created programs and partnerships to allow small business owners to "reclaim" public streets as a way to increase placemaking and vibrancy, as here in Ankeny Alley. **ABOVE:** Charleston, South Carolina, wrote the first Historic Preservation Code, but has been open minded about allowing well-proportioned, compatible contemporary design to evolve as a complement to the city's historic fabric. *(All images © CRAFT Development)*

City of Phoenix Adaptive Reuse Program Eligibility

TO QUALIFY FOR ASSISTANCE, buildings must meet the following criteria:

→ Be an independent structure permitted prior to 2000

→ Be a change of occupancy or significant change in use

→ Be a change that incorporates the entire building

→ Be a building that is up to 100,000 square feet with tiered relief as follows:

- **Tier 1:** 5,000 square feet maximum. This can include an addition to the existing building. The addition cannot exceed 50 percent of the square footage of the existing building and a combined total of 5,000 square feet.

- **Tier 2:** Greater than 5,000 square feet to 25,000 square feet.

- **Tier 3:** Greater than 25,000 square feet to 100,000 square feet and Large Scale Commercial Retail as defined as "big box" (Mercantile Occupancy) in the zoning ordinance.

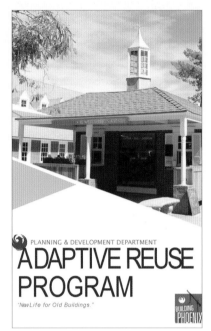

PLANNING & DEVELOPMENT DEPARTMENT
ADAPTIVE REUSE PROGRAM
"New Life for Old Buildings."
BUILDING PHOENIX

leveraging staff who are familiar with the challenges faced by adaptive use projects, building reuse becomes a more viable option for a developer, architect, or investor considering locations and development options.

ADOPT A COMPREHENSIVE ADAPTIVE USE PROGRAM

Adaptive use ordinances, whether applied citywide or used as an overlay, bring together incentives along with flexibility in building and zoning codes, removing unnecessary barriers to reuse projects. (To read more about the city of Phoenix's Adaptive Reuse Ordinance, see the success story on the Phoenix Office of Customer Advocacy in chapter 12.)

Jurisdictions considering an adaptive use incentive program should also adopt supportive policies into their comprehensive or general plan. The following 10 policies can serve as guidelines:[10]

- **Policy 1:** Promote adaptive use as part of broader goals supporting historic preservation, economic development, and environmental sustainability and resilience.

- **Policy 2:** Recognize the social, economic, and environmental value of older buildings.

- **Policy 3:** Incentivize building reuse at a neighborhood scale to encourage activation of a cohesive district of older buildings.

- **Policy 4:** Eliminate or allow nonconformance with certain development regulations that would make adaptive use of eligible buildings infeasible, including such standards related to parking and loading, height, density, floor/area ratio, and open space.

- **Policy 5:** Encourage adaptive use projects to provide space for a mix of uses.

- **Policy 6:** Prioritize the review of adaptive use projects through interdepartmental coordination.

- **Policy 7:** Allow alternative building and fire code compliance for eligible adaptive use projects able to demonstrate an alternative means or method of protecting public health, safety, and welfare.

- **Policy 8:** Allow alternative compliance with public works standards, where alternative compliance will protect public health, safety, and welfare.

- **Policy 9:** Adopt a zoning overlay outlining specific provisions to incentivize adaptive use.
- **Policy 10:** Add policy identifying in general terms areas of the jurisdiction where adaptive use incentives could be applied.

Adopting an adaptive use ordinance as a zoning overlay will allow the ordinance to be integrated as a cohesive chapter into most zoning regimes. Jurisdictions wishing to implement an adaptive use program would adopt the zoning overlay as a chapter in their zoning code, identify districts or neighborhoods where adaptive use is desired, and amend the zoning map to show the overlay areas. Adoption of both the text and mapping amendments are discretionary and administrative approvals, which will require approval by the local legislative authority, such as the city council. The following are important incentives to include in the text of the adaptive use ordinance:

- **Density:** The ordinance should allow projects to exceed the maximum density established by the local zoning code for the site provided the adaptive use project is in compliance with any minimum residential unit size standards.
- **Setbacks:** The ordinance should allow existing building setbacks to remain and be considered legally nonconforming.
- **Height:** The ordinance should allow the height of the structure, if it exceeds the maximum height of the zoning district, to remain and be considered legally nonconforming.
- **Loading zone:** The ordinance should not require a new loading zone if the existing building does not have one.
- **Parking:** The ordinance should not require any new parking spaces for any converted use within the existing footprint of the building. Parking requirements pose one of the most common and most significant barriers to building reuse. If parking requirement waiver or reduction is appropriately targeted, and specified, this incentive can change the equation for reuse and have a powerful effect on development patterns. If a full waiver of parking requirements for the portion of the building that has a converted use is seen as overly generous given the development climate of a jurisdiction, the jurisdiction may opt to reduce parking requirements or allow off-site parking at a specified distance as a more limited incentive.
- **Alternative fire code regulations:** Subject to the approval of the fire official, the ordinance should allow the use or occupancy type of an eligible building to be changed as part of an adaptive use project without conforming to all requirements of the locally adopted version of the Existing Building Code, provided the new or proposed use is equally or less hazardous, based on life and fire risk, than the existing use. Whenever practical difficulties are involved in carrying out the provisions of the local fire code, the fire official should have the authority to grant modifications for individual cases, as long as such modifications do not lessen health, life, and fire safety requirements.
- **Alternative public works standards:** Jurisdictions may choose to adopt incentives specific to their local infrastructure and streetscape. For example, a jurisdiction could choose to relax street tree regulations, or sidewalk improvement requirements for adaptive reuse projects, or allow existing nonconforming driveways, alleys, or rights-of-way to remain unchanged.

CONCLUSION

This chapter covers the most typical challenges developers face in each area, including zoning, parking, building codes, and common conflicts between various regulations. It lays out a variety of recommendations city governments and public officials can implement to better support and encourage the kind of small development that can help to revitalize a community and make it more attractive to investment, more sustainable, and more livable.

The Fair-Haired Dumbbell, Portland, Oregon *(© Pete Eckhert)*

the
projects
and
people
building *small*

small
success
stories

With rising interest in how to build better places, how to make better use of limited land and financial resources, and how to elevate second- and third-tier communities to compete in a rapidly changing marketplace, *small* is attracting a number of followers and actors interested in contributing in some way to the solution.

Studying lessons learned from specific projects—the signature ULI case study method—is always valuable. But because *small* requires an unconventional attitude toward real estate, telling the story of the *people* engaged in small development provides insights that go beyond traditional project analysis.

The following pages tell six unique stories that capture the spirit, motivations, passion, and creative solutions generated by people and agencies that have committed their talents and time to realizing the potential of *small*.

Upstart and entrepreneurial developers such as Kevin Cavenaugh of **Guerrilla Development** in Portland, Oregon, and the partners of **Pivot Project** in Oklahoma City demonstrate what commitment, passion for great places, tenacity, and creativity can yield when applied to their local communities and building *small*.

One of the more enlightening discoveries in the research for this book is the **Phoenix Office of Customer Advocacy (OCA)**. The OCA provides an exemplary story of a public agency that at one time made small development all but impossible. However, through committed leadership and outreach, the city changed the agency's policies, its regulations, and, most important, its *culture* so the OCA could become a productive partner with small developers looking to transform the sprawling city's underused midcentury assets through a series of neighborhood-scale interventions.

Amid the renaissance occurring in Detroit, one enterprising nonprofit has led the way for years in the transformation of the Midtown district—acting as advocate, facilitator, convener, cheerleader, and when required, developer of last resort. **Midtown Detroit Inc.** has consistently created or initiated transformative projects that started the flywheel spinning for block-level regeneration, and for new investment once the potential had been demonstrated.

MassDevelopment, the quasi-public Massachusetts development authority that manages all local and statewide bond financing, has created the Transformative Development Initiative (TDI), a uniquely targeted program for catalyzing regeneration of smaller cities under stress due to loss of their economic base. TDI accomplishes its goals by directing some investment toward attracting and supporting small developers as the vanguard of hope and reinvestment in these challenged communities.

The final profile focuses on the work of one individual—Eve Picker—whose aptly named firm **Small**

The following pages tell six unique stories that capture the spirit, motivations, passion, and creative solutions generated by people and agencies that have committed to realizing the potential of small.

Change is the first-of-its-kind capital intermediary leveraging groundbreaking crowdfunding legislation to allow an average citizen to invest in projects in his or her own community. This critical effort provides an alternative path through which small developers can build better where big capital is uninterested in going.

GUERRILLA DEVELOPMENT
keeping it *small*

AT A GLANCE

Guerrilla Development Co.
PORTLAND, OREGON

→ **DEFINING IDEA:** Every relationship matters

→ **ASSET CLASS:** Mixed use—new construction and adaptive use

→ **ENTITY TYPE:** S corporation (umbrella entity), limited liability companies (project entities)

→ **FOUNDED:** 2000

→ **STAFF SIZE:** 8

→ **OWNER:** Kevin Cavenaugh

→ **PROJECTS:** 17, totaling 236,000 square feet

→ **PROJECTS UNDER MANAGEMENT:** 16

AS IS THE CASE WITH MANY A GOOD FOUNDING STORY, there was not a Day One for Kevin Cavenaugh, the charismatic and counterculture founder of Portland, Oregon–based Guerrilla Development.

After studying architecture at the University of California, Berkeley, Cavenaugh moved to Sacramento, took a job as an architect in training, and bought a house. "I wanted to live in a dynamic, younger, creative, affordable city that had some neat vision and was going somewhere," he says. But Sacramento in the late 1980s and early 1990s was not that city. "There didn't seem to be any urban planning rhyme or reason. All building was done just to increase the tax base, so 'build whatever you can.' That didn't feel right to me."

He left Sacramento for the West African country of Gabon and a stint in the Peace Corps. Returning to the United States and Portland two years later, he took up work once again as a designer. But this time he became increasingly concerned about the number of unenlightened developers working in the field. These were developers who cared solely about returns and being sure not to go overbudget. "Is this all there is?," Cavenaugh asked himself.

While pondering this question, Cavenaugh was also buying and fixing up houses to rent or sell. He sold one to Francesca Gambetti, a client of Fletcher Farr Ayotte, the architecture firm where Cavenaugh worked. Through Gambetti, a developer with Sheils Obletz Johnson, Cavenaugh learned how to be a developer. Over a 20-minute coffee conversation, she showed him that the work he was doing fixing up houses *was* real estate development. She shared her pro forma with Cavenaugh—the same pro forma he uses to this day, with a few slight modifications. (He also makes it available on his website to help other aspiring small developers.) "Once I realized that I already was a developer just buying and fixing

up houses, it demystified the concept of owning 'phase 0'"—the term Cavenaugh uses for the initial development phase during which a developer figures out what the project is all about.

Cavenaugh's first development other than small remodel jobs was the Box + One Lofts, a mixed-use project in Portland with four lofts, a live/work space, a wine bar, and a bakery/coffee shop. Cavenaugh was able to pull off the project with the support of his bosses at Fletcher Farr Ayotte, he says, underscoring a theme for small developers—the need for partners, either financial or intellectual. While continuing to work for the firm, Cavenaugh secured the construction loan, hired a contractor, got the project built, and in the process won a handful of awards.

By being proactive and deciding to own phase 0, Cavenaugh went from doing seismic upgrade details for a Portland high school to being an award-winning small-scale developer.

OPPOSITE: *Top:* Outdoor patio at The Zipper, one of Guerrilla Development's neighborhood-transforming projects. *(© Brian Foulkes)* *Bottom:* Cavenaugh speaks to SSDF 11 attendees from the courtyard of his home at The Ocean *(©2017 Jim Heid)* **ABOVE:** Streetfront of New New Crusher Court, former auto repair shops converted to small, locally owned shops. *(© Herman Jolly)*

Cavenaugh explains the change. "It was hilarious because I was the exact same person I was 10 months earlier, but because I didn't like playing the 'designer card,' I decided to go a different route,

> *"We decided to tackle gentrification completely internally by redefining the word enough."*

and that route was small-scale development," he says. "But now suddenly people thought of me as something completely different. And yet I was still the same designer I had been, just designing and building for myself instead of others."

MISSION AND PURPOSE

Guerrilla is focused on creating inventive and experimental projects that use both hemispheres of the brain: its projects require creative design solutions as well as detailed financial analysis, both of which the team at Guerrilla carries out. Finding a balance between those two elements is a key to making a project sing and finding success. Cavenaugh's team understands this balance and knows how to carry it out. Guerrilla creates buildings that prove good design and good financial returns are not mutually exclusive. It measures success by the social capital its projects produce as well as by the asset value they generate.

After the 2016 presidential election, the firm shifted its intellectual capital to address a common challenge of small success—gentrification. Members of the Guerrilla Development team decided to change their approach and toggle between their heads and their hearts. "We've got the 'head' stuff down, but how do we do things like 'reverse gentrification,' or as we now like to say, 'gentlefication'?," Cavenaugh asks. "How do we do things like weave in social capital to all of our projects? How do we create equity in a neighborhood instead of bringing it into just our coffers?" These are the questions with which the team is currently grappling.

Gentrification is the biggest topic Cavenaugh talks about with his team. "By definition, I am a gentrifier," he says. "Now my job is to figure out how I can do that

without displacing. How can I improve a neighborhood physically and give it a richer variation of tenant mix, yet not displace the current residents?" Cavenaugh believes strongly that small-scale developers need to be aware of gentrification, consider it, digest it, and figure out how to fix it.

This is the focus of Cavenaugh's newest projects. "We decided to tackle gentrification completely internally by redefining the word *enough*," he says. Cavenaugh's investors in more conventional projects might see industry-standard preferred returns of 8 to 9 percent. But by offering lower returns like 5 or 6 percent to investors in these new projects, Guerrilla is able to shift every dollar that would have been additional profit into lower rents for tenants, specifically for commercial tenants that would otherwise be displaced by new, pricier rents. The projects remain very profitable, he says, and the investors love being a part of something bigger—making a difference in the neighborhood and keeping locally owned, locally run businesses in place. This creates projects that have a soul and improve a community.

PORTFOLIO AND PROJECT TYPES

Some of Guerrilla Development's projects include the following:

- **The Ocean**, the adaptive use of a former strip center to serve as space for microrestaurants with a shared seating area;
- **The Zipper**, a ground-up restaurant incubator with experimental lenticular art (created on an accordion-like folded surface showing a different image from the left and right), deployed along its entire facade;
- **Dr. Jim's Still Really Nice**, an adaptive use, social-capital-turned-architecture project that turned a livery stable into four lofts with 9,500 square feet of space and an interior courtyard; and
- **The Fair-Haired Dumbbell**, a corridor-free creative office space in a six-story, 56,400-square-foot office building organized as two medium-sized, canted buildings connected by a skybridge.

ORGANIZATION SIZE, STRUCTURE, AND ROLES

Guerrilla Development is a 21st-century company that operates within a midcentury model. Cavenaugh refers to his company as being rooted in 1958 values. "By that I mean at five o'clock you have to go," he says. "No one works after hours and no one works weekends. You don't have a company cellphone, and I will never send an email after five o'clock—not any day." However, during work hours, Cavenaugh's team is focused entirely on Guerrilla Development and the work at hand.

Guerrilla's team of eight (including Cavenaugh) takes on a wide variety of roles. For instance, staff members have strong financial, construction management, asset management, and accounting skills. Cavenaugh's goal is to do as much work as possible in house while hiring people with "big brains" and

ABOVE: *Top:* Cavenaugh's residence, carved from the former back storage buildings at The Ocean. *(© Brian Foulkes) Bottom:* Before development. *(© Kevin Cavenaugh)*

with little pertinent experience. "I don't play by the normal rules, so I don't want a full head of expectations," he says. "I'd rather teach you my way."

An example of the work ethic and varied expertise is Anna Mackay, Guerrilla's former project lead for investor relations, business development, and marketing. Her background is in architecture, woodworking, and carpentry. "We have a really good time working hard," she says of Guerrilla. The firm's small size "helps us to stay tight, focused, integrated, and, frankly, humble." Cavenaugh's enthusiasm for what the built environment can do for communities is contagious, MacKay says. "He has an uncanny ability to nurture our ideas, which are born out of the extension of the seed that he plants. He's not ever holding us back from taking the kernels of the original ideas and seeing how far out they can go." Consistent with the entrepreneurial ethos Guerrilla Development nurtures, Mackay left in 2020 to start her own development firm, Sister City.

Guerrilla's annual operating budget is $600,000, and the primary revenue sources are development fees, property management, and income from properties. Asked to break down the operating costs, Cavenaugh says, "It varies so much by the year, with steady growth. In 2019 it was costing us $52,000 per month to keep the doors open, but with some 'skinnying down' we are now running about $44,000 per month. Of that, 20 percent comes from man-

agement fees, 2 percent comes from administration fees, and the balance comes from development fees. However, that does not include the $4,000 per month that comes in from existing building cash-flow distributions. In 2020, these monthly distributions, along with distributions from projects currently under construction, were roughly $36,000."

SHARING THE SUCCESS

Guerrilla is an idea and concept with little in the way of capital assets outside of a lease, some computers, desks, and chairs, Cavenaugh says. All the properties developed by Guerrilla are owned personally by Cavenaugh, not Guerrilla. In January 2017, Cavenaugh took his portfolio and split his ownership, keeping half and putting the rest into a new vehicle called the Guerrilla Fund. The Guerrilla Fund operates as a holding fund for ownership interest from which phantom shares are allocated to employees. The employees do not have an ownership interest in the properties, but they have rights to income earned by the properties and to a portion of the sale price (if the properties are ever sold).

"It's important to not accept the ways things are normally done," Cavenaugh says of his motivation for the program. "In the commercial real estate industry, it's about wealth creation, usually on an individual basis. But for me, we're all working for the same thing. We should all share in that same

ABOVE: Guerrilla strives to include local artists in its work, as in this mural along the side of The Zipper that changes depending on the vantage point of the viewer. (© Brian Foulkes)

outcome. The typical CEO of an American company currently makes 475 times their average employee, when in 1958 the ratio was eight to one. I'm trying to get closer to that with the fund. I won't know for sure until a handful of years have passed, but someone had to try to develop a different model."

GETTING PROJECTS DONE

When looking for new projects, Cavenaugh focuses on identifying areas of Portland where real estate is appreciating at a higher rate than the average market in the city. "Once you identify the neighborhood, then you literally just comb it," he says. "You identify raw land or a building with a big parking lot or a dilapidated building that still has good bones. You find something that you see a vision in or merit in that others might not necessarily see."

More than half the time when he identifies a project with an inspiring phase 0, the land or building is not for sale, he says. When that is the case, Cavenaugh does research to identify the owner and where he or she lives. "I actually prefer not writing letters," he says. "I prefer going to their house and knocking on their door or calling them, introducing myself, saying, 'Hey, you've got a really wonderful piece of property, and I love it.'" Many of the owners Cavenaugh contacts are used to hearing the exact opposite about their properties. People tell them that the property is falling down, it's junky, it's an eyesore, and that they need to do something with it in order to not lose more money, he says.

Cavenaugh explains to the owners why their land is wonderful, the vision he sees for the site, and the inherent potential the site has. He is not afraid to share a large portion of his vision with the owners, even if it means they might take his idea and develop the property themselves. "If you do that, then you will make the city better, and I'll just buy the building down the block, which is great," he says. "Nothing

that we do is magic. It's just hard work. So if someone else wants to work as hard alongside me, all the better." It's common for Cavenaugh to develop five or six properties in a neighborhood before going to look for a new area of Portland to invest in.

Guerrilla is not trying to hit home runs with its projects, he says. "We're tiny and nimble, and we do small scale quick, slapping singles to right field. We just get on base and get up to bat again. And we have more ideas than we have time." The team is not interested in spending five years on a project, and because of that the group of decision-makers at the table is kept small.

FINANCING PROJECTS

As a result of the Great Recession of 2007–2008, Cavenaugh went from having a net worth of $4 million in 2007 to being underwater by $1 million. "In the recession, I was completely taken out at the knees," he says. Loans for several of his buildings needed to be restructured, and at the time Cavenaugh had no choice but to sell those buildings at

> *"In the recession, I was completely taken out at the knees. . . . I only knew, pre-recession, how to play offense; I didn't know how to play defense. Now I know how to play defense."*

very low prices. "It took me a good two years to get back onto dry land, to get back to zero. I only knew, pre-recession, how to play offense; I didn't know how to play defense. Now I know how to play defense."

The main thing that has changed for Cavenaugh is how he finances his projects. Before the recession, he had no investors and owned 100 percent of his projects. "I used a lot of smoke and mirrors," he says. "We used leverage and a lot of chutzpah, and got loans I couldn't get today and that got my projects done." Today, Cavenaugh has investors and 42 long-term, high-net-worth individuals with whom he shares ownership of his projects.

Cavenaugh describes the financing for his projects this way: "The structure of each deal is typically 8 percent preferred returns for the investors. Then once they get theirs, I—and the fund—get our 8 percent," he says. "Once everybody is at 8 percent, every extra dollar of income gets split on a pro rata basis. There is no waterfall, and I don't build to sell. My developments are structured like nice and boring annuities." Consistent with Guerrilla's objective to help the industry think differently, the pro forma for each of his projects is available for download at the individual project profiles on Guerrilla's website, guerrilladev.co/projects.

Cavenaugh says he has had coffee with more than 200 potential investors. "It's just like a date. I know at the first date if there will never be a second date, because if their only goal is yield, they'll be unhappy with me and I'll be just as unhappy with them," he says. Aligning investor needs with Guerrilla's purpose is a key consideration. Guerrilla's investors who do not have a personal stake in a project care deeply about the types of projects the company pursues. Cavenaugh spends a significant amount of time making sure that he knows each investor well, that they know him, and that they are happy with all aspects of the project's returns—financial and social.

Cavenaugh also nurtures relationships with his lenders. John Maher, vice president at M&T Bank, was the first person to approve a loan for Cavenaugh after the recession. Because of this, Cavenaugh now goes to him for every loan. Maher describes Cavenaugh as a "breath of fresh air in his style and, of course, his projects. They are so creative and unique, it makes it really fun to step outside the box a bit and help him do these cool projects." Maher says one of his favorite things to do is tour one of Cavenaugh's properties with him because he finds the mutual admiration between Cavenaugh and his tenants inspiring. "He is so good at developing and maintaining these relationships that there seems to be an endless supply of tenants wanting to get into his projects. As a banker, that is very reassuring," Maher says.

Guerrilla was one of the first small firms to finance portions of its projects through crowdfunding. Its first crowdfunded offering was for The Fair-Haired Dumbbell, which is located in the heart of the Burnside Bridgehead neighborhood. The offering closed in December 2016 with a targeted investor annual rate of return of 8 percent over a period of three to five years. With a minimum investment in this Regulation A offering of $3,000, the project attracted 118

ABOVE: Guerrilla created 5,000 square feet of new open space by peeling the roof off former warehouses at New New Crusher Court. The "found" space serves as a central amenity and source of daylight and natural ventilation for tenant spaces that surround the courtyard while also creating increased value for the remaining leasable square feet. *(© Brian Foulkes)*

people, with investments ranging from that minimum to $234,000. Crowdfunding made up $1.5 million of the total $18 million project capital stack.

In 2018 Guerrilla Development used crowdfunding to raise $300,000 for Jolene's First Cousin. The offering, with a $3,000 minimum investment, sold out in 68 hours. The project consists of two two-story buildings on a single lot in the heart of the Creston-Kenilworth neighborhood with a total of six spaces—three retail businesses, two market-rate lofts, and one space containing 11 rooms in a single-room occupancy (SRO) arrangement. SRO renters will secure their spot in Jolene's First Cousin for $290 a month. Half the rooms will be offered to the general market on Craigslist. The others will be filled with working homeless people—an arrangement made possible through collaboration with Guerrilla's partner JOIN, a Portland-based nonprofit that produces a newspaper and uses other media to create income opportunities for people experiencing homelessness and poverty.

DISTINCTIVE STRATEGIES

Commercial tenants are a crucial piece of the puzzle for Guerrilla Development. "I'm a bit of a serial entrepreneur, and I run away from national franchise tenants or large institutional tenants," Cavenaugh says. "For the most part, I do small quirky buildings, and I have small quirky mom-and-pop tenants."

He looks for tenants who are just starting out and perhaps have one other venture or none at all. "I don't care about stability the way most care about stability. If I look at you and I believe in you and your business model, then I'm excited to get you into my building and I really want you to succeed." From Dream Cakes in New Crusher Court and Rubinette Produce Market in the Shore to the Pie Spot in The Ocean, Cavenaugh's tenants are examples of the important role small businesses play in creating projects that produce strong financial returns as well as social capital for a neighborhood.

Cavenaugh has taken no formal development classes; everything he has learned has been from being in the field. All his projects involve long-term commitments and, as he explains, he "loves not even knowing what the rules are." As noted, unlike most developers, Cavenaugh makes his pro formas public. "There's no magic to it. It's not proprietary knowledge. It's just math, really simple algebra."

As a designer, Cavenaugh knows his strengths and his weaknesses. "I know that I do 'warm modern' or lowercase 'm' modern," he says. "I don't do a lot of steel and glass. I like volume. As a guerrilla developer, I'm happiest when I'm creating interesting spaces for not much money." In many projects, Cavenaugh has blurred indoor and outdoor space through architectural features such as a roll-up door, but now he thinks perhaps he has overused that detail.

As a designer or developer, Cavenaugh does not want to be known for a signature detail or signature project for fear that his work will become generic and predictable. "The only formula that I do is really high-level right-brain/left-brain, head/heart, redefining *enough*," he says. "That's the formula. There are no architectural details that necessarily define that formula, that description."

LEARN MORE

GUERRILLA AND ITS PROJECTS

→ **Guerrilla Development Co.**—guerrilladev.co

→ **The Zipper**—guerrilladev.co/projects/#/the-zipper

→ **Dr. Jim's Still Really Nice**—guerrilladev.co/dr-jims-still-really-nice

→ **The Fair-Haired Dumbbell**—guerrilladev.co/projects/#/the-fair-haired-dumbbell

PIVOT PROJECT
building a firm

Pivot Project Development LLC

OKLAHOMA CITY, OKLAHOMA

→ **DEFINING IDEA:** Connecting community through thoughtful development
→ **ENTITY TYPE:** Limited liability company
→ **FOUNDED:** 2014
→ **STAFF SIZE:** 7
→ **PARTNERS:** Jonathan Dodson, Ben Sellers, David Wanzer, and Candace Baitz
→ **PROJECTS:** 20

IT WAS JONATHAN DODSON'S 34TH BIRTHDAY when David Wanzer and Ben Sellers delivered the best gift he had ever received—a signed contract for the Tower Theatre. The iconic building had fallen into disrepair, and it was this 30,000-square-foot, mixed-use project that kick-started their partnership.

The three had met through ULI Oklahoma. For several years, Wanzer and Sellers would separately drag Dodson, at that time a banker, to look at various buildings around Oklahoma City, scope out neighborhoods, and examine underused parcels. At times, the pair would take Dodson to look at the same project, both asking him to lend money for a deal. At first, Dodson just recommended that the two work together. However, as each left his respective job—Sellers leaving the U.S. Department of Housing and Urban Development, Wanzer his design/build practice, and Dodson the banking field—they decided they were better off joining forces to form Pivot Project Development LLC. They committed themselves to creating a company focused on connecting community through real estate development.

OPPOSITE: The iconic Tower Theatre *(top)* is one of Pivot Project's signature projects. Using a complex "capital cocktail" that included historic tax credits, Pivot restored the movie theater, built in 1937, as a series of food and beverage outlets and offices while retaining the original theater for 1,000-seat music performances *(bottom)*. *(All images © Joseph Mills Photography)* **ABOVE:** Town House was Pivot Project's first housing endeavor and helped convert a disinvested single-room-occupancy hotel into 19 new contemporary apartments. *(All images: Pivot Project)*

MISSION AND PURPOSE

Three years after its formation, Pivot Project had grown to include a portfolio of more than a dozen projects, all focused on the urban core of Oklahoma City, a second-tier city of 655,000 people. The goal of Pivot Project—to develop projects that are financially successful and that have a positive impact on the revitalization of neighborhoods—is accomplished through a concurrent focus on the block, the street, and the neighborhood. The partners care deeply about the communities in which they develop and show that commitment by living in the surrounding neighborhoods—working in them, shopping in them, and investing in them. "We are not chasing random deals in the suburbs just to do deals," Wanzer explains. "We all live in the neighborhoods around all of our projects."

PORTFOLIO AND PROJECT TYPES

Projects in Pivot Project's portfolio range in size from 3,500 to 30,000 square feet for commercial developments, 14 to 50 units for multifamily projects, and $1 million to $10 million in total development costs. The firm's portfolio of work includes diverse projects,

ABOVE: Sunshine Laundry repurposed a 17,000-square-foot industrial laundry facility as a microbrewery, a restaurant, and offices *(top)*. The Stonecloud Brewing Company occupies the former open industrial floor *(bottom left)* and its taproom is in the former drive-thru *(bottom right)*. *(All images © Timothy Hursley Photography)*

from the Tower Theatre, a $7.5 million music and specialty entertainment venue, to Classen 16, a $10 million mixed-use retail and residential project in the Plaza District, which has 48 market-rate apartments and 3,000 square feet of retail space. Twelve of the company's 20 projects involve adaptive use and a mix of retail, residential, and office uses.

Though Pivot Project does not explicitly focus on environmental concerns or certification under the Leadership in Energy and Environmental Design (LEED) program, by pursuing adaptive use and historic renovation projects, it is recycling and repurposing existing buildings. This, according to the U.S. Environmental Protection Agency, is the greenest type of development of all. By default, this approach supports sustainability, efficiency, and revitalization.

FIRM SIZE, STRUCTURE, AND ROLES

Pivot Project has a staff of seven: in addition to the three partners, there is a development manager, a property manager, an accountant, and a bookkeeper. The three founders share the role of creating the vision for the company and recently have worked to make the operations more efficient: Wanzer has focused on creating operational standards; Sellers has shifted his focus to analysis, underwriting, and asset review; and Dodson has turned his attention to building the firm's equity and tenant base.

Each project is led by one partner alongside the development manager. For each project in its portfolio, Pivot Project serves as the managing member, with different equity investors involved in each deal. Each project is its own single-asset limited liability company with a standalone mortgage and a standalone operating agreement. From each of its projects Pivot Project receives development fees, which range from 5 to 10 percent of all hard and soft costs (excluding acquisition), depending on the complexity of the project and partnership structure. In addition, the company may receive consulting fees

if the project receives historic tax credits or other tax credits; this fee, which is based on the amount of nontraditional capital raised, ranges from 3 to 5 percent of the funding.

GETTING PROJECTS DONE

Pivot Project builds its project pipeline in multiple ways to maintain deal flow and make sure the company can seize opportunities as they arise. The deals are either self-generated—partners identifying buildings with hidden value and capturing that value—or respond to tenants or clients that come to the company with their needs.

It is not uncommon for Dodson, Wanzer, and Sellers to chase a project or site they would like to develop for several years before a deal can be fashioned. In some instances, it has come down to an owner approached by the partners trusting Pivot to responsibly and historically redevelop a property to which the owner has a personal attachment. The partners keep their eyes open for opportunities and value that others might not see, which may include sites not on the market. Often their projects are on the edge of a hot neighborhood or district. They also consider how a creative capital stack—incorporating historic tax credits, New Markets Tax Credits, tax increment financing, or other tax approaches—as well as specific tenants can create value not yet recognized. They then begin the process of creating an opportunity for themselves.

It is not uncommon for the partners of Pivot Project to chase projects or sites they would like to develop for several years before a deal can be fashioned.

In other cases, a Pivot Project client will request a particular setting or type of building. In one instance, the team acquired three buildings in the urban core adjacent to a future streetcar line in response to such requests. A law firm, a brewery, and a food market were each looking for space in the city's Midtown

neighborhood in the urban core, and Pivot Project was able to collaborate with each of the three tenants to agree on the terms of a project that made sense for all parties involved, before acquisition of the three buildings.

When deciding whether to move forward with a specific deal, the Pivot Project partners consider three main factors:

- **Does this project fit within our mission?** Will the finished product help spur or continue neighborhood revitalization?
- **Will the project work financially?** Will the project be able to attract investors, obtain bank debt, and meet the requirements of any other funding sources?
- **What additional risks and benefits does the deal have?** For instance, if the first two criteria are met, are there any other factors such as timing or tenant opportunities that should be considered?

Pivot Project's success can be attributed in part to the fact that the partners know their city and its neighborhoods. "We live very low to the ground," says Wanzer. "We know our streets, our buildings, the people."

FINANCING PROJECTS

Pivot Project typically develops projects with the intent of holding them and building long-term wealth. After its first three years in business, it had a core inventory of assets, some of which are irreplaceable because of their distinctive architecture or location. The team stresses the importance of having good relationships with its lenders and investors. As Pivot Project continues to grow, it is focused on finding investors that are concerned with a triple bottom line—projects that perform socially, environmentally, and economically.

DISTINCTIVE STRATEGIES

In several of its developments, Pivot Project has partnered with its tenants. For instance, the Sunshine Laundry building, erected in 1929, had been vacant for 30 years and had no roof and several trees

ABOVE: 2×2 is a microhousing development consisting of four detached, single-family homes with a shared driveway. (© *Joseph Mills Photography*)
OPPOSITE: Classen 16 is a 48-unit rental housing development with street-level commercial space. (*Allford Hall Monaghan Morris Architects*)

growing out of the concrete floor. After its historic rehabilitation, the building is occupied by Stonecloud Brewing Company, which operates a brewery and taproom at the site, as well as the Pivot Project offices. Pivot Project formed a partnership with the owner of Stonecloud and made him a partner in the real estate, creating an owner-occupied building and reducing the risk to the lender.

The 1212 Hudson project, a 28,000-square-foot retail and office development in the Midtown neighborhood of Oklahoma City, was developed through a partnership between Pivot Project and Resolution Legal Group, a local law firm. Resolution Legal invested capital in the redevelopment project, making it an equity partner as well as an anchor tenant. This aligned the financial interests of the landlord and tenant, creating a longer-term view for the project's success.

Pivot Project also has partnered with tenants of locally owned businesses that may have limited access to capital for investment but whose good name and brand will help anchor a project. At its 2.7-acre

East Point renovation project along the NE 23rd Main Street Corridor project, the tenants have a 15 percent ownership stake in the real estate they are leasing as long as they fulfill the terms of their lease. This was made possible through a public/private partnership with the city of Oklahoma City. This represents the evolution of an approach taken previously by Pivot

The team takes land or buildings that have sat vacant for years and redevelops them into engaging projects, increasing pride and honoring the neighborhood where each property is located.

Project—partnering with tenants in the real estate ownership. It allows small business owners to profit from what they are helping create.

Generally, the city and the neighborhoods in which Pivot Project works support the firm's projects and ethos. This is in part because the team takes land or buildings that have sat vacant for years and redevelops them to become engaging projects that connect with the community. Increasing pride and honoring the neighborhood where each property resides is a goal of each project.

OFFICE OF CUSTOMER ADVOCACY

regulatory change

AT A GLANCE

City of Phoenix Office of Customer Advocacy

PHOENIX, ARIZONA

→ **PURPOSE:** To offer development guidance, streamlined processes, shorter time frames, and cost savings to customers looking to adapt older buildings for new business uses

→ **ENTITY TYPE:** Local government agency

→ **FOUNDED:** 2008

→ **STAFF SIZE:** Six: started with three in 2008; fourth added in 2018 to focus on small businesses along the light-rail corridor; two more added in 2019

→ **CONTACT:** Sam Allen, Office of Customer Advocacy program manager

→ **PROJECTS ASSISTED SINCE FOUNDING:** Case management for more than 195 small businesses to convert existing buildings to accommodate a new occupant; general assistance to hundreds more seeking development guidance, interdepartmental coordination, or plan assistance

BEFORE THE GREAT RECESSION, staffers at the Phoenix Development Services Department (DSD, which later merged with Planning to form the city's Planning & Development Department) were accustomed to hearing complaints from developers and business owners that building downtown presented overwhelming burdens. Little new development was going on in the city center at the time, and the surrounding neighborhoods had their fair share of vacant and abandoned buildings.

The city began investing in large-scale development projects such as a new convention center and a sports arena. Land in Phoenix became more valuable than the buildings that sat on that land, often leading developers to raze structures to capture the residual land value. The combination of a zoning code that indirectly favored suburban development types, a rigid building code that made adaptive use more burdensome than new construction, and a department built on a cost-recovery model—its operating budget had to be covered by collected development fees—made redevelopment of existing buildings for new uses almost impossible.

Through a combination of grassroots organizing, the education of elected officials and city management, and the pure determination of small-scale developers, business owners, and concerned residents, the city was finally persuaded to take a hard look at the conundrum it had created.

According to Kimber Lanning, founder and director of the nonprofit business advocacy group Local First Arizona and one of the biggest champions for creation of the city's Office of Customer Advocacy (OCA), there was an "entire legion of renegade building inspectors holding entrepreneurs' heads in a toilet." Other staff members within the DSD were also initially unsupport-

OPPOSITE: Phoenix OCA assisted the sponsor with realizing Sip Coffee and Beer Garage, a former drive-thru oil change garage adaptively repurposed as a coffee/bar restaurant that incorporated the basement pit (formerly used for oil changes) into a bar. *(OCA)*
ABOVE: Previously home of the Phoenix Chamber of Commerce, this building underwent an adaptive use renovation with the assistance of the Phoenix OCA. It is now the Cobra Arcade, serving as the center of Phoenix's nightlife while offering craft beers, clever cocktails, and vintage arcade games. *(OCA)*

ive of adaptive use and infill development. "They were defensive, offensive, and refused to change," she says. Local First Arizona became one of the biggest champions for creation of OCA.

FIRST STEPS

The first step the campaign took was a half-day conference about adaptive use and small-scale development, held at City Hall. Lanning recruited speakers from outside Phoenix who were experts in

series of simplified processes, code/ordinance changes, and code clarifications that would save developers time and money on adaptive use projects while maintaining building safety. Concurrent with the task force's efforts, city staff members completed training on the International Existing Building Code to ensure its consistent application on adaptive use projects.

To ensure that the task force focused on revising requirements that would benefit the adaptive use customer, input was solicited from a customer focus group and the Downtown Artists Issues Task Force. The arts community was attracted to downtown as a place where artists could add character and value and where low rents were available for their workspaces

Recommendations emerged from four working groups: code related, site related, process changes, and education.

economic development, the International Existing Building Code, and preservation of older buildings. Also, three of the city's most popular business owners whose businesses were housed in adaptive use buildings spoke frankly about how hard it was to open their businesses. The conference started buzz in the community around these issues. In addition to the conference, Lanning worked with stakeholder groups that had never vocally supported small-scale development and adaptive use in Phoenix. Both the Americans with Disabilities Act (ADA) community and the fire department went before City Council to push for policy and procedural changes that would support adaptive use.

In response, the City Council, Mayor's Office, and City Manager's Office requested in 2008 the creation of the Adaptive Reuse Task Force, made up of representatives of those offices and the City Council, as well as the city departments covering development services, community and economic development, neighborhood services, fire protection, historic preservation, planning, streets, and water services.

The task force brought downtown advocates together with neighborhood associations to look at codes, policies, and procedures that could be implemented downtown to make smaller-scale projects more feasible. Specifically, the task force proposed a

and galleries. Members of that community wanted the adaptive use program to allow them to make minimal investments in properties while adding to the revitalization of downtown. Design professionals, small business owners, community leaders, and representatives from the artist community who had direct experience with adaptive use were invited to the focus group to share their perspectives and recommendations.

Using the feedback received, the task force created a work plan consisting of a list of recommendations and gave a variety of city departments responsibility for implementing and tracking the progress of each item. The DSD coordinated with the relevant city departments (fire, historic preservation, water, and streets) to implement code and policy changes to support identified adaptive use projects, tracking the progress and reporting back to the City Council and the task force on the effectiveness of the policy revisions.

Work plan items were arranged under four working groups: code related, site related, process changes, and education. Members of each of these four working groups created policies that were carried forward and ultimately approved by the City Council to establish a pilot program. The effects of those policies were then tracked for each pilot project, and the time or cost savings were monitored to determine whether the policies had the intended

positive effects. The education component, for instance, included training plan review staff and educating partners in other city departments, as well as significant outreach to inform the small business and development community about the adaptive use program and its benefits.

2008 PILOT PROGRAM

A pilot program, based on the Adaptive Reuse Task Force's work plan, was put in place in April 2008, focusing on a two-square-mile area of downtown Phoenix. Eligible buildings had to be 2,500 square feet or smaller, be built before 1960, and be designated for commercial use. The pilot program implemented specific code and ordinance relief recommended by the task force. For example, parking and fire sprinkler requirements were relaxed, and projects were allowed to participate in a streamlined plan review process with dedicated time on the public hearing agenda.

The 15 projects included in the pilot program—most were restaurants, galleries, or multiuse projects—saved an average of 4.5 months of work time and $16,000 in fees. Given this success, the City Council approved a permanent Adaptive Reuse Program in October 2008.

MISSION AND PURPOSE

The Adaptive Reuse Program is administered by the Office of Customer Advocacy, part of the Phoenix Planning & Development Department. The OCA is considered one of the most comprehensive agencies of its kind in the United States. Its staff members work to determine an adaptive use project's eligibility for one of three tiers of regulatory relief and help applicants as they work through the development process, providing them with a central point of contact. OCA staff members provide guidance and support to small business customers new to the development and permit process, as well as assistance with pre-project research, identification of plan submittal requirements, coordination between the design team and city staff, and resolution of technical issues.

The Adaptive Reuse Program encourages reuse of buildings and in many cases provides regulatory relief for reuse. Proportionality guidelines, as well as administrative changes to the Phoenix building and fire codes, helped establish development requirements based on the scope and scale of a project. This provided transparency and consistency from the standpoint of both the customer and the plan review staff to establish required improvements and determine project feasibility. The program offers development guidance,

---

ABOVE: A women-owned automotive care business, 180 Degree Automotive incorporated community space and an art gallery into the design and operations of an auto care facility. *(OCA)*

streamlines processes, reduces project development time, and enables cost savings to those looking to adapt older buildings for new business uses.

ORGANIZATION SIZE, STRUCTURE, AND ROLES

Since its inception, the OCA has undergone several staffing structures to find a workable team and format. Today, after a decade of operation, the office is made up of a program manager, two project managers, a light-rail advocate/planner, an engineering tech, and a chief engineering tech.

The program manager oversees the office with support of the deputy director of the Planning & Development Department, ensuring that the policies and procedures are being followed correctly and consistently. The agency also engages in outreach and interdepartmental coordination on projects. The project managers provide the majority of the case management to design professionals, developers, and business owners. The engineering tech and chief engineering tech conduct research and process plans for expedited commercial plan review services. These services include permit by appointment and permit by inspection, which allow minor scopes of work to be submitted and approved quicker when they are undertaken in a space consistent with the intended end use, such as when a renovation does not include a change of occupancy, structural work, or a building expansion.

GETTING PROJECTS DONE

Over the past decade, the Adaptive Reuse Program has been expanded to include areas outside downtown Phoenix and all buildings built before 2000. Most recently, the city has seen increased interest in use of the program in areas served by light rail; redevelopment and adaptive use have naturally followed reinvestment along the existing Central Avenue and Camelback Road light-rail corridors. The program also created an opportunity for revitalization of structures throughout the city for a variety of uses, including adapting a church designated as historic for use as a gym; using multiple homes to serve as restaurant, office, and retail space; and encouraging a wide range of arts projects.

In 2013, Phoenix approved annual fee-relief incentives totaling $100,000 for adaptive use projects. Any design professional, developer, or owner can submit to staff an application for a project to receive up to $7,000 to offset the cost of commercial plan review and permit fees. An application is submitted for each plan review and permit, allowing program staff to track the amount of incentives used per project and in the program as a whole. Through mid-2020, the program has provided more than $517,000 in incentives and 195 projects have been completed, with dozens more in the pipeline. Over $50 million in commercial reinvestment has occurred since the program's debut.

ABOVE: Phoenix's Culinary Dropout at the Yard is the successful adaptive use of a former motorcycle garage as a beer house and cocktail bar that serves classic food in a fun, laid-back environment with yard games and live music. *(OCA)*

DISTINCTIVE STRATEGIES

Adaptive use policies associated with the OCA include case management; regulatory relief covering site, civil, building, and life safety requirements; streamlined development processes; and $100,000 in fee incentives.

One innovation is the program's tiered approach to incorporating regulatory relief into projects. Tier 1 projects—those smaller than 5,000 square feet—receive the greatest relief from code compliance. Tier 2 projects are 5,000 to 25,000 square feet; the city has seen more projects in this range in areas south of downtown such as the warehouse district, which has become known for its tech corridor and office conversions. Relief for Tier 3 projects (25,000 to 100,000 square feet) focuses on finding new uses for regional and neighborhood shopping centers amid the national trend of changing retail norms in an era of increased online shopping.

The city has specific adaptive use programs and policies associated with building and life safety, building occupancy, site and landscaping, and civil and traffic requirements. Among those policies are the following:

- The Neighborhood Services Department agrees to extend time frames for enforcement of code violations as long as continued progress is being made to correct them on a monthly basis.
- The Zoning Ordinance was amended in 2009 to ease off-street parking standards for adaptive use projects of 5,000 square feet or less for a building at least 25 years old.
- Proportionality guidelines are applied to site, civil, parking, and landscaping requirements, allowing developers to use what is already on site if the impact of the project is small.
- A self-certification program eliminates plan review by allowing a registered professional to take responsibility for, and to certify, a project's

compliance with building code, standards, and ordinances. Depending on the scope of the project, permits can be issued within one to five days. The expanded program includes inventory, salvage, landscape, and parking lot plans by landscape architects; and grading, drainage, and parking lot plans by civil engineers. Eligibility is not determined by building size—the program was expanded to include most buildings over 25,000 square feet—though staff members

> *Building small is inherently challenged by regulatory barriers, but Phoenix's OCA provides a replicable model of cross-disciplinary and multi-stakeholder solutions that cut through bureaucratic inertia.*

audit projects to ensure that the design professionals are meeting all necessary building safety requirements. The threshold for an automatic audit includes buildings of 25,000 square feet and more. An authorized architect or engineer assumes all liability for site and building design, bypasses the standard plan review process, and obtains a permit in three days.

In an era during which building small is inherently challenged by regulatory barriers, Phoenix's OCA provides a replicable model of cross-disciplinary and multistakeholder solutions, removing bureaucratic inertia and creating a positive partnership between the city and small developers. Though many cities possess a richer stock of historic or architecturally significant structures, Phoenix has emerged as a national leader in the area of adaptive use. By addressing both code challenges *and* the culture of personnel involved in the review and approval process, the OCA provides a model for communities desiring to make better use of existing building stock and create more unique spaces that foster and support small, local businesses.

MIDTOWN DETROIT
the nonprofit entrepreneur

AT A GLANCE

Midtown Detroit Inc.
DETROIT, MICHIGAN

→ **PURPOSE:** To support the physical maintenance and revitalization of the Midtown Detroit neighborhood while working to enhance public awareness, appreciation, and use of the district; and to encourage creation of new mixed-income housing, an increase in the number of visitors to area attractions, new commercial activity, and infrastructure investments throughout the Midtown/New Center/TechTown districts

→ **ASSET CLASSES:** Hospitality, office, retail, mixed use, mixed income
→ **ENTITY TYPE:** Local nonprofit planning and development organization
→ **FOUNDED:** 2011
→ **STAFF SIZE:** 8
→ **CONTACT:** Sue Mosey, executive director
→ **PROJECTS:** 10 projects totaling 320,000 square feet
→ **PROJECTS UNDER MANAGEMENT:** 7

MIDTOWN DETROIT INC. (MDI) was established in 2011 when the University Cultural Center Association (UCCA) and New Center Council merged. These predecessor organizations focused on the Midtown/New Center districts of Detroit, a roughly one-by-three-mile neighborhood to the north of and adjacent to downtown. Rich with historic resources and a fine-grained block pattern, the area was perceived by UCCA and New Center Council to be ripe for redevelopment, offering opportunities for historic preservation and adaptive use.

Like much of Detroit, the neighborhood had suffered considerable disinvestment since the 1970s. UCCA and New Center Council were formed to encourage development of new mixed-income housing, increased numbers of visitors, new commercial investment and activity, and infrastructure investment.

MISSION AND PURPOSE

MDI is a 501(c)(3) nonprofit planning and development organization that supports the revitalization and physical maintenance of the Midtown Detroit neighborhood while also working to enhance public awareness, appreciation, and use of the district.

Since 2000, the organization has raised more than $100 million for a variety of initiatives. Moving beyond the marketing role played by most neighborhood-based nonprofits and business improvement districts, MDI has engaged in a wide variety of entrepreneurial efforts. These include

- restoration and conversion of six historic homes to serve as a boutique hotel;
- renovation of more than 60 commercial facades throughout the district;
- development of the Midtown Loop, a greenway trail;
- execution of various streetscape enhancement projects;
- creation of an arts district;
- acquisition and redevelopment of key gateway properties throughout the neighborhood, such as green spaces, parks, medians, and larger developments;

- construction of two community gardens;
- development of New Center Park and a number of other public green spaces;
- facilitation of funding for more than 40 residential developments providing more than 2,000 units of new housing;
- assistance to more than 150 local businesses with technical aid, site location, and financing; and
- administration of the Live Midtown and Stay Midtown residential incentive programs.

One of the most important roles MDI played in the neighborhood, especially early on, was demonstrating the potential of the market to other developers and showing how small development creates enthusiasm and passion for an area. As a nonprofit catalyst, MDI has developed real estate projects that show others how development in the area can work, producing space that can get leased and have value. For example, MDI developed a 30,000-square-foot office building for companies and organizations working in community revitalization in Detroit. The building is fully leased with credit tenants that pay market rents.

Susan Mosey, executive director of MDI, says that by developing a significant number of smaller, mixed-use developments, the nonprofit has laid the groundwork for much larger, well-capitalized developers to build and accelerate value in the neighborhood much more quickly. It is clear that the neighborhood would not be what it is today if it were not for MDI and other small developers that were the early risk

OPPOSITE: Elise Fields, chief operating officer of Midtown Detroit Inc., facilitates a neighborhood discussion about future plans and ways to bring new investment to the neighborhood. *(© MDI)*

takers and set the stage for the district being able to live up to its potential.

Beyond physical construction and renovation of properties, MDI has developed a comprehensive advertising campaign for the district that publicizes housing options, promotes cultural events, and connects people to Midtown museums, theaters, galleries, restaurants, and stores—an effort embodied in MDI's signature arts events: Dlectricity and Noel Night. These initiatives have proved successful and continue to attract new residents and visitors to the area.

MDI has more than 200 dues-paying members representing the area's corporations, businesses, community organizations, and cultural, academic, medical, and service institutions. More than 150 representatives from member organizations actively participate in MDI activities through committees, which include Public Space Development and Maintenance, Community and Economic Development, Security, Marketing, and Special Events. These committees have been responsible for the completion and/or operation of more than 40 programs and projects in the Midtown district.

PORTFOLIO AND PROJECT TYPES

MDI's real estate projects typically range from $2 million to $10 million in total cost and from 3,000 to 23,000 square feet in size. MDI develops hospitality, office, retail, mixed-use, and mixed-income projects, in addition to public spaces such as community

ABOVE: Known as 644 Selden, or the Smith Welding Supply Company building *(top)*, this is one of three properties purchased and renovated by MDI as part of the larger Selden Innovation Corridor revitalization. MDI has been leading efforts with local funders and developers to create a walkable, innovative, and creative corridor along Selden Avenue. The completed renovation of 644 Selden and the newly created Selden Courtyard *(bottom)* are now home to Smith & Co. restaurant (a nod to the former tenant), eight residences, and a future commercial use on the second floor. Selden Courtyard is ecofriendly and offers a public gathering space for the adjacent businesses and residents. Programming of the space was anticipated to begin in 2021. *(All images © MDI)*

gardens, parks (programmed and unprogrammed), streetscapes, and greenways.

MDI has established about 28 limited liability companies for all its real estate holdings and partnerships. Many of its projects are collaborations with other developers or local agencies. MDI uses a variety of real estate models—sometimes acquiring a property to sell it for a complementary development, other times acquiring property and creating a joint venture with another developer to execute the project. If it is a mission-related project, MDI typically will develop the project on its own.

ORGANIZATION SIZE, STRUCTURE, AND ROLES

MDI has a staff of eight, with additional part-time staff supporting the various programs and initiatives. MDI's real estate operation is staffed by Mosey and chief financial officer Cari Easterday. Mosey develops the concepts and works on partnerships, vision, and fundraising; Easterday closes the loans and manages the technical back-of-house work related to projects.

Mosey is supported by a 40-member board of directors and a 10-member executive committee, plus subcommittees that determine the direction of the organization. Building an organization with staff members who have expertise in a variety of areas is critical to MDI's ability to carry out its organizational strategy. Also driving MDI's hiring practices is the knowledge that community and economic development does not happen overnight and requires a staff with longevity and commitment to the work.

GETTING PROJECTS DONE

Early on, Mosey and her team worked hard to develop strong relationships with national and local community development financial institutions (CDFIs) to figure out how to use their capital effectively to move projects forward. She also leveraged her relationships with small businesses, philanthropies, advocacy organizations, the city of Detroit, private developers, and other stakeholders in the neighborhood.

Today, representatives of developers and businesses visit Mosey's office every day to ask about opportunities in Midtown. Whereas 10 years ago a call from a commercial broker looking for space would have been unheard of, today Mosey has more than 30 commercial brokers who call regularly with clients looking for space. "It's a very different game now," she says. In 2019, the district had only 7 percent commercial vacancy and 2 percent residential vacancy. In 2008, residential vacancy was 8 percent.

MDI conducts small-scale planning in what it calls micro-district areas. The organization will "tackle a 10-block area or a three-block area or a five-block area, not something too big—an area with a lot of disinvestment," Mosey says. "And then we start to work on finding private-sector partners, CDFIs,

> *MDI uses a variety of models—acquiring property to sell for complementary development, creating a joint venture with another developer to execute the project, or developing its own mission-driven projects.*

and other nonprofit partners who all want to come in and tackle a small district." MDI has historically employed this micro-district approach as its major strategy and continues to do so today. MDI will convene all the stakeholders, conduct workshops and lead efforts to create a planning strategy, and then work to implement it. Often the public sector will play a part, perhaps to carry out an element of the strategy involving transportation or mobility. Planning for each micro-district engages different partners and stakeholder groups.

When looking for real estate development partners, MDI is interested in furthering relationships with those who have some level of experience, taste,

FINANCING PROJECTS

Funding for MDI's projects can be grouped in the following major categories:

- **CDFIs:** These funds come through either direct lending or program-related investment the CDFIs get from large foundations. These investments are low-interest long-term loans that the CDFIs get for projects such as green grocers, health care clinics, or mixed-use, mixed-income development.
- **Foundations:** Foundation funding has been used in the past to support predevelopment and equity in order to start a project. Typically, the mission of the project must align with the foundation's mission. These funds have included recoverable grants and program-related investments.
- **Local public sector:** MDI has received funding through loans from the city's economic development agency, the Detroit Economic Growth Corporation; the Detroit Planning Development department; and other city agencies for affordable housing, hospitality, and other types of infrastructure programs and projects.
- **State of Michigan:** A state program provides funding that serves as subordinated debt and helps fill the capital stack between what a lender will provide for a project and what MDI needs.
- **Federal tax credit programs:** MDI has used New Markets Tax Credits, historic tax credits, and low-income housing tax credits to help fill the equity stack for projects.
- **Conventional sources:** MDI has used equity and debt from senior lenders such as CDFIs or the U.S. Department of Housing and Urban Development (HUD).

MDI has an annual operating budget of $3.5 million, which is largely funded by local anchor institutions, MDI members, and foundation partners. Development fees are typically deferred and paid out of cash flow. Each project has a capital stack that looks different from that of all the projects that came

and understanding of the market. MDI wants to partner with developers "who understand stacking capital and realize they're not going to get the kind of returns they could get in some suburban markets," Mosey says. Many MDI partners are attracted by opportunities for longer-term appreciation, as well as motivated by a personal connection with Detroit.

MDI has had unsatisfactory experiences with some partners in the past. These were "folks who were not established or didn't have enough development infrastructure to carry their part of the partnership," Mosey says. Learning from these mistakes, she emphasizes the importance of vetting all development partners and the development team, from the architects to environmental companies. "It's worth spending a lot of time vetting those people upfront before you enter into any relationships," she says. "We're more cautious today than we used to be about that." MDI examines its potential partners in terms of financial strength, infrastructure, and staffing in order to ensure that they have the capability and capacity to carry out the type and scale of development MDI is considering doing with them. MDI also looks at whether its partners have strong management skills and a demonstrated track record with a similar project.

ABOVE: West Willis Street is home to many locally owned shops and restaurants, including Avalon International Breads, a pioneer business in the Midtown district. MDI worked with the city of Detroit to remove the rights-of-way in this area, creating the opportunity for businesses to use their sidewalks for patios, outdoor spaces, and events. *(© MDI)*

before it, but typical funds include HUD loans, tax credits, grant funds, subordinated debt, and senior debt, among other types of capital.

DISTINCTIVE STRATEGIES

As a nonprofit, MDI has built a lot of value by taking considerable risk—atypical for a nonprofit. "We're able to take more risk on the front end if we think there will be a catalytic or transformational impact," Mosey says. "We also can play a role in acquiring buildings that we think are key to the district even if we sell them later or codevelop them with others in order to make sure there is consistency with the broader vision."

In 2016, MDI sent a consumer survey to every address in the district—about 9,000 households—asking residents what kind of services, goods, and price points they wanted in their community. Residents told MDI they thought there were too many boutique shops and other businesses that did not meet their day-to-day needs and that they could not afford. Other residents spoke of wanting a movie theater, a good 24-hour diner; affordable retail shops, salons, and apparel stores; a general goods store; and more grocery options. Using those results, MDI is targeting the types of retailers the neighborhood wants. For instance, in recent years the district has attracted more moderately priced, high-quality restaurants that are more affordable than the chef-driven restaurants already in the neighborhood.

Mosey wishes that MDI had conducted the broad-based consumer survey earlier. Historically, the high vacancy rate in the neighborhood gave prospective businesses multiple choices of location. Now, only a handful of spaces are available, some of which are controlled by MDI.

One strategy MDI employs is to reserve well-located storefront retail space in the district for women-, minority-, or immigrant-owned businesses. In some cases, MDI master leases space and in others it offers low-cost space in MDI-owned properties. This strategy ensures an inclusive mix of goods and services.

MDI also runs Stay Midtown, a rental incentive program for low-income residents. Through this program, MDI provides a housing subsidy for households whose rents have become a burden. The subsidy lasts up to three years, during which MDI tries to find the household a long-term housing option that is of high quality and fits into its long-term budget. The program has supported 160 low-income households since its launch in fall 2016.

Stay Midtown and MDI's support for local businesses are both proactive steps the organization is taking to combat gentrification and displacement.

MDI provides another glimpse into how building *small* can be a strategic neighborhood strategy that is attuned and adaptable to address the downsides of gentrification, embodied in displacement of and unaffordability for existing residents as neighborhoods are "discovered" and their character and grit find new fans with more disposable income. MDI uses a combination of strategic planning, executed at a micro scale; a commitment to partnerships of all

> *MDI provides another glimpse into how building* small *can be a strategic neighborhood strategy that is attuned and adaptable to address the downsides of gentrification.*

types and sizes; and the capacity to take on considerable risk. Its success helps breed more success as its efforts and projects—as well as the demonstrated transformation of the neighborhood—attract more partners, who in turn now have greater access to more capital.

For communities around the country where neighborhoods have little recent investment but high-value building stock and urban fabric, MDI provides a model for how building *small* can be an effective tool for transformation.

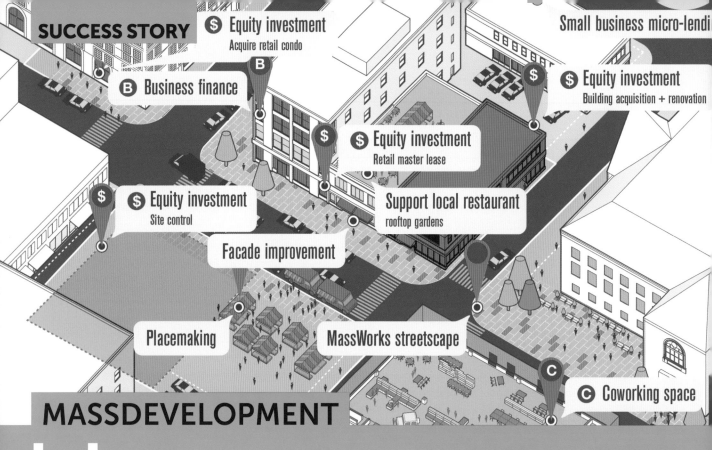

$ Equity investment
Acquire retail condo

B Business finance

$ Equity investment
Retail master lease

$ Equity investment
Site control

Facade improvement

Placemaking

MassWorks streetscape

Support local restaurant
rooftop gardens

Small business micro-lendi

$ Equity investment
Building acquisition + renovation

C Coworking space

MASSDEVELOPMENT

big agency embraces *small*

AT A GLANCE

MassDevelopment's Transformative Development Initiative
BOSTON, MASSACHUSETTS (HEADQUARTERS); PROGRAMS IN GATEWAY CITIES ACROSS THE COMMONWEALTH

→ **PURPOSE:** To accelerate economic growth in focused districts in Gateway Cities, working with cross-sector partnerships to engage community members, implement local economic development initiatives, and spur further public and private investment

→ **ENTITY TYPE:** Statewide program housed in MassDevelopment, the state's quasi-public finance and development authority

→ **FOUNDED:** 2014

→ **PROGRAM STAFF SIZE:** 9

→ **LEADERSHIP:** Noah Koretz, program director; Daniel Rivera, MassDevelopment president and chief executive officer

→ **TOTAL PROJECTS/INVESTMENT:** During the program's first five years, investment of about $17.8 million in the TDI districts through technical assistance, real estate investments, grant programs to accelerate local markets, full-time staff to work in the districts, and other initiatives

MASSDEVELOPMENT'S TRANSFORMATIVE DEVELOPMENT INITIATIVE (TDI) works to concentrate economic development activities, resources, and investments within designated neighborhood areas, known as TDI districts, to create a critical mass of activity that inspires investments by local residents, entrepreneurs, and businesses, as well as additional private development. The program works with cross-sector partnerships to engage community

members in actionable planning and implement local economic development initiatives. The use of program resources is coordinated within the comprehensive partnership and community planning facilitated by the TDI fellow, a dedicated fulltime MassDevelopment employee assigned to each district.

The program is deployed in TDI districts for two to four years. During this time, the goal is to assist the progress of catalytic investments and seed the long-term practices and relationships that will support inclusive local economies, which create jobs and provide wealth-building opportunities. In addition to partnership development, TDI focuses on place-based solutions and implementing incremental improvements to the built environment as one component of neighborhood revitalization.

This high-touch program is also designed to create, and then demonstrate, replicable redevelopment strategies for use throughout the state. In this way, TDI serves as an innovation lab to test approaches and grant programs in Gateway Cities, such as collaborative workspaces and placemaking projects, before expanding them statewide.

MISSION AND PURPOSE

MassDevelopment, formed in 1998 as a quasi-public agency of the commonwealth of Massachusetts, works with businesses, nonprofits, financial institutions, and communities to stimulate economic growth across the state. MassDevelopment achieves

this mission by providing loans, tax-exempt financing, grants, and real estate services to eligible communities, organizations, and projects.

As part of its statewide focus, MassDevelopment has a history of supporting cities and towns both within and outside metro Boston. The Massachusetts Institute for a New Commonwealth (MassINC), a public policy think tank, originated the term "Gateway Cities" in 2007 to describe medium-sized urban municipalities that anchor regional economies in the state. These cities typically have postindustrial economies, have consistently served as gateways for immigrants entering the country, and have not always shared in the recent economic successes of

OPPOSITE: MassDevelopment takes an integrated approach to regeneration of gateway cities, combining capital, building local capacity, and catalyzing small physical improvements. *(Massachusetts Development Finance Agency image)* **ABOVE:** TDI helped activate this formerly vacant alley in downtown Springfield with new shops and regular programming organized by the Springfield Business Improvement District. *(© 2018 Springfield BID "White Lion Wednesday" Beer Garden)*

the metro Boston area. Since 2008, Massachusetts has formally recognized 26 Gateway Cities as defined by population, average household income, and educational attainment.

In 2013, MassINC developed a set of proposals and recommendations for these cities in a report titled *Transformative Redevelopment*, which outlined a series of economic development suggestions and tools, including a MassDevelopment fund that would work to revitalize Gateway Cities through execution of a variety of new real estate–focused proposals. The ensuing legislation to establish the fund outlined support in the form of technical assistance, staff capacity, and specific real estate investments.

Based on these recommendations, the Massachusetts Legislature in August 2014 created the Transformative Development Fund, which partially funds TDI within MassDevelopment. The final legislation also included a program to fund collaborative workspaces in the Gateway Cities. All 26 Gateway Cities were eligible for the program, and in 2014 after a competitive application process, MassDevelopment designated areas—known as TDI districts—in 10 of those cities for the three-year pilot program. In 2018, MassDevelopment solicited a second round of applications, ultimately extending six districts from the first round and introducing four new districts in Chelsea, Fitchburg, Lawrence, and Worcester, as well as early-stage partnership development work in Chicopee and Fall River.

TDI has been funded through a combination of MassDevelopment and state resources. The Transformative Development Fund includes dollars from MassDevelopment's general and restricted funds—which are capitalized by earned income from loans, bond fees, and property sales—supplemented by state operating and capital funds.

TDI is designed to advance customized local work plans that draw from a comprehensive transformative development toolbox. The agency's slate of finance programs, real estate services, and related state

resources, as well as broad experience in these cities, shaped the breadth of TDI. MassDevelopment built TDI in the six months after the legislation's passage and has improved and adapted the program over the past five years to meet community needs. Instead of relying on annual grants and single transactions, the agency deploys its TDI programs—technical assistance, investments and grants, local staff capacity, and more—through a variety of activities and investments in a small, focused area, building momentum to help catalyze long-term sustainable redevelopment. The vision of TDI is a connected network of Gateway Cities in which sustainable, restored market conditions more accurately reflect the promise of their communities.

ORGANIZATION SIZE, STRUCTURE, AND ROLES

MassDevelopment has a statewide staff of about 175 people. TDI itself is headed by Noah Koretz, director of transformative development, who oversees both Boston-based staff members focused on TDI as well the TDI fellows, who are based in their TDI districts and are dedicated to economic development in those cities. Members of MassDevelopment's real estate department (led by executive vice president Cassandra

ABOVE: In downtown Holyoke, college students and community farmers are working side by side to grow produce inside two 40-foot shipping containers—fully outfitted with hydroponic farming technology—that were purchased with a TDI equity investment. *(Massachusetts Development Finance Agency image)*

McKenzie) and the community development department, members of which are based in regional offices across the state, also support various TDI initiatives in their regions.

PORTFOLIO AND PROJECT TYPES

Rather than focus on single solutions, TDI knits together a variety of resources to catalyze a culture of co-investment in which several constituents—public, private, nonprofit, and others—come together to invest in their neighborhoods. TDI is designed to be nimble, responding quickly to the local needs of a designated community using the resources available through MassDevelopment.

One of the program's organizing elements is the TDI district, a unique designation of a small area—with a diameter of about five minutes' walking distance—identified by a cross-sector local partnership. With a TDI district designation, these areas are eligible for additional local staff in the form of TDI fellows, technical economic development assistance, small grants to boost community engagement and local market development, and real estate investments.

A second organizing element of the program is the TDI partnership. Each district must have a local partnership with representation from the public, private, and nonprofit sectors. This group serves as the lead agent for directing work in the TDI district. Within their application to the program, the partnerships commit to a long-term engagement to implement a vision for district revitalization. The cross-sector nature of the partnership helps ground the work outside politics or election cycles, which is important to sustaining momentum. Although TDI is time-limited in nature and functions like an accelerator program, the redevelopment visions that the partnerships work to address often have a longer-term focus.

TDI brings a range of resources to designated districts:

- **TDI fellows**—entrepreneurial economic development professionals who work for two to four years with the TDI partnerships every day in the TDI district. As MassDevelopment employees, the fellows act as connectors and organizers, working with local leaders and stakeholders to encourage the establishment of new and growing businesses and activities to enliven the district.

- **TDI technical assistance**—direct third-party consultant services designed to build earlier planning efforts and drive an implementation-focused, market-building approach in the district. TDI has provided a wide range of technical assistance to districts, including urban design plans, market strategies, retail activation

The vision of TDI is a connected network of Gateway Cities in which sustainable, restored market conditions more accurately reflect the promise of their communities.

strategies, sustainability studies, and community visioning reports.

- **TDI local**—small grants supplied to TDI partnerships in support of inclusive market development. The most recent round of grants, designed to support and improve local small business programs, has helped small businesses and property owners in the districts improve facades and storefronts, and has helped subsidize the lease of retail spaces to activate new businesses. TDI local grants, which range from $10,000 to $75,000, are provided on an annual basis. They are awarded to fiscal agents within the TDI districts, who then distribute the funds through a local program identified in the TDI local grant application. In some cases, the grants are distributed through existing local programs; in others, new local programs and guidelines have been created to administer the funds.

- **TDI peer-to-peer**—workshops, resources, and events aimed at fostering collaboration and a collective knowledge network across Gateway Cities. TDI partners, community leaders, and fellows across districts convene to visit each other's TDI districts, share lessons learned and topic area knowledge, participate in skill-building activities, and create implementation-oriented resource guides and case studies.

- **TDI creative economies**—with the support of the Barr Foundation, TDI offers a competitive grant program for art and other creative industry projects aimed at catalyzing economic development and neighborhood revitalization, and a multiyear program for graduated TDI districts aimed at building a sustainable arts infrastructure in a city as a mechanism for supporting economic growth.

- **TDI challenge**—financial support upfront to municipalities that commit to making a change in policy, process, or ordinance that will directly advance the goals of the TDI partnership work plan. Once that change is complete, TDI partnerships receive additional funding for programs or projects that the new policies make possible.

- **TDI investments**—equity investments to help advance "stuck" properties in the districts that perpetuate or contribute to negative perceptions of the community or region. These properties have the potential to spur transformative development in and around a TDI district, but face significant hurdles for financing without a TDI investment. Current investments include:

  » **8–12 Stearns Square**, a former nightclub at the heart of the Springfield TDI District, an area undergoing significant public and private investment as the city's dining and innovation district;
  » **526 Main Street in Worcester**, a former pawnshop whose redevelopment is critical to advancing the TDI partnership's vision for transforming the city's Theatre District;
  » **335–337 Dwight Street in Holyoke**, an 8,550-square-foot, three-story historic brick building located at a key gateway into the Innovation District and TDI district; and
  » **A container farm project** at 150 Race Street in Holyoke that brings workforce development and urban farming to a highly visible, formerly vacant lot downtown.

While each TDI district has access to the preceding "TDI toolkit" resources, the use of these resources is tailored, according to the TDI partnership's work plan, to address unique local challenges and advance community priorities. An instructive case study is the Springfield TDI District, which MassDevelopment established in 2015 based on the local public/private partnership's vision of creating a downtown dining district in the blighted area between Union Station (opened in 2017) and the MGM Casino (opened in 2018). The partnership wanted to explore ways to increase foot traffic, add restaurants and amenities for new market-rate housing, and increase the visibility of investment opportunities.

In Springfield, first TDI steps included program-sponsored technical assistance, such as urban design strategies for the public realm, and provision of a market strategy and investor prospectus to help attract new restaurants, retail businesses, and other development. MassDevelopment also provided Springfield with a TDI fellow, Laura Masulis, and has improved local small business support though TDI local small grants.

Successful partnership efforts in Springfield so far have included the following:

- **Pop-up holiday market.** A month-long pop-up to test the viability of retail uses in a formerly vacant alley has resulted in a permanent retail location that was occupied by the Shops at the Marketplace, a cluster of women-owned businesses. Despite some turnover due to the pandemic, new businesses continue to be opened in this location, bringing retail business downtown. No direct grants were made to the Downtown Springfield Holiday Market, but Masulis supported the effort through business recruitment, small business development support, and promotion and marketing. About $10,000 in private funds was dedicated to the initial pop-up holiday shop and programming; another $65,000 in private money funded startup costs, capital improvements, and renovations associated with permanent tenancy.
- **Make-It Springfield.** A community workshop space for local makers, artists, entrepreneurs, programmers, students, and enthusiasts to make, create, and share their skills and tools, Make-It Springfield provides a platform for community members of all backgrounds to learn new skills, build relationships, launch businesses, and inspire one another. This community space, which, like the Shops at Marketplace, started as a one-month pop-up, celebrated its fourth anniversary in summer 2018. Make-It Springfield was initially funded with a $13,000 TDI grant that leveraged additional partnership funds to support operations and programming. Masulis has provided continued support for community management, operations, and marketing. In addition to the TDI funds, Make-It Springfield received grant money from the University of Massachusetts, a Collaborative Workspace seed grant from Mass-Development, a rent subsidy from the property owner, and matching funds from the MassMutual life insurance company for strategic planning. Make-It Springfield has established itself as its own institution with a membership structure, board, and executive director.
- **The Springfield Downtown District Loan Fund.** Capitalized by the city through the U.S. Department of Housing and Urban Development Section 108 Loan Guarantee Program, the fund, totaling $1.5 million, is for design, construction, equipment, and working capital for full-service restaurants in the city's dining district. Loans range from $50,000 to $200,000.

OPPOSITE: *Left:* TDI partners and community members work in small groups during a storefront activation peer-to-peer learning workshop. *Right:* TDI helped activate this predevelopment site as a pop-up beer garden and performance venue in Brockton. Sales data from the project, known as PROVA! ("proof" in Cape Verdean Creole) has helped prove the market for downtown dining and a brewery. *(All images: Massachusetts Development Finance Agency images)* **ABOVE:** Carlos Peña, founder of the social enterprise Paper City Clothing Company, cohosted a design and screen printing workshop at Make-It Springfield. The workshop, funded by the Springfield Local Cultural Council, produced youth-designed and printed T-shirts that were a typography collage of Springfield street and neighborhood names. Excess inventory was sold at Make-It, with the proceeds dedicated to supporting future programming. *(Make-It Springfield)*

- **Weekly farmers market and beer garden.** The Farm to Marketplace farmers market and the White Lion Wednesday outdoor beer garden are held during the summer at the Shops at Marketplace. The Springfield Business Improvement District operates this programming.

- **Pedestrian-friendly streetscape improvements.** These included traffic-calming curb extensions as part of the Stearns Square and Duryea Way restoration and revitalization project. MGM Springfield is also providing funding for the lighting of underpasses, street trees, and murals as part of an overall downtown revitalization. The Stearns Square and Duryea Way project includes decorative lighting and string lighting, a first for downtown Springfield. Downtown activation planning funded through TDI technical assistance efforts helped inform the lighting concepts, among other improvements.

- **Public art.** These efforts include a movie night, mural painting, and interactive art in Stearns Square funded by a TDI places grant. Following the TDI project, the Springfield Cultural District launched a downtown-wide utility box mural program. The city also started a public arts program with Community Development Block Grant funds, which led to creation of a mural in the district. Finally, the Springfield Department of Parks and Recreation funded movie nights in parks around the city following a first showing in Stearns Square.

- **Advances in restoration of Stearns Park.** Through the Stearns Square and Duryea Way renovation project, which includes $1.2 million in municipal investment, progress has been made on the restoration of historic Stearns Park. The first phase of the project opened in fall 2018, with a final grand opening scheduled for spring 2019, and the investment has already resulted in new tenants, restaurants, and investments in the surrounding area.

- **New businesses opened or relocated in the TDI district.** These businesses include 211 Worthington Pub, Art e' Pizza, Cajun on the Go, the Ethnic Study, Granny's Baking Table, Hot Oven Cookies, Nosh Café, Snapchef, and White Lion Brewing. The work of the TDI fellow and of the local partners to educate property owners, businesses, and investors about the market, facilitate introductions, and support business development—and in some cases, startup costs—was critical in attracting these businesses downtown. Other projects underway in TDI districts include J.M. Lofts, the mixed-use redevelopment of a historic building in Haverhill with new revitalizing local businesses in its retail spaces; Beyond Walls, a downtown public art installation in Lynn; the Brockton Young Professionals Group, a networking group for young professionals to advance ideas for the city and increase civic engagement; and the redevelopment of St. Mary the Morning Star in Pittsfield, a key church campus in the district now slated for redevelopment. For St. Mary the Morning Star, TDI fellow Sika Sedzro connected developer David Carver with MassDevelopment's lending team, which provided a $385,000 bridge loan to help Carver buy the property and line up financing for its development.

FINANCING PROJECTS

Over the program's first five years, from 2015 to 2020, MassDevelopment has invested $17.8 million in Gateway Cities through TDI-specific programs, including grants to coworking spaces, redevelopment of key buildings, and funds for placemaking activities. Through internal assessment and data collection, the agency has classified the relationship between the TDI program and public and private investments within the districts:

- A "TDI-influenced" investment is defined as an investment that would not have been made (at all or at its current scale, location, timing, or use) but for the direct involvement of a TDI resource or in response to specific TDI technical assistance efforts and program activities within the district. Using this definition, the agency has identified more than $56 million of TDI-influenced public and private investments in 16 TDI districts.

- In addition, the agency has identified more than $80.5 million of TDI-assisted investments in the 16 TDI districts. These TDI-assisted investments were supported in their implementation by some significant TDI involvement but would have happened—though perhaps with different outcomes—without the involvement of the program.

DISTINCTIVE STRATEGIES

Because of continued disinvestment in the commonwealth's Gateway Cities, some key challenges that MassDevelopment aimed to solve were a lack of local staff capacity and lack of financial resources. Thoughtful public policy from gubernatorial administrations, the legislature, and civic institutions led to Gateway Cities becoming the focus of numerous programs. Some efforts yielded planning strategies, but the lack of local capacity resulted in little implementation of complex, systemic urban redevelopment efforts, and many years of well-intentioned, yet isolated, state investments in these communities generated limited long-term impact.

When MassDevelopment formed TDI, its goal was to take a novel, incremental, fine-grained approach to development, rather than focus on one large investment. As a result, TDI aggregates many small investments from various sources to support existing assets and catalyze more activity.

An example of a low-cost, tactical investment that has catalyzed private investment can be found in Peabody, where a $10,000 grant resulted in a new permanent use for a downtown space and helped inspire a culture of trying varied approaches to activate a space. That creative culture shows itself in the many placemaking efforts and events that the local Peabody TDI Partnership has funded since the success of the TDI places grant, including pop-up ice bars, markets, and pubs.

The following is the step-by-step story of the initial $10,000 TDI places investment in Peabody:

- The TDI partnership identified a desired new use for downtown: a coffee shop.

- The partnership applied for and received TDI places funding: $3,200 for a pop-up parklet (outdoor seating), the success of which led to another $6,800 TDI places grant for a pop-up café (the "coffee shop experiment" inside a vacant storefront).
- The pop-ups opened in June 2016; Jaho Coffee & Tea occupied the space over the summer.
- Jaho Coffee & Tea did not permanently locate in the space, but when Northeast Arc, which offers job training to people with disabilities, expressed interest, Jaho acted as a resource and was able to support the permanent tenant during its startup phase.
- Northeast Arc was able to move into the space over the course of just a month to open Breaking Grounds Café in October 2016. As of publication, this business is going strong and has become an important local destination on Main Street.

Through TDI, MassDevelopment works to more effectively use, integrate, and add to existing state economic development tools and efforts in challenged local economies. TDI's philosophy of co-investment and adding capacity in the form of the TDI fellows brings all stakeholders together to counter the negative cycle of disinvestment, providing a push toward prosperity by building collective ownership of the future. This collective ownership is shifting perceptions and building momentum in places like Lynn, where a mural festival has grown into an organization with four full-time positions focused on arts and culture downtown; in Springfield, where planning led to a change in an outdoor dining ordinance and investment by small business owners; and in Gateway Cities across the commonwealth, where community leaders—engaged through the work of the TDI partnership—continue to operate, scale, and build off initiatives that began during their neighborhood's years in the Transformative Development Initiative.

SMALL CHANGE
funding *small*

Savers Village
📍 Newark, NJ

Work-force housing designed to turn tenants into home-owners.

$1,000 minimum investment

> Affordable workforce housing
> Building wealth for tenants
> Annual preferred return
> Profit-sharing after investment returned

Sharswood
📍 Philadelphia, PA

A mixed-use Opportunity Zone project set to transform a community. Change the game.

$751,250 raised

> For $2,500 invested, $14,500 expected back
> 16% targeted IRR
> Opportunity Zone tax benefits
> 10-year projected term

AT A GLANCE

Small Change
PITTSBURGH, PENNSYLVANIA

→ **DEFINING IDEA:** To fill a missing piece of the capital stack for developers tackling transformative neighborhood and community real estate development projects

→ **ENTITY TYPE:** A holding company and three subsidiaries, all of which are limited liability companies

→ **FOUNDED:** Winter 2016

→ **STAFF SIZE:** Team of three staff, seven consultants, and two advisers

→ **FOUNDER AND CEO:** Eve Picker

→ **TOTAL PROJECTS FUNDED:** 15 funded, with five offerings funding in winter 2020

→ **TOTAL PROJECT FUNDS RAISED:** $3.5 million as of end of 2020

EVE PICKER BELIEVES THAT GOOD DESIGN is for—and should be accessible to—everyone. With her background as an architect, city planner, real estate developer, and community development strategist, Picker has a deep understanding of how cities and urban neighborhoods work and how they can be revitalized. And her experience as a publisher, presenter, and instigator for the urban good make her an influential voice for positive change in cities everywhere.

In 2003, Picker tackled the redevelopment of a historic, architecturally significant building in Pittsburgh that had sat vacant for 15 years. The seven-story structure was badly deteriorated, with a gaping hole in the roof, water damage throughout, and little left to salvage but the exterior walls. Picker struggled to fund the project. Traditional financing was difficult to come by because the neighborhood was blighted, the market was soft, and no investments had been made in the community for many years. A local bank was willing to lend only 40 percent of the total project cost. Funding the project required 12 sources of financing, including a variety of loans and grants from authorities and agencies committed to redeveloping the city and the neighborhood.

As difficult as it was to finance the project, securing capital for redevelopment projects only became more difficult for small-scale developers when, in 2005, the first Bush administration severely reduced Community Development Block Grant funding. The reduction left cities and urban development authorities with less money and less certainty on which projects to fund. Soon afterward, in the wake of the foreclosure crisis, banking became more regulated, and community banks continued a decades-long trend of consolidation through mergers or acquisitions by larger banks, further removing them from the communities they had been created to serve.

These factors exacerbated the challenge of funding neighborhood-scaled projects. Banks sometimes shy away from projects involving aging structures deemed "too far gone" or those located in untested markets. In addition, underserved communities often lack similar buildings on which to base an appraisal for a bank loan—another test development projects must pass to receive financing.

"We're in a time when the value of cities is taking on new meaning. This renaissance is in part due to the transformative and creative power of smaller developments, all of which have an incremental impact," Picker says. "Despite this clear trend, institutional capital continues to be centered on conventional and formulaic projects. These are not the projects that cities and communities need [in order] to innovate and change. It's a shame that communities seeking to reinvent themselves must work so hard to find sources of funding that will support these finer-grained and sometimes game-changing projects."

In the meantime, the success of crowdfunding sites such as KickStarter and Indiegogo had not gone unnoticed. However, beyond philanthropy, there was a large segment of the population that was clamoring to be investors, and for that to happen, changes had

"We're in a time when the value of cities is taking on new meaning, due in part to the transformative and creative power of smaller developments."

OPPOSITE: *Top:* Rendering for 3451 Benning, a food hall under construction in Washington, D.C. The developer raised over $300,000 in new equity using Small Change's crowdfunding platform. (© *Neighborhood Development Company*) *Bottom:* Sample of offerings from the Small Change investor portal. (© *Small Change*)

What makes Small Change different?

MOBILITY

You can invest in projects that are walkable, bike-able and close to transit.

COMMUNITY

You can invest in projects that make places complete - with room for everyone to live, work and recreate.

ECONOMIC VITALITY

You can invest in projects that catalyze local economies and keep dollars close to home.

LEARN MORE

to be made to securities laws. Enter the Jumpstart Our Business Startups (JOBS) Act, signed into law in 2012 by President Barack Obama to encourage the funding of small businesses by easing several U.S. securities regulations and adding a new one. Perhaps the most important changes enacted were to allow issuers of securities—those raising money—to market those securities through advertising rather just soliciting participation behind closed doors, and to allow nonaccredited investors to participate. These constituted a catalytic change.

An individual accredited investor, as defined by the Securities Act of 1933, must have a net worth of at least $1 million, excluding his or her primary residence, and an annual income of $200,000. The definitions vary slightly for married couples or companies, but regardless, only 3 percent of the U.S. population fits this definition. Permitting nonaccredited investors to invest allowed the remaining 97 percent of the population to participate in investment activity from which it previously had been excluded.

To accomplish this shift, the JOBS Act of 2012 assigned the U.S. Securities and Exchange Commission (SEC) the task of changing two securities regulations, Regulations D and A, and writing a new one,

Regulation Crowdfunding (Reg CF). These changes took four years to complete, with updates to Regs D and A going live in 2013 and 2015, respectively, and Reg CF going live in May 2016.

With rules published, the investment crowdfunding industry unfolded. Although the first round of rule changes to Reg D was still limited to accredited investors, they permitted advertising to the general public, and investment crowdfunding platforms began to emerge. Among the earliest real estate platforms to appear using this rule were Fundrise, Patch of Land, and Realty Mogul.

In mid-2015, changes to Reg A, which had required approval of each offering memorandum by each state, eased the way for private companies to raise up to $50 million—an increase from $20 million—from the public, including nonaccredited investors.

And finally, Reg CF went live in 2016, representing the first step toward true democratization of investment. Reg CF permits anyone over age 18 to invest in qualified projects, but requires a serious commitment by any platform wishing to use this rule to raise money. A platform must be registered with the SEC as a "funding portal" and be a regulated member of the Financial Industry Regulatory Authority (FINRA), a

ABOVE: In keeping with the hallmarks of *small*, Small Change looks at a set of goals broader than just economic returns.
(© *Small Change; images: © 2014 John D. Norton [left and right], and iStock [center]*)

not-for-profit organization authorized by Congress to protect American investors by making sure the broker-dealer industry operates fairly and honestly.

Each funding portal must follow the rules and guidelines for introducing unsophisticated investors to the world of investing. Offerings must be written in plain English, educational materials must be provided, investors must be notified of their investment activities at multiple points in the investment process, and many other rules meant to protect unsophisticated investors must be followed. In exchange, markets are now open to people who never before had the opportunity to invest.

All these things together have created a seismic shift in investment activities and the beginnings of an investment crowdfunding industry.

With the promise of Reg CF, Picker saw an opportunity to help fill the funding gap for smaller developers by adding new access to debt and equity to build the capital stack. This gave both emerging and experienced developers an opportunity to be part of the change they wanted to see in their community. The result: the Small Change platform, currently the only registered funding portal focused on real estate in the United States.

"My goal as a developer has always been to tackle projects that will make significant change," Picker says. "But choosing projects in struggling neighborhoods brings financing challenges. I know there are many other developers struggling with this same challenge; they reach out to us at Small Change every day. I see great potential for these innovative and nonformulaic real estate projects to raise funds through the emerging equity crowdfunding industry. I believe that every day people are hungry to support developers making change where they live. And that's a powerful statement."

THE NEW COMMUNITY BANKING

Small Change has carved out a specific space—at the confluence of crowdfunding, social change, and urbanism—to provide missing finance in underserved neighborhoods. "Central to Small Change is my belief that everyday people can invest in, and help bring to fruition, important projects in forgotten places," Picker says.

In Small Change's use of the JOBS Act securities regulations to help developers, sometimes the offering follows conventional Reg D standards and sometimes Reg CF rules. But a recent innovation of Small Change is the ability to provide developers and their projects a "side-by-side" offering—both Reg D and Reg CF.

Reg CF places limits on how much any investor, whether accredited or not, can invest annually, while Reg D, although only available to accredited investors, does not limit investment amounts. By marrying Reg CF and Reg D in this side-by-side approach, Small Change has created a seamless investor flow and expanded the opportunity for larger contributions.

For all the promise the equity crowdfunding world holds, this is not a simple business. As a member of FINRA, Small Change is subject to audits and must conduct business much like a broker-dealer does. Documents and emails are "write once, read many" (WORM) archived—meaning they cannot be altered—and key employees are registered as "associated persons."

"What we're doing is serious stuff. We're listing projects on our platform that everyday people can invest in. It's appropriate that this is regulated," Picker says. "There are rules to follow. But in exchange the JOBS Act of 2012 provided us with an opportunity to expand the system of capital to fund projects that were simply ignored before. There used to be more than 15,000 banks in this country. Through decades of mergers and consolidation, there are now less than 5,000. In the absence of what were once locally focused banks, crowdfunding has the opportunity to become the new community banking."

SIMPLIFYING THE EXPERIENCE

The requirements and processes Small Change takes on are complicated, but the team has worked hard to simplify the experience for both developers and investors. Regulation CF requires that the platform's

Successful Change

SMALL CHANGE HEARS FROM NEW DEVELOPERS ALMOST EVERY DAY. Since it was launched, more than 1,000 developers have reached out seeking alternative financing. Their projects range in size from $80,000 to $50 million and span practically every state in the country.

In line with its mission, Small Change's success stories vary in project type and size but share the common theme of community impact. Representative projects include the following:

- **STARTER HOME TWO, 3609–3613 S. SARATOGA.** Part of a series of projects developed by OJT (Office of Jonathan Tate) in New Orleans through a program called Starter Home, this early Reg CF project (the first on the Small Change platform) consisted of two new single-family homes located on constrained sites in an inner-city neighborhood undergoing transition.

- **TINY HOUSE.** A planned "tiny house" was poised to introduce inexpensive, entry-level tiny homes to an underserved Pittsburgh neighborhood while serving as a pilot project for local nonprofit cityLAB Inc. Because the project was the first of its kind, it was impossible to get the appraisals of postconstruction value required for a bank loan. Small Change raised $100,000 for Tiny House LLC, which funded the construction loan for cityLAB. The result introduces a new infill housing type while spurring neighborhood development. As a result of this project, the city of Pittsburgh subsequently introduced a tiny house/accessory dwelling unit beta overlay district in this neighborhood.

- **BUVINGER BUILDING.** Shawn Kichline, principal of Oxide Real Estate Development LLC, had gained experience working for large development companies before deciding to branch out on his own. He needed $240,000 in equity for his first project—renovating a historic, three-story structure located in a vibrant and rapidly evolving retail corridor in Pittsburgh. Small Change investors provided him with funds for the project, helping him turn his vision into reality.

"That building put the developer in business," Picker says. "With that project under his belt, he is now doing more projects, including another nearby parcel, and there's development going on all around the site. It's a pretty big change we helped implement."

In 2018, Kichline refinanced the building and investors received a handsome 21 percent internal rate of return.

- **BENNING ROAD MARKET.** Inspired by a Portland retail development called The Zipper, this distinctive project in the River Terrace neighborhood of northeast Washington, D.C., is geared toward foodies, hipsters, and others through its diverse array of offerings. Located along a major retail corridor, the project expands a single-story retail building to create 6,800 square feet of ground-floor retail space and 4,400 square feet of mezzanine space. The project is intended to spur a vibrant group of community-oriented projects that combine retail, residential, and public space.

ABOVE: Oxide Development's Buvinger Building was an early project to use Small Change's platform, raising $300,000 in equity for the project. (© Oxide Development)

information be understandable on the first reading. This is something Picker appreciates, given her belief that investing should be accessible to everyone.

"I'm a reasonably sophisticated real estate investor myself, but there are times when even I don't understand the content on some investment platforms," Picker says. "Who knows what 'capital stack' means except developers? Our goal, and the purpose of Reg CF and its 'plain English' rule, is to make sure that the average, everyday investor can easily understand the terms of the project or business they are investing in."

To keep it simple, Picker's team "tries hard to keep our glossary to a minimum," she says, and works with each developer to ensure that the terms of the offering are explained to investors in the simplest way possible.

Beyond being understandable, the site is extremely user-friendly. It takes less than 60 seconds and just a few steps to invest on the Small Change website. This is by design.

"The site is absolutely transparent," Picker says. "We're open for investment to anyone over the age of 18, and there's no fee to join. This is an unprecedented way to invest in real estate." Small Change launched with a test project in 2015, but once the Reg CF rules were published, Picker found she had to rebuild the platform. It was not until the end of 2016 that Small Change became a registered funding portal. Since relaunching its platform in 2017, the company has expanded its following to 20,000 and its active account holder list to more than 1,700, which is growing daily.

Picker and her team have also endeavored to make the experience seamless for developers. Preparing an offering typically requires the help of an expensive SEC attorney. Instead, she has prepared a complete set of offering templates with her lawyer, so developers need only fill in the blanks. Additional resources, such as an FAQ page, help developers determine if their project is ready to list and offer answers and resources for each step of the process.

"We've worked really hard to design a set of resources which solve a classic dilemma for developers: they want to find new ways to raise money, but their projects are already complex enough," Picker says. "Adding in a securities offering can be a lot of additional work. Our goal is to create access to deeper funding for those who might not have the ability or time to put everything together on their own."

The offering pages on the Small Change website tell an important story—why the project matters, who the developers are and why they believe in their work, what neighborhood the project is located in, and how these elements work together. Unlike companies with numbers-laden institutional investment offerings, Small Change uses video, great photography, and eye-catching graphic design to communicate a sense of positive and creative energy.

To get it all done, Picker leads professionals—in-house and outside advisers—with expertise in and emphasis on deal flow, technology, communications and outreach, operations, content and special projects, SEC counsel, finance, bookkeeping, accounting, and compliance, as well as real estate development, technology, and the law.

STAYING TRUE TO MISSION

Small Change is focused on projects that are transformative and creative and that make cities better. To stay true to this mission, the company created the Change Index, a proprietary system illustrating the impact a project has on its surroundings. The Change Index uses data points—such as an area's walkability and bikeability, public transit access, proximity to green space, availability of commercial and cultural amenities, and other measures of quality of life—to gauge a project's potential.

"We're focusing on opportunities that not only have the potential for a financial return but also do some good." Picker says. "We care about the impact a building makes on a place and on the people who occupy it."

In addition to using the Change Index, the Small Change team vets projects to determine their viability, reviewing everything from the business plan and existing market forces to the project's readiness and timeline, along with the developer's background. A project must make sense before the opportunity for investment is presented to the public.

THE WAVE OF THE FUTURE

Since the real estate equity crowdfunding industry began, the market has grown dramatically. By 2014, $1 billion had been raised globally through investment crowdfunding platforms. By 2017, that number had risen to $5.5 billion, and the World Bank predicts that $93 billion will have been raised by 2025. Reg CF has had a slower start. Since mid-2016, over $160 million has been raised, but only 2.2 percent of that has been for real estate projects. All funding portals other than Small Change are focused on business offerings, not real estate.

Picker is certain more growth, maturity, and transformation are on their way. "There is a huge need for financing transformative and creative projects, evidenced by the large pipeline of developers we see coming to Small Change," Picker says. "I truly believe that equity crowdfunding is the future of capital formation and will help to finance impactful projects in cities and towns everywhere."

SMALL CHANGE INDEX™

MOBILITY

COMMUNITY

ECONOMIC VITALITY

Mobility		Community		Economic Vitality	
Urban location	✓	Street life	✓	Underserved community	✓
Walkable	✓	Third Place	✓	Jobs Created	✓
Bike friendly		Park or Plaza	✓	Incubator	
Business Corridor	✓	Building reuse or infill	✓	Diverse workforce	✓
Public or other transit		Affordable housing	✓	Green features	
Fix your own transport		Fresh food access	✓	Even more green	
Transit oriented development		Minimized site disturbance		Reduced parking	✓

SMALL CHANGE INDEX™

MOBILITY

COMMUNITY

ECONOMIC VITALITY

Mobility		Community		Economic Vitality	
Urban location	✓	Street life	✓	Underserved community	✓
Walkable	✓	Third Place	✓	Jobs Created	✓
Bike friendly	✓	Park or Plaza	✓	Incubator	
Business Corridor	✓	Building reuse or infill	✓	Diverse workforce	✓
Public or other transit	✓	Affordable housing		Green features	✓
Fix your own transport		Fresh food access	✓	Even more green	
Transit oriented development		Minimized site disturbance	✓	Reduced parking	

ABOVE: Small Change uses a proprietary "index" to convey to investors the anticipated triple-bottom-line performance of each investment: the Change Index for Innovation Houses *(top)*, a nonprofit housing/leadership project in Chicago, and for 3451 Benning *(bottom)*, a food market in Washington, D.C. *(All images © Small Change)*

Perspectives on Making Change

IN STARTING SMALL CHANGE—and throughout her career—Eve Picker has learned lessons that can benefit both private developers and the public sector. For new developers interested in raising funds, she stresses the importance of taking an honest look at their projects.

"The first time you do real estate development, it takes a while to sort through it, and it's not very clear who will help," Picker says. "And if you're doing something unusual and it's the first in your community, it likely won't be easy to get a bank loan. Really think through the numbers—you're going to have tax, insurance, maintenance—and understand what the income stream will look like. Be honest about the project's viability and business plan. The story matters, but the numbers tell a story, too, and they have to work."

Picker also emphasizes the value of thinking differently. For example, she is working with a first-time developer who pulled together funding from tax credits, grants, and other resources to make her project work. "She put together a perfectly viable plan for something a bank would never look at," Picker says. "That's what it takes: if you want to do something different, you have to think different."

Picker encourages the public sector to embrace change as well and to stay connected with potential funding sources for developers interested in building in their communities.

"When I built my portfolio years ago, I couldn't guess which banks would be supportive," Picker says. "The local Urban Redevelopment Authority worked hard at relationships with local banks, which was extremely helpful for me. If your community wants incremental development—places people are drawn to—stand beside the developer and help them. It's not always about the money; it's about the relationships."

When it comes to making positive change, it takes a positive outlook. Throughout each chapter of her career, Picker has found the following traits to be helpful.

→ **CONTINUAL LEARNING**: "As a developer, I learned to read contracts carefully. With Small Change, I've learned a lot about a sector I knew nothing about when I started. I'm a maker, so it's been an interesting process to take dense, difficult-to-read regulations and break through to their meaning to create a simple solution."

→ **PROBLEM SOLVING**: "As an architect, I learned how to solve problems—to really develop something from nothing. That's key to the work we do at Small Change."

→ **PATIENCE**: "I worked with a lot of community development corporations when I was younger and learned I had to be patient. Not everyone has the same skills or moves at the same pace, and it takes time to gain understanding and get on the same page."

→ **HUMOR**: "Bizarre things happen in development, so you have to keep your sense of humor with you."

ABOVE: Eve Picker, founder of Small Change. (© *Small Change*)

small
case
studies

Small comes in a rich variety of building types, uses, and locations—from dense urban downtowns, to suburban arterial strip centers, to small-town neighborhoods. The case studies profiled here were selected to illustrate the diversity and power of *small*. How it contributes to building and renewing neighborhoods, and how it can be built new or repurpose down-but-not-forgotten building stock. Most important, these projects are meant to demonstrate how we can build better places—and create valuable real estate—by fitting into community context, rather than overwhelming it.

Oslo is a small, ground-up, multifamily infill development with units designed for sharing. Targeted to young adults seeking affordability, the project was the redevelopment of an underused site of just over an acre located in a lively and increasingly unaffordable neighborhood of Washington, D.C.

The Newton, located in the Uptown neighborhood of Phoenix, is a mixed-use rehab of a rambling mid-century building that was home to a restaurant in a reemerging neighborhood, along the new transit line. The rehabbed development creates energy with its mix of retail, food and beverage, office, and event space.

The Tomorrow Building in downtown Chattanooga is a conversion of a hotel into furnished micro-unit apartments. The development provides housing for entrepreneurs and other young professionals drawn to the city's designated "innovation district," thereby expanding the district's population beyond its nine-to-five workers.

Chophouse Row is a mixed-use redevelopment comprising office, retail, and apartments in a 43,500-square-foot assemblage of small buildings. It is located in the Capitol Hill neighborhood of Seattle, one of the city's most vibrant areas. The project fills in the "missing teeth" of a block.

AF Bornot Dye Works, in central Philadelphia, is a redevelopment of three abandoned factory buildings. The transformation includes 17 apartments and ground-floor commercial uses that synergize the residential component. The project was financed using an innovative mix of public and private sources as well as crowdfunding.

> *These projects are meant to demonstrate how we can build better places—and create valuable real estate—by fitting into community context, rather than overwhelming it.*

rethinking residence

OSLO | WASHINGTON, DC

OSLO IS A NINE-UNIT MULTIFAMILY rental apartment development on a central-city infill site in the Shaw neighborhood of Washington, D.C. The project has been positioned to appeal to recent college graduates and millennials who want to share a large apartment as a preferable and cost-effective alternative to renting a studio or one-bedroom unit. The building offers three units with three bedrooms and six units with four bedrooms, with typical unit sizes ranging from 970 square feet to 1,410 square feet.

DEVELOPMENT BACKGROUND AND THE SITE

Ditto Residential was founded in 2008 by Martin Ditto, who is the company's chief executive and leads all its development activities. He is responsible for procuring acquisitions and investment opportunities, as well as overseeing design direction and growth strategy. He previously worked in development at Bozzuto and Monument Realty, two prominent developers in the Washington area. Ditto Residential began with the development of a single home on an urban lot, and it has grown steadily since then.

With Oslo, Ditto set out to build something a bit different from the typical Washington apartment building. He notes, "We wanted to get into a little trouble, make money, and be successful, . . . but break the mold, something that was not just what everyone else was doing." Ditto was familiar with shared-housing concepts that had been developed in Portland, San Francisco, and Seattle and bought the site with the idea of building an apartment building using the shared-housing idea.

The 5,520-square-foot site when acquired consisted of an old, obsolete, nonhistoric nine-unit brick apartment building that covered the front half of the midblock site; the back half was used as open space and parking. The space between the front of the building and the street is owned by the city and is not included in the site size calculation. Although located in the middle of the city block, the original

building had eight-foot setbacks. This was an attractive feature that allowed Ditto to develop a building that capitalized on natural light by placing windows on all four sides of the structure.

The walkability of the neighborhood and its location one block from the Shaw Metro station and about a 12-minute walk from downtown D.C. were two additional appealing features of the site. At the time of the property acquisition, Shaw was already seeing rising land values and a good deal of new development, so Ditto Residential was not a pioneer when it entered this market.

The seller was a local property owner who owned numerous small buildings in the area. The sale was

---

OPPOSITE: Oslo, a small, nine-unit, infill apartment building that features a distinctive modern facade, is designed to appeal to young people who want to share an apartment. *(Michael Wilkinson, 2015)* **ABOVE:** The living area of one of the four-bedroom units that faces the street features large floor-to-ceiling windows. *(Patrick Ross, 2015)*

an off-market transaction in 2012, a time when the market was active and several firms were bidding on the site. Ditto Residential paid a retail price, acquiring the site for $1.28 million. At the time of acquisition, Ditto did not know exactly what the final product would be or what it would cost to develop, although the developer was able to calculate rough square footage costs and revenues based on the zoning.

Even though the site had by-right zoning, because the company was making major changes to a nonconforming existing building, conforming to zoning requirements was a challenge. This was caused primarily by some initial uncertainty regarding how much of the building foundation needed to be retained to preserve the existing zoning rights, which allowed for a nine-unit building with a height limit of 40 feet. Ditto eventually determined that the zoning allowed the company to demolish most of the building, but Ditto needed to retain the foundation to a level four feet above grade to maintain the zoning rights. Getting to this final zoning interpretation was not simple, however, and took some time and expertise.

Planning for Oslo began in November 2012, and the site was purchased that December. Design

proceeded throughout 2013, construction financing was arranged in November 2013, construction began that December, and the project was completed in November 2014.

DEVELOPMENT FINANCE

Development costs for the project totaled $4.85 million, comprising the site acquisition cost of $1.28 million, $2.74 million in hard costs, and $831,000 in soft costs, including $190,000 in overhead costs for the development staff. The project was financed with $1.25 million in equity capital, 50 percent from Martin Ditto and 50 percent from a private real estate investor that he connected with via family when he started the company. The private investor is a 30-year real estate investor who had been involved in a variety of real estate projects before this one.

Financing also involved a $3.6 million construction loan from Capital Bank, a Maryland-based institution that has been an active lender to smaller development startup companies in the area. Martin Ditto has worked with Capital Bank on a majority of its projects since he founded the company. He noted that this early and strong banking relationship with an important banker was instrumental in the company's growth. The loan was arranged with an 80 percent loan-to-cost ratio and covered both acquisition of the property and development of the building.

Permanent financing was obtained from Sandy Springs Bank, a Maryland institution, in spring 2015 after the project was stabilized for 30 to 60 days. The permanent loan totaled $5.35 million and is structured as a seven-year adjustable-rate mortgage loan. At the time of the refinancing, the property was valued at $7.25 million.

While the project encountered some construction delays (discussed below), it has ultimately been financially very successful for its investors. "It was a home run from a financial perspective," notes Ditto. The permanent financing allowed both equity investors to get their equity back after the permanent financing was put in place, and the owner partnership—1734

ABOVE: A rendering of the building highlights the cellar level, the floating entry bridge on the second level, and the upper levels sheathed in fiber-cement board. *(DEP Designs)*

6th Street LLC—expects to hold the property for some time. "We will get the most value out of this property by holding it long term," says Ditto.

PLANNING AND DESIGN

The program for the project increased the overall square footage on the site while still conforming to the nine-unit and 40-foot height limit required by zoning. To accomplish this, the developers and designers focused on the specifics of the zoning and came up with a plan that allowed them to build a three-story building with a below-grade fourth level. The footprint of the new building was also expanded toward the rear, and the new building footprint is about twice the size of the previous one.

With the addition of the lower-level floor and the larger footprint, the new four-level building is more than twice the size of the old one: the built area increased from nine units in 5,400 square feet to nine units in 12,800 square feet. The height of the building is 39 feet 8 inches.

The objective of the design was to create a high-design, transformative residential building that provides young professionals a great living experience at a reasonable cost through a shared living concept. The zoning on the site supported this objective and the shared-housing concept: since the zoning requirements focused on the number of units and not the square footage, the designers used the shared-housing concept to create a building with large units of three and four bedrooms that was highly marketable to millennials. Large units like this would likely not have been marketable if not positioned as shared living units.

Martin Ditto had met the architect, Chuong Cao of DEP Designs, when they worked for different firms, and they both founded their own firms in 2008; they have worked together on at least six projects before Oslo. Ditto brought Cao to the site, even before it was purchased, to discuss its potential. At the outset, the principal program element was that there would be nine units; the size, number of bedrooms, and configuration of the building were yet to be determined.

Foundation and structural features. The principal issue the developer and designer faced was how to fit a larger building onto the site—including a new lower level—given the zoning requirements and the fact that they were required to retain the foundation of the building. It took considerable time and effort to properly interpret the zoning requirements.

The developer eventually determined that only 48 inches of the above-grade foundation needed to be retained, rather than two stories, which was the company's initial assessment. This allowed the addition of a lower level, removed some of the design constraints Ditto and Cao were facing, and allowed for value engineering. The zoning stipulated that if the finished ceiling of a unit in a basement level is less than four feet above the exterior grade, then that floor area is not applicable to the overall floor/area ratio calculation. The exterior grade in this case is the original grade at the front and rear of the building.

In addition to the three stories above grade, a cellar level was created to maximize the building density. To accomplish this, the developer actually built a new foundation under the existing one, with the cellar level partially below grade. Soil was removed from the middle of the site to lower the grade and create lighted walkways, allowing the cellar-level units to feel like above-grade units and providing individual exterior unit entries.

Building the new foundation itself was a challenge. Four feet of foundation above grade had to be maintained, and that foundation went three or four feet below grade. To create the new lower level, Ditto Residential had to dig below the existing foundation and underpin it. The new foundation ties into the old foundation, with a new footing below the existing footing (tied with reinforcing bar); a new concrete slab was also added at the base. Ditto Residential also had to underpin the neighbor's foundation, a two-story wood-frame building abutting the property line.

Because of the foundation challenges, the developer needed to get the structural and mechanical engineers involved very early on. In fact there was a robust dialogue among the developer, architect, engineers, and contractor early in the process about which elements of the old building to keep and which to replace. The finished building itself is wood-frame construction.

Windows on all sides. Because the site offers eight-foot setbacks around the entire building, the new structure was able to provide large windows on all sides, ensuring that all units offer a lot of light; every room of the building has at least one window. The lower-level units have patios on the north side, and the two top-level units have balconies on the back of the building, all with large windows. The front units facing the street have large signature storefront-like windows, which are a significant feature in the overall image of the building.

The window pattern on the lower level was affected by the existing foundation masonry facade and differs from the window patterns above. The designers sought to use the existing openings in the foundation wall so as not to compromise the foundation structure.

Unit layouts. The building includes nine apartment units, six of which are four-bedroom units of about 1,410 square feet, and three of which are three-bedroom units of about 970 square feet. All three-bedroom units are on the ground-floor terrace level, and all have large, private patios. The four-bedroom units are on the upper three floors—two per floor—and have an extra-large living room/common area; units on the two upper levels at the front have large floor-to-ceiling windows.

Each bedroom, bathroom, and closet module was designed to fit into a square, and all are the same size throughout the building. Thus each renter receives roughly the same bedroom, bathroom, and closet, minimizing the need for tenants in the shared living units to set different rent levels for different rooms.

The overall layout divides the building into halves consisting of two "bars"—one with public spaces (living rooms and kitchens) and one with private spaces (bedrooms and bathrooms). This design created efficiencies in the plumbing layout and construction. Most of the bedrooms and bathrooms are located along the north wall of the building in a long bar. The living room and kitchen areas are along the south wall, where the entrances are also located.

Wall system, footbridge, and construction delays. The wall system for the building is an important feature of the design. The wall is a structural system in itself, independent from the building structure, and this particular system, because of its small size, required considerable project management skills to put in place. The developer and architect chose Nichiha Illumination Series fiber-cement siding panels for the sides of the building, primarily for their resilience, beauty, and modern look. Furthermore, the Nichiha system is a rain screen, a breathable building skin that creates a healthier building environment.

A floating footbridge was also chosen to provide access to the second-level units and to the stairwell entrances that provide access to the third and fourth levels. The footbridge and the wall cladding served together as primary entry features for those visiting the building, becoming a kind of second front for the building.

The developer, however, had never worked with the Nichiha material before and discovered there were uncertainties regarding how best to install it. As a result, the installation was delayed, which in turn delayed installation of the floating bridge on the second level; Ditto Residential could not finish the bridge until the wall was finished.

Facade and building front. One of the most unusual and striking features of the structure is the two-story glass curtain wall on the front of the building. This glass curtain wall spans about half of the upper two levels of the building and is a key element in establishing the modern nature of the building design. But the facade also includes lattice on about half of the upper two levels as well, softening the look and paying homage to the residential character of the neighborhood. The lower part of the facade also features lattice as well as smaller windows.

This pattern of mixing glass with lattice serves to break the facade into separate and distinct components. The lattice was used to make the building more contextual and provide an appropriate scale. The mixture of glass and lattice also separated the building facade into base and top and divided the building horizontally and vertically.

Visitors to the building can gain access to the building from the front via stairs that go down to the lower level or up to the footbridge level. The lower level is gated and locked at both the front and back to restrict access and cut-through traffic.

Parking. Three surface parking spaces, located at the rear of the building, are rented separately from the residential units. The existing zoning requires one space for every three units. The trash and recycling bins are also located in the parking area.

MARKETING AND MANAGEMENT

The building website promotes the following key features of the building:

- It is a brand-new building.
- Every bedroom has its own bathroom.
- Modern design, space-efficient units, minimalist features.
- Kitchen with stainless-steel appliances, including a stove, oven, dishwasher, fridge/freezer, and large basin sink.
- Large walk-in showers.
- A space-saving, stackable washer and dryer in every unit.
- There are windows everywhere. We are talking about a lot of light.
- A small community. You (should) know your neighbors. There are only 33 of you.
- Three off-street parking spaces behind the building are available for rent.
- Amazing location in Shaw. Great restaurants, bars with people you want to talk to, some of the best music venues in the city. And the building is a block from the Shaw Metro station.

One goal of the marketing is to attract people who do not want to live in a large building—those looking for more of a boutique experience. Part of the appeal of the offering is that it allows tenants to "get in on something social," notes Jamie Weinbaum, chief operating officer of Ditto Residential. "The units are communal and the building is communal. Our tenants want to be in a boutique, curated experience. That goes with the idea that we are trying to provide."

Marketing and leasing. As noted, permitting and construction issues affected final delivery of the project. Building occupancy, originally planned to start in August 2013, was delayed by three months until just before Christmas, which is historically a slow season for leasing.

"That was not an ideal scenario," notes Weinbaum. "Leasing apartments at that time of the year was extremely challenging. We knew we had to be creative. We knew we had to have a guerrilla campaign around really bringing groups together. Our long waiting list had shrunk due to the time of year. With events and mixers, we were really doing a lot of matchmaking."

ABOVE: The foundation and lower level of the building during construction.

A little less than three months later, by the end of February, the project was fully leased. Notes Weinbaum, "That exceeded our expectations." The introductions and the personal touch were very important in the quick lease-up. The fact that only nine units needed to be leased was also helpful.

To find tenants, the marketing team leaned heavily on craigslist, the place where most people look for shared-housing offerings in Washington. This was very cost-effective because craigslist is free. More traditional apartment marketing sites were also used, as were flyers placed at graduate schools and area bars and coffee shops. The project's website marketing offers assistance with group formation: "Looking for only a room? Let us know! We're happy to help you find a few roommates." Initial leasing was done in-house by the development team.

Unit pricing. Three-bedroom units rent for about $3,640 per month ($3.75 per square foot), and four-bedroom units rent for $5,310 per month ($3.76 per square foot); the cost to rent a room in a three- or four-bedroom unit at Oslo ranges from $1,200 to $1,350 per month. While the per square foot rents are comparable between the three- and four-bedroom units, the per room rent is higher in the four-bedroom units because these units offer a much larger common living area.

These rents compare favorably with one-bedroom units being offered in the area, which typically rent for $1,800 to $2,200 per month. Oslo does more than just offer a less-expensive alternative: many individuals in the market like the social aspects of group living as well. The developer did find that three-bedroom units were easier to lease than those with four bedrooms.

Tenants and tenant turnover. Creating groups to lease units was necessary at the beginning and was an effective initial lease-up strategy. However, once these groups are formed and units are leased, the units tend to stay leased to the group even as individual tenants move into and out of the unit.

When Ditto Residential began leasing, only one full tenant group had signed a lease; all other units were filled by renters who had been introduced to one another through the Ditto marketing effort. The developer notes that this most likely would not have been the case had lease-up occurred during a different time of year.

Ditto Residential signed two six-month tenant leases in the beginning, but when those leases came up for renewal, everyone stayed. Since then the building has maintained 100 percent occupancy. Full occupancy is expected to continue: in this type of shared housing, rooms may turn over frequently, but part of the group typically stays and finds another person to rent the room.

Notes Martin Ditto, "The likelihood of three or four tenants moving out at the same time is relatively low." Each person's name is on the lease and each is responsible for the lease of the entire apartment, not just his or her own room. Notes Weinbaum, Oslo has attracted a "broader [tenant] age range than we originally thought." The tenants are not just recent college graduates, but also people in their 30s. Oslo is the only apartment building currently owned by Ditto Residential, so management and maintenance of the building is handled by an outside firm because it was not cost-effective to manage the building in-house.

OBSERVATIONS AND LESSONS LEARNED

In retrospect, it seems obvious that a shared-housing multifamily concept could work in Washington, but when the project started, many observers were skeptical. College students often live in shared apartments near campuses, and Washington, D.C., offers many rowhouses that are rented and shared by single people. However, the idea of developing a new and very modern apartment building in the city that targeted the millennial market with this shared concept was relatively new and innovative. Ultimately, the project was able to tap into an underserved market and be successful. Ditto Residential has at

least four other projects underway in the city using the shared-housing concept.

Using custom and nontraditional materials in a modern building design can be challenging. At Oslo, some initial uncertainty about how to install the facade material led to delays in project completion. It is best to thoroughly research and understand the materials being used and how they should be installed well before construction is underway. And if problems do occur, they should be addressed immediately to avoid costly delays.

Zoning requirements on redevelopment sites, even where the use remains the same, can be complicated and confusing. Ditto Residential began the project with the belief that the zoning required the project to retain more of the foundation than was ultimately required. It took some time and legal wrangling to sort this out, which created initial challenges for the planning and design. A full and thorough zoning assessment is essential at the outset to understand what is allowed and required from existing zoning.

When working with older buildings, it is best not to depend on the structure or foundation being square, plumb, or level, and to be prepared for the problems these irregularities will create. Ditto Residential had to be creative to make the building walls straight when the foundation wall was not. A convex wall would have been noticeably odd for the building.

Design matters. The large front windows, the floating access deck, and the exterior material all served to distinguish the project and draw attention to the building. Ditto saw the building attract a lot of interest because of the design. Being very thoughtful about the design and layout of a nontraditional unit is also essential, especially regarding the size and proportionality of the living space and the kitchen space. Ditto Residential invested more in finishes and materials than it originally planned, but this turned out to be worthwhile and is expected to reduce costs for maintenance.

Timing the initial lease-up is critical for a building with multi-bedroom programming. Ditto Residential missed the prime window for leasing and as a result had to get creative to lease the building during the winter. Although the company succeeded in this effort, opening in the spring or summer when the leasing cycle is most active would be preferable.

Location is very important for shared-housing developments like Oslo. Shared housing works best where residents can walk and bike and easily reach transit. Easy access to neighborhood amenities, such as restaurants and grocery stores, is also a key feature. Oslo is located about one block from a Metro station; the neighborhood also offers bus lines, shared cars, and bike sharing; and downtown Washington is a 12-minute walk away. Many bars and restaurants are located nearby on Seventh Street.

The design process works best when it is collaborative. The robust dialogue and investigation of issues—among the developer, the architect, the engineers, the contractor, and the marketing team—led to an innovative but superior product. Notes Cao, "If your process is thorough and sincere and dynamic, being bold and being creative is not a risk."

ABOVE: Oslo at night. *(Patrick Ross, 2015)*

granular infill

CHOPHOUSE ROW | SEATTLE, WA

CHOPHOUSE ROW IS THE LAST PHASE Of a multiyear redevelopment of a cluster of properties in the Pike-Pine neighborhood of Seattle. Completed in spring 2015, Chophouse Row is a small-scale, mixed-use project that includes 25,317 square feet of office space, 6,379 square feet of retail space, and three penthouse apartments totaling 4,795 square feet; total gross building area is 43,543 square feet. The development includes a mix of vintage and modern structures, a pedestrian alley/mews that provides a walk-through connection from 12th to 11th avenues, and a courtyard and pedestrian plaza at the center of the block that ties together Chophouse Row and the other properties on the block.

Granular and *incremental* are words not often used when discussing urban redevelopment—but they are both key concepts in Liz Dunn's approach to development and redevelopment. Chophouse Row is a carefully crafted infill development project in the heart of the Pike-Pine neighborhood of Capitol Hill. The project is part of a larger, block-sized redevelopment effort—the 12th Avenue Marketplace—that consists of six separate parcels that have been acquired, redeveloped, and knit together over a 15-year period by the firm Dunn & Hobbes LLC, a small Seattle-based developer focused on small-scale infill projects in urban village neighborhoods.

The Chophouse Row portion includes a mix of loft office space, a retail marketplace, public space, and residential penthouses. The project combines a two-story former auto parts store building, built in 1924, with a new seven-story steel-and-concrete tower that features five levels of open-plan office workspaces along with floor-to-ceiling windows and exposed steel framing. Three residential penthouses are located on the top floor of the tower. A pedestrian alley and midblock plaza provide frontage for retailers and for pedestrian strolling and gathering areas; they also connect Chophouse Row to other 12th Avenue Marketplace properties.

THE SITE AND THE IDEA

The block where Chophouse Row is located consists of about 12 separate parcels once occupied primarily by low-rise commercial buildings. Starting in 1999, Dunn, principal of Dunn & Hobbes, acquired six of those parcels, including the Piston & Ring Building, the Pacific Supply Building, the Manhattan Building, the Agnes Lofts site, an auto parts building, and a surface parking lot. The first three properties were individually renovated between 2000 and 2006, a surface parking lot was developed into loft apartments over a restaurant in 2007 as Agnes Lofts, and the last two properties—the auto parts building and an adjacent surface parking lot—were combined to implement the Chophouse Row project, which was completed in 2015.

The first four of these properties face onto 12th Avenue, and the latter two—now Chophouse Row—face onto 11th Avenue. In addition, a seventh parcel, an adjacent vintage 1916-era office building—known as the Baker Linen Building and facing onto 11th Avenue—was acquired in 2014 (and recapitalized in 2015 through a separate investor capitalization). The overall project spans almost 500 feet of frontage that wraps around three streets—11th Avenue, East Pike Street, and 12th Avenue. The entire property is collectively known as the 12th Avenue Marketplace.

OPPOSITE: A view of the original restaurant in the old auto parts building, viewed from a mezzanine level above. The new restaurant is using much of the same interior features. *(Tim Beis)*

The Pike-Pine corridor is one of Seattle's vibrant pedestrian areas, with a combination of historic building stock and new developments full of local restaurants, bookstores, live music venues, galleries, cafés, apartments, and innovative office tenants. The area offers an abundant housing supply, with more than 1,500 new residential units under construction or in permitting.

PLANNING AND DESIGN

Dunn's approach to planning and development has been heavily influenced by her experiences while living in Toronto, Paris, and London, each of which, she observes, "[is] very granular, at least in their center cities, and small-scale development defines much of those cities. On any given urban block in those cities you will find five to 10 older buildings, and those urban blocks thrive. . . . I have always been a fan of what I call 'skinny infill' development—filling in the missing teeth on a block rather than demolishing it. My entire business is defined by rehab paired up with skinny infill, and Chophouse Row is an example of both."

Several parcels on the southern portion of the block are not part of the project, including a Ferrari and Maserati auto dealer showroom and an associated parking lot.

The site for the Chophouse Row parcel is about 10,000 square feet (0.23 acres), while the overall 12th Avenue Marketplace site is about 38,000 square feet. A large portion of the Chophouse Row site was occupied by a two-story, heavy-timber building that was constructed in 1924 as an auto parts store. From the mid-1980s until 2013, the building was divided into band practice rooms supporting Capitol Hill's robust alternative music scene. The other half of the site was a surface parking lot, where a Victorian-era rooming house had been demolished in the 1960s.

The project is located in the Capitol Hill neighborhood of Seattle, less than one mile from downtown Seattle. Two blocks from the new Broadway streetcar and four blocks from the new Capitol Hill light-rail station, the location is transit- and pedestrian-friendly.

The plan. A master plan for the 12th Avenue Marketplace site was developed in the early 2000s by Lesley Bain, now principal of Seattle design firm Framework, when she was with Weinstein A+U. The plan governed the initial phases of development, including the mews and courtyard concepts, but it also provided for the removal of the auto parts building and the construction of a new apartment building in its place.

Because of the 2008–2010 recession, during a hiatus that occurred between the planning and development of the 12th Avenue properties and the 11th Avenue properties, the market changed, and a zoning change was implemented for the area. Such changes led the developer to shift the plan to an office-oriented concept. The new overlay zoning, with incentives to keep facades and structures that have character, led the developer to integrate the auto parts building into the plan; the zoning change

---

ABOVE: Chophouse Row as seen from 11th Avenue. The entrance to the alley is on the third bay on the left and connects to the courtyard in the back (*Lara Swimmer*)

also gave the developer an additional floor of development rights.

The plan that resulted integrates the two-story 1924 auto parts building with a new seven-story steel-and-concrete structure, and the new building is set back from the older building. The plan incorporates a public pedestrian alleyway, which runs through one of the three bays of the original auto parts building, and a midblock courtyard. These pedestrian areas are lined with retail and restaurant uses that connect Chophouse Row to several adjacent commercial buildings and to 12th Avenue.

Design team. The design for Chophouse Row involved a collaboration between two Seattle architecture firms, Graham Baba Architects and Sundberg Kennedy Ly-Au Young Architects (SKL). Both have previous experience working together and a shared philosophy about urban design and adaptive use. Both firms are small—each has fewer than 25 employees—and both were located in the 12th Avenue Marketplace as tenants. Dunn & Hobbes was also located in this space, so they all worked closely and collaboratively on a project located right outside their doors. Jim Graham, principal with Graham Baba Architects, first got involved with the project when Dunn acquired the parcels in 1999 and hired him to conduct a survey and inventory of the parcels that had been acquired.

The project team comprises architects who are from both offices and who work on a common database. Graham Baba focused on the ground-level marketplace and retail and restaurant aspects of the project while SKL, as executive architect for the building's shell and core, focused on the office and new construction aspects.

Old and new structures. Principal objectives of the plan were to preserve and adapt the two-story building on the site and to provide attractive pedestrian spaces within the project. To accomplish these objectives, one bay portion of the existing structure—which includes a facade of three bay portions—was reconfigured to become the open-air

The project design integrates construction of a new steel-and-concrete loft office structure over a preserved smaller 1924 heavy-timber-and-masonry auto parts building.

pedestrian alley. The north bay of the building, on the left when facing the building, has been opened up to both the street and the sky to create the pedestrian alley/mews that provides access to the courtyard at the interior of the block.

The project design integrates construction of a new steel-and-concrete loft office structure over the preservation of the smaller 1924 heavy-timber-and-masonry auto parts building. The original structure now includes an opened-up two-story interior and a partial mezzanine level. The new structure above is roughly L-shaped and includes a five-story section in the front that is adjacent to the existing building along the street. A seven-story section weaves through, over, and behind the rear portions of the existing building. The complex includes retail space and restaurants on the first two levels of the existing building, office space on levels two through six of the new structure, and three penthouse residential units on the seventh floor of the new structure.

The intent was to juxtapose a modern design against the old structure and to keep many structural elements—wood beams, steel brace frames, metal decks—exposed.

Seismic elements include a concrete shear core in the new building and a braced frame structure that comes down through the old building. The architects had to clip the old building to the new one, but they used the new building to help support the old structure.

To gain an extra story of height, the developer needed to set the new building back from the original building. As a result, the various setbacks allowed for a deck off the third floor and another from the sixth floor, both of which serve as amenities for the office tenants on those floors.

Mews and courtyard. The development provides for dedication of a large portion of the site—about 3,500 square feet—to a unique public "mews" (pedestrian alley) and midblock retail courtyard, which, in turn, enhanced the opportunity for new entrances, new retail space, or both, in five existing adjacent buildings in the 12th Avenue Marketplace. The midblock courtyard was expanded by carving away the back portion of the auto parts building.

What the alley and courtyard allowed the developer to do was create 160 linear feet of additional retail and restaurant frontage. Because the courtyard has

become a vibrant place, Dunn has begun converting the backs of the 12th Avenue buildings into front-of-house retail space. The original courtyard increased threefold in size, and eight different buildings have frontage and fire exits onto the courtyard.

The scale and height of the mews, together with the exposed structural elements, invite visitors to enter. The northernmost column bay width of the original 1924 Chophouse building was about 12 feet, which was perfect for the alleyway. The architectural framing, the texturing, the lighting, and the numerous small tenant spaces along the mews help draw the pedestrian in. The mews and courtyard have emerged on social media as a favorite photo backdrop.

Wood decking taken from parts of the demolished old building was placed on the outer wall of the mews, which further adds to the texture of the space. When entering the mews, visitors can also see

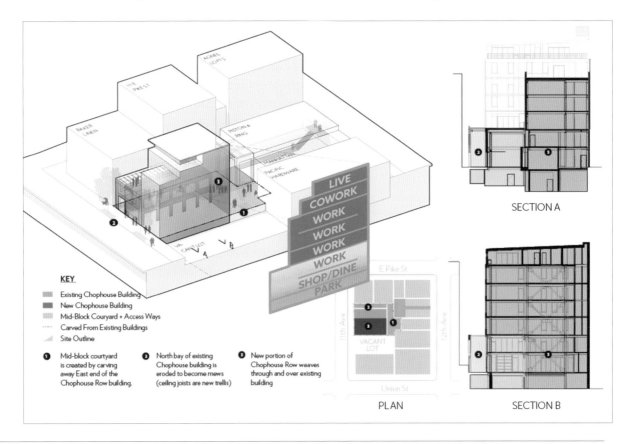

KEY

▨ Existing Chophouse Building
▪ New Chophouse Building
▨ Mid-Block Couryard + Access Ways
--- Carved From Existing Buildings
◢ Site Outline

❶ Mid-block courtyard is created by carving away East end of the Chophouse Row building.

❷ North bay of existing Chophouse building is eroded to become mews (ceiling joists are new trellis)

❸ New portion of Chophouse Row weaves through and over existing building

SECTION A

PLAN

SECTION B

ABOVE: A rendering of the block, the massing, the plan, and the building section. *(SKL Architects)*

the second level of the restaurant that faces 11th Avenue, which makes it more interesting at night.

Office space. The project includes 21,080 square feet of net rentable office space on five floors—three full floors and two half-floor mezzanines. The building features floor-to-ceiling windows, open floor plans, and high ceilings. The fourth floor is occupied by the Cloud Room, a member-based shared workspace and social club. The office space is reached through an entry off the courtyard that leads to an internal corridor through the building; additional access is provided through the bake shop at the front of the building. That shop also leads to the same corridor.

Retail space. About 5,328 square feet of net leasable retail space in the Chophouse Row building is in an open market configuration, with two tenants facing the street, four on the alleyway, one on the courtyard, and one on the internal corridor. In addition, completion of the courtyard allowed construction of a courtyard-level mezzanine above the basement of one adjacent building; that mezzanine is now used as a 900-square-foot doggie daycare and retail shop. It also allowed the conversion of office space in another adjacent building to a 700-square-foot barbershop, and the conversion of the "back of house" of a former restaurant space on 12th Avenue to a skin care salon.

Penthouse apartments. Three residential penthouses of about 1,300 square feet each, with large walk-out terraces, are located on the top level of the office building. Development of the penthouses involved a different structural approach: light-gauge metal framing sits on a concrete deck located on the roof of the office building. The three apartments total 3,901 square feet of rentable area; the gross building area for the apartment space is 4,795 square feet.

Parking and storage. The project has about 7,000 square feet of space for storage and parking on one underground level. The city did not require that parking be provided on the site. The buildings on the site already had basements, which the developer connected underground so that all the parking for 12th Avenue Marketplace is integrated and the entire complex needs only two parking entrances, one of which is at the center of the Chophouse Row building facade on 11th Avenue.

Only 12 parking spaces are provided for the office and apartment tenants of the Chophouse Row portion of the complex. Visitors to the retail and restaurants must use street parking or other garages if they arrive by car. Storage space is provided for 16 bikes; lockers and shower facilities are also available for bike commuters and runners.

DEVELOPMENT FINANCE

Founded by Liz Dunn in 1997, Dunn & Hobbes LLC specializes in the adaptive use of existing buildings, as well as new construction, including multifamily, office, and retail uses.

Investors. Dunn assembled the 12th Avenue Marketplace site using a combination of her own capital along with capital from friends and family investors. She used this capital and additional investor capital to redevelop the first four properties on the site. When the time came to develop the Chophouse Row portion of the project, Dunn connected with Heartland LLC to find additional investors.

Heartland is a real estate advisory and investment firm that created Heartland Investment Opportunities (HIO), a program that connects informed, forward-looking investors and capital partners with small- to medium-scale, best-in-class local developers and operators. As Deva Hasson, principal and investment director for the firm, notes, "Heartland recognized that, coming out of the recession, there were individuals in the Seattle area that were interested in coming back into direct real estate investments, but wanted to do it in a way and in a product type and with sponsors that they were proud to be affiliated with."

Those investors wanted to put their money to work where they could see it and touch it, and they wanted their investment to have a positive impact on their own community. Heartland formed HIO to address this market niche and began connecting with sponsors with a track record. Dunn & Hobbes was one of the firms that matched the profile.

Heartland targets $2 million to $10 million equity projects for the HIO investors. The firm's interest in Chophouse Row was based largely on Dunn and her strong track record. Heartland also appreciated that the investment involved a combination of existing performing assets as well as new construction. About 45 investors are in the 12th Avenue Marketplace deal, and each has typically invested $50,000 to $200,000.

The project presented an interesting assemblage for investors, including existing assets—with current cash flow and relatively low risk—and a new construction component, with no current cash flow and with higher risks. The project also offered a blend of several uses. Dunn believed that the more people investing, the more advocates there would be for the project. Democratizing the financing was part of the investment strategy, and investors actually visit and patronize the project.

Recapitalization plan. Dunn's objective in seeking financing was not only to finance the Chophouse Row project, but also to restructure the financing of the entire 12th Avenue Marketplace assemblage, to provide capital to help monetize her position in the existing assets, and to provide the equity needed for the new component. In the recapitalization, some existing investors in the original 12th Avenue Marketplace deal made new investments because many had a close relationship with Dunn. A number of investors are real estate professionals in their own careers.

The total cost of the Chophouse Row project, excluding land, was just over $14 million. The land was purchased by the original ownership entity in 1999 for about $900,000 ($90 per square foot). The land is valued today at about $4 million ($400 per square foot), but at the time of capitalization in late 2013 and early 2014, the land was contributed to the project at a value of about $2.4 million ($240 per square foot).

The financing combined the recapitalization of about 70,000 square feet of existing retail, office,

and residential space with the new Chophouse Row office space, ground-floor retail space, and penthouse residential units. Heartland raised about $5.6 million in equity from accredited investors to fund the recapitalization and expansion of the 12th Avenue Marketplace as a whole. As such, most of the existing investors in the other buildings were brought into this recapitalization. Heartland is also a co-investor together with the equity investors that it brings to the project.

Financing and ownership structure. Broadly, the financing structure has involved a managing member, the sponsor; a nonmanaging member, the investor entity; a platform entity; and project entities.

Two single-purpose project entities, each wholly owned by the platform entity, have been formed to own the properties as follows: Agnes Piston LLC owns Agnes Lofts and the Piston & Ring Building, and Pacific Chop LLC owns the Pacific Supply Building, the Manhattan Building, and 11th & Pike (Chophouse Row). Those assets were financed separately because of the legal lot configuration and because financing costs were different for each asset type.

Agnes Lofts and the Piston & Ring Building are on a single legal lot, and the Pacific Supply and Manhattan buildings and the 11th & Pike site are on another single legal lot. The financing was structured such that if the platform entity should encounter a need for additional cash, whether for construction cost overruns or startup costs associated with 11th & Pike or other reasons, the sponsor would be obligated to contribute up to $500,000 of additional capital.

The development costs (including land) for Chophouse Row upon completion came to $16.4 million, higher than the original estimate of $14.4 million. Construction cost overruns were around 15 percent, plus a five-month delay in opening. However, higher-than-anticipated rents allowed the developer to offset the costs, and in anticipation of a larger permanent loan, the construction loan was increased during construction from $10.7 million to $12.4 million because rent deals consistently exceeded the pro forma.

Equity and debt. Capitalization for the development of Chophouse Row involved about $4 million of equity and $12.4 million of debt (see data table for details), plus $750,000 for closing costs and working capital. Urban Shelter LLC (Liz Dunn) provided 51 percent of the equity, and HIO 12th Avenue investors provided 49 percent.

Construction financing was provided by HomeStreet, a patient, locally based national lender. The partnership with this type of lender was key to working through all the complexities of the project. The construction loan was around 75 percent loan to cost on the new construction, and the loan-to-value ratio was 70 percent across the whole project. There was no mezzanine debt in the capital stack. HomeStreet also provided permanent financing upon project stabilization.

Returns. The leveraged 10-year internal rate of return for the investors was originally projected to be 13 percent; as of early 2017, it was 11 to 12 percent. The stabilized cash flow after debt and expenses is around $940,000 per year. The priority return to investors is slightly below the 10 percent target because of the construction delays and overruns.

Sustainability. Sustainability features include radiant heat, natural cooling (office windows that open), high-efficiency ventilation, a high-performance building envelope using a continuous exterior wrap of rock-wool insulation combined with state-of-the-art glazing, adaptive use at the building and materials level, a green roof/water management system, and a highly walkable location with a high density of transit options and on-site bike facilities.

TENANTS, MARKETING, AND MANAGEMENT

All of the commercial spaces were leased before construction was completed. The office portion of the building achieved a new benchmark for market rents in the Capitol Hill neighborhood, with rents in the range of $24 to $28 per square foot. The retail portion, which attracted a mix of restaurateurs and several innovative retail entrepreneurs, has achieved rents in the range of $34 to $37 per square foot. The residential penthouses were rented within three months of the project opening, with typical rents of around $4,800 per month for a 1,300-square-foot unit, or $3.69 per square foot.

ABOVE: The midblock courtyard, with Chophouse Row on the right and the previously redeveloped 12th Avenue Marketplace buildings on the left. *(Andrew J.S)*

Office tenants. Office tenants include Anvil Studios, a product design firm; Cloud Room, a shared workspace provider, including the offices of Dunn & Hobbes; Glympse, a technology firm focused on mobile tracking apps; Mazlo, the developer of a suite of mobile apps for personal development in areas such as parenting, stress management, relationships, and sleep; and Tectonic, an experience design/software development firm.

The Cloud Room has become more of a hub than expected. It includes a lounge, a bar, and an outdoor terrace. Both members and the developer program events in the space, including guest speakers, and some of the traditional office tenants have chosen to become paying social members of the Cloud Room community.

Retail tenants. Chophouse Row involves a carefully recruited retail mix built on the principle of supporting small, local, unique businesses. They include Amandine, a bakery; Empire Espresso, a coffee shop; Marmite and Upper Bar Ferdinand, a pair of restaurants; NICHEoutside, a garden and

housewares shop; Kurt Farm Shop, an ice cream and cheese business; Honed, a jewelry boutique; and Sundry, a juice bar and bodega.

Several other restaurant and retail tenants also face onto the courtyard from surrounding buildings, including the Scotch Pine barbershop, the Cake skin care salon, and Play on the Hill, the doggie daycare and retail shop in the Manhattan Building that was built and opened in conjunction with the completion of Chophouse Row.

One setback for the development was that the anchor restaurant at the front facing the street—Chop Shop—failed after a year of operation. The space has been leased to Marmite, a French café that focuses on casual dining and carryout and features soups and broths.

Leasing and marketing. Dunn & Hobbes relies largely on its own leasing efforts and found many of the office and retail tenants through Dunn's connections and network of technology and broker contacts and friends. Notes Dunn, "I spend a lot of my time on leasing . . . searching for the tenants I want or choosing between tenants, determining which is going to be the best fit. I like to get a feel for who the tenant is."

Small tenants are a big part of the plan. "What tenants starting a small business probably care most about is their total monthly rent bill, not what rate they are paying on a per-square-foot basis," Dunn notes. Creating and leasing smaller spaces has allowed the development to attract small retailers that generate sufficient rental income per square foot to provide the shared spaces and amenities that are needed to make the project work, such as the mews, events, and restrooms, as well as heating, ventilation, and air conditioning.

As part of the marketing approach, the project was positioned as something unusual and different from the typical downtown Seattle office building. Even before the project was built, there was an expectation that the space would be "cool." It took time to attract the first tenants, but the office and retail

ABOVE: A mixture of old and new buildings can be seen from the interior of the Marmite restaurant, including the horizontal seismic bracing that was included in the structural design. *(Tim Beis)*

space was 100 percent leased before construction was completed, and the residential units were leased within three months of opening.

Property management and events. Dunn & Hobbes manages the property from its on-site office. The mews/courtyard is a privately managed space that is open to the public from 7 a.m. to 11 p.m. Notes Dunn, "We can program all kinds of crazy events without needing a permit. This is a way to help people discover the project if they haven't been here, and it creates foot traffic." Events include monthly art walk happenings and a weekly Wednesday night farmers market from 4 p.m. to 8 p.m.

OBSERVATIONS AND LESSONS LEARNED

Incremental infill development can take extra time and effort, and it requires a dedicated developer who is committed to staying with the project over an extended period. Done well—and with patient capital—such development can be profitable and have a positive impact on the urban environment.

Chophouse Row is the final puzzle piece in a half-block redevelopment scheme that, in the end, looks like it has simply evolved—which, in fact, it has, but under the guidance of a strategic plan from one developer with a vision over a 15-year period. Notes Graham, "One of the most exciting things about this project is the way that it, in a very patient manner, played to a long-term master plan that had an effect on its block in the neighborhood."

Working with older buildings is always challenging and full of surprises. Notes Graham, "The complexities of a project [like this] are more than you can understand [at the onset] of the project. Some of the complexities, even with the deepest due diligence, won't be known. There was not enough contingency for these unforeseen variables in the budget."

Notes John Kennedy, principal at SKL Architects, "[If we had it to do over], we might have spent more time with the existing building and measured it more thoroughly and investigated further. Once

we opened up walls, we found things like wood columns that were two or three inches on an angle that we weren't expecting, and we had to deal with that during construction. It would have been better to deal with that earlier in the design phase." This unexpected building issue affected the placement of the steel framing for the new building.

Heartland believes that many small investors are looking for investment opportunities like Chophouse Row, but it takes more work and time to arrange this financing than it does to arrange financing with one large institutional investor. There are benefits, however, in that the developer can exercise more control when using small investors rather than large institutional investors, who may have their own vision for the project that they want to enforce.

Also, from a capitalization structuring perspective, notes Deva Hasson, principal and investment director at Heartland, "The priority return structure was helpful; it provided investors with a healthy return [and reduced their risk]." Also, she notes, it is important to "communicate and align investors with goals [for the project]."

Overall, despite the complexity of a mixed-use project, having a mix of residential, retail, and office uses has been beneficial. For example, the residential portion of the project, though small, has greatly contributed to the overall profitability of the project and has helped offset other high-cost aspects of the project that required more complex structural engineering and design features. "The capitalized income value of those three units is approaching $3 million, and it probably added only about $1 million to the budget to add that floor to the project," notes Dunn.

While some developers might have tried to remove the old buildings on the site and build new ones in one big phase, notes Kennedy, the 12th Avenue Marketplace "is much more granular and the interplay [between old and new] is really wonderful." There are easier and perhaps more profitable ways to go about developing a site like this, but those approaches likely would not have resulted in the richness of the environment that has been created.

cultural icon reborn

THE NEWTON | PHOENIX, AZ

THE NEWTON IS AN 18,599-SQUARE-FOOT mixed-use retail, dining, office, and events building in Uptown Phoenix, Arizona, housing an independent bookstore with a beer, wine, and coffee bar; a home and garden store; a chef-led restaurant; a small office; and spaces for meetings and events. It was built within a renovated restaurant/banquet facility whose midcentury modern architecture and old-fashioned cuisine made it a local landmark for 40 years.

Every Phoenix resident of a certain era knew about Beef Eaters, a renowned steakhouse that restaurateur Jay Newton opened in 1961 on Camelback Road. It was housed in a quintessential midcentury modern rambler: its post-and-beam roofs spread in a sawtooth profile of low vaults, sitting atop exterior walls of local red adobe bricks. Inside, the restaurant embraced the era's love for kitsch with tartan carpet, oak-paneled walls, and British antiques, such as shields and suits of armor.

SITE AND CONTEXT

The Newton is located in Uptown Phoenix, less than five miles north of downtown and just off the intersection between two of Phoenix's signature roads—Central Avenue and Camelback Road. Camelback Road runs east–west across the north side of Phoenix, coming to prominence in the 1930s and 1940s as resorts sprang up around its namesake Camelback Mountain. The mile of Camelback spanning Central Avenue was nicknamed "Architects' Row" in the 1960s, both for the many architects (including several protégés of Frank Lloyd Wright) who rented offices there and for the midcentury modern curiosities that they built in their midst.

Interest and investment in Uptown Phoenix were reinvigorated following the 2008 opening of the Valley Metro light-rail line, which runs along Central through midtown and then turns west onto Camelback in Uptown. The rail line overcame initial skepticism to become America's 13th-busiest rail transit system, with many riders going to or from

Arizona State University's campuses in Tempe and downtown Phoenix. By 2009, Uptown was one of the first neighborhoods to show signs of life after a deep recession; a restaurant row emerged on Central in what had been a cluster of low-slung midcentury office buildings.

Not long after Beef Eaters closed, California investor Tes Welborn bought the abandoned restaurant with no immediate plans.

OPPOSITE: Southern Rail's patio seating along Camelback Road. **ABOVE:** The renewed monument sign. *(Both images: Venue Projects LLC)*

THE IDEA

Venue Projects' principal Lorenzo Perez had grown up in the neighborhood, had attended high school a few blocks away, and had recently launched a retail development career with the Windsor, a restaurant on Central Avenue. In 2010, four years after Beef Eaters had been abandoned and in the depths of the downturn, city officials introduced Perez and his business partner, Jon Kitchell, to Welborn with the hope that someone could rescue the building. They agreed to meet with the owner, look around the property, and brainstorm a few ideas for it.

When the door creaked open, Perez and Kitchell gasped. "It was stopped in time: the tables still had linens on them, the Old English shields were still on the walls." Welborn hired Perez and Kitchell as consultants to document the property's condition through as-built drawings and engineering assessments, to facilitate community outreach meetings and draw up a vision board, and to serve as a local contact.

Right out of the gate, neighbors came forth to share their memories and stories about the building. It became clear that the site was, Perez says, "an ideal place to create something that said something about central Phoenix and its heritage. It had the potential to revive what Beef Eaters was: a community gathering space where people come together around food." It was adjacent to a burgeoning restaurant district, was less than a quarter mile to two new light-rail stops, and the excitement expressed during outreach demonstrated its loyal following.

Yet there was also a lot wrong with the site. The dilapidated building's condition was worsening as its leaky roof failed, and as vandals, thieves, and squatters targeted vacant structures across foreclosure-wracked Phoenix during the recession. Extensive demolition would be necessary to remove dozens of interior partitions and to let in natural light. It was located three blocks west of Central Avenue, a longstanding dividing line that separated it from the

ABOVE: Southwest Gardener sells a colorful array of home and garden items. *(Andrew Pielage)*

wealthier east side of town. It was also far too large, says Perez: "The sweet spot for restaurants today is around 2,500 or 3,500 square feet, but what do you do with the rest of the building?"

The answer that emerged from the outreach meetings was somewhat vague. People liked the idea of retail and other commercial uses, as well as informal spaces that invited gathering and lingering, but the off-the-beaten-path location could make those a tough sell. The idea was alluring, but Perez just could not see the project penciling out. So Welborn went back to market with the property, listing it at $2.1 million.

A year later, Perez and Kitchell were giving a presentation about renovating an old 1940s retail building into the Windsor restaurant. In the audience was Cindy Dach, one of the owners of Changing Hands bookstore, a local institution that had served the college town of Tempe since 1974. After the talk, she approached Perez and Kitchell with an idea: she liked their style and wanted them to help Changing Hands with its longtime search for a second location in central Phoenix. The owners envisioned about 5,000 square feet of retail space for books and gifts; a beer, wine, and coffee bar with light fare; a space for some of the more than 300 events the store hosts each year; and a location where they could share synergies with creative neighbors. Ideally, all of those features should be in an interesting old building on the light-rail line, so that customers from across the valley (including Tempe) could easily visit for events. Even more of a stretch: the bookstore, having been displaced from downtown to south Tempe by rising rents, wanted to have an ownership stake as well.

Not long after missing out on a site across from the city's central library in midtown, Kitchell had "an idea so contrarian that we fell in love with it: an iconic bookstore in the iconic Beef Eaters building." Sure, it was west of Central, and "you had to get past the smell to see the possibilities," but the bookstore was a perfect fit for the concept that Venue had envisioned. He went back to Welborn with an offer to purchase the Beef Eaters property and was able to negotiate a substantially reduced acquisition price.

The next step was to find a complementary restaurant anchor. Perez and Dach reached out to contacts in the local restaurant scene to ask which chefs might entertain the notion of expanding into Beef Eaters. During a tour of the space, chef Justin Beckett, his wife Michelle, and their business partners Scott and Katie Stephens were noncommittal, but "you could see the reaction on their faces when they walked through," says Perez. After a few meetings with Venue and Changing Hands to explore the idea further, Southern Rail restaurant soon signed on—and with both anchor tenants and co-owners in place, The Newton was off and running.

DEVELOPMENT TEAM

Perez was first intrigued by the opportunities that development presented while studying architecture in college. He had been working at a print shop and took an internship at one of its customers, Kitchell Contractors. Sam Kitchell founded that firm in 1950, and it grew to become one of the state's largest construction companies. One of Kitchell's largest clients was DMB, a developer of master-planned communities. While working with DMB, Perez realized that "the developer has ultimate creative control" over a project.

Just as Perez and Jon Kitchell left Kitchell Custom Homes at the end of 2007 to start Venue, the Phoenix real estate market went into free fall. Perez and Kitchell spent much of 2008 meeting with bankers and investors to present their vision, seemingly for naught. Their first project was done entirely with equity from friends and family. Especially at that time, "the hardest deal you'll ever do is your first one," says Perez. "Once they can taste, touch, and feel what you're getting at, it gets easier."

"A lot of people will think you're nuts," says Perez, "but we were lucky to cross paths with somebody who bought in and listened." That banker was Steve Curley of Alliance Community Bank, whom Perez remembers once calling to say, "My bank went under. I'm at a new bank—but I think you're on to something, and I want to stay in touch." Venue went on to close five transactions with Alliance in the following years.

DESIGN AND CONSTRUCTION

The Newton is an almost-square, 135-by-150-foot building on a 220-by-250-foot corner lot. Busy Camelback Road runs along its southern edge, and quieter North Third Avenue runs along its eastern edge. Beef Eaters had a narrow front yard along Camelback and a porte-cochere within a parking lot along Third. The parking lot extends along the alley on the north side of the building, and the building abuts the western lot line.

Redesigning the building did not involve just slicing up a single-tenant structure into one that would house four. Rather, the goal of creating a gathering place meant fostering connections between tenants with different design priorities, between patrons of different businesses, and between the building and the outdoors—what Perez calls "a sense of constant discovery as you move through" the building. Architect John Douglas points out that the design came together "with tenants who were committed from the very beginning. Having lots of people involved was both the biggest challenge from an architectural standpoint and the best feature of the process. It gave personality to the whole development. . . . The building has multiple layers of meaning to many different people."

The restaurant space along the front, facing Camelback, is mostly new construction within what had been the front yard. Adding onto the front makes the building's zigzag roofline more prominent from the street, while also helping improve the pedestrian-friendliness of what remains a wide, automobile-dominated arterial. Putting the restaurant out front, says Perez, "screams 'people gathering place' to folks who are riding by on the train." It also allowed an efficient new kitchen to be built along the building's blank side wall, without having to untangle the web of utilities that underlay the far-too-large old kitchen. A covered patio with an outdoor fireplace and bar fills the building's front corner, where Beef Eaters once had an outdoor lounge; sidewalk tables (with umbrellas and a deep overhang for shade) fill a raised patio in the front. A reviewer for *Phoenix New Times* called the interior aesthetic "rustic-meets-Steampunk," with steel accents and distressed wood combined with vintage elements from Beef Eaters like half-round black-leather booths and chandeliers. In one corner is a residentially scaled private dining room, located in what had been Jay Newton's front office.

The bookstore fills most of the space that had been the original dining room and bar; it is set back from the street but has most of the building's parking lot frontage. Its minimalist, open layout highlights a fireplace that was the centerpiece of one dining room and now anchors the children's section, offering a ready perch for story times. The bookstore's storage and receiving area is located in the building's interior, near the meeting rooms, and its office and beverage storage are within a former wine cellar that was excavated into a full-height basement. (An earlier plan had specified a mezzanine instead, which proved costlier once the lost selling-floor space was considered.) Many of the store's fixtures were rescued from a shuttered Barnes & Noble, repainted, and mounted onto casters to maximize flexibility when accommodating events. Out front, under the old porte-cochere, the damaged Beef Eaters sign lives on as a mold set within the entrance walkway's concrete.

Southern Rail's bar offers indoor and outdoor service.

The Commons, the 1,885-square-foot former banquet hall, sits in the middle of the pinwheel. Its wide hearth and twin chandeliers were carried over from Beef Eaters and are now surrounded by skylights and glassy openings to both the bookstore and the restaurant that connect it to the present. One entire wall is open to the rectangular First Draft Book Bar and can be closed off during events by lowering windows that span the entire opening. (The bar itself is made from redwood reclaimed from Beef Eaters' outdoor trellis.) The opposite corner has windows and a door that look into the restaurant's bustling kitchen. Between events, the room functions as a public lingering space adjoining the bookstore's bar.

Southwest Gardener, a garden and home boutique, lines most of the back wall, taking space that was part of the kitchen. It has a solarium-style entrance off the side parking lot that glimmers with brightly colored decorations. A glassy hallway leading back from the Commons accesses the two small meeting rooms and office. The meeting rooms are 300 square feet and 575 square feet, and they are separated by a movable partition that can be opened to create an 80-seat proscenium theater ideal for author talks.

Perez refers to the gut rehabilitation process as "peeling the onion." Even though Venue's team had done as-built drawings and engineering feasibility in 2010, the old building continued to reveal new secrets, and designs were altered after demolition had wrapped up. Haphazard additions were especially surprising; demolition of a rear storage room uncovered three different parking slabs sitting beneath it. Ultimately, the building was stripped down to its frame, and the roof, which still smelled of cigarette smoke, was replaced. At one spot over the old kitchen, structural damage to the roof's trusses caused by a 1970s storm had simply been covered up. Exposing and repairing the roof also permitted skylights to be inserted at strategic points to brighten the cavernous interior.

APPROVAL PROCESS

The site is zoned C-2 Intermediate Commercial, with a transit-oriented overlay. The proposed uses fit within the existing zoning, with the minor exception of the outdoor dining. City officials, including the mayor and local council members, actively facilitated and shepherded the project since they saw how popular and transformational it could be. Perez had "a direct link to the mayor's office and a whole team that parted the seas for us."

One instance where that came in handy was when it came time to resurrect the Beef Eaters' monument sign, a landmark along Camelback Road that is easily

as tall as the building. A sign inspector was holding up the process, and one call to the mayor's office was enough to defuse the situation.

DEVELOPMENT FINANCE

Perez and Kitchell's vision of creating a community at The Newton extends even to its financing. Its tenants are not just sending rent checks, they also serve as coinvestors, codevelopers, comanagers, and community anchors.

The acquisition price for the building was substantially below the listing price, which had fallen from $2.1 million to $1.1 million. Venue's first offer in mid-2012 was for $900,000 in cash, a price that required short-sale negotiations with a lender. That offer was accepted but fell through at the last minute, as the short-sale lender refused to extend the contract to accommodate continued negotiations with the restaurant. A few months later, after the restaurant deal was finalized, an even better purchase price of $850,000 was negotiated and closed in early 2013.

The total development costs for The Newton came to $3.5 million, which was financed with $700,000 of equity and $2.8 million of debt.

ABOVE: Changing Hands defies the odds in an era when brick-and-mortar booksellers are not considered credit tenants. (*Andrew Pielage*)

Equity. The Newton's anchor tenants were also its codevelopers and coinvestors. The project LLC has three classes of equity, with more-preferred classes having lower risk but higher par values. Venue Investments contributed $200,000 for 40 percent of the equity. It is the managing member of the LLC and fully guarantees its debt. The individual owners of the bookstore and restaurant (but not the corporate entities) each contributed $150,000 for 20 percent ownership stakes. They have limited management authority and limited liability. Douglas (the architect) and Kitchell's sister each contributed $100,000, for 10 percent passive ownership stakes that have no exposure to a default.

Perez says that this arrangement "aligns your interests. It was a sign of commitment [to lenders] that they were all in with us—but other developers do question your sanity." Making tenants also co-owners does means that "you need to be more balanced and empathetic" when negotiating leases, Perez says. The leases have a base rent that ramps up over the first three years, plus a percentage of sales. The leases are arm's-length transactions with the tenants' corporate entities.

"I was on board the minute [Venue] brought it to my attention," says Douglas. "They asked if I would like to be a partner, and I said there's no way I'm not going to be partner, which was a first for me." His firm's offices are in a building that Venue reconstructed, and he had worked with the Kitchell company for decades.

Changing Hands' customers were so enthusiastic about its expansion that the bookstore ran a successful campaign on crowdfunding site Indiegogo to help raise funds for its buildout. The campaign raised $90,000 in donations during the 2013 holiday season in exchange for items like T-shirts and tote bags.

Senior debt. Alliance Bank, a community bank, made a $1.6 million first-lien construction loan on flexible terms: a three-year interest-only period and 20-year amortization, and no prepayment penalties. Venue had a good track record with Alliance, and the bank was "willing to do [this deal], but only up to a certain amount," says Perez. He'd have to go out to find a mezzanine loan before starting construction.

Junior debt. Like the first lease signed, the second mortgage came about serendipitously. Perez was speaking on a panel, and another panelist said The Newton could be a poster child for the new investment fund she was launching. It turned out that the Local Initiatives Support Corporation (LISC) and Raza Development Fund (a community development

ABOVE: Southern Rail's bar offers indoor and outdoor service. *(Venue Projects LLC)*

financial institution affiliated with the National Council of La Raza) had just launched a $20 million fund—since renewed with an additional $30 million commitment in 2015—to provide gap financing for equitable-development projects in the Valley Metro light-rail corridor.

LISC has shown remarkable flexibility with its loan. A year in, the project was meeting its pro forma, but operating cash flow was still tight, so LISC offered to expand its initial credit. When the permanent financing fell short of fully taking out both mortgages, LISC still wanted to stay tied to the project and refinanced $177,000 of its loan as a small second mortgage.

Additional outside investors made $400,000 in debt and $100,000 in equity investments to cover construction price escalation that had occurred while the project was going out for loans in 2013.

MANAGEMENT AND MARKETING

The property is managed by a committee comprising Venue Projects and the two anchor tenants. Venue manages the site's day-to-day operations, but the partners meet monthly to discuss strategy, programming, problems, social media and outreach, big decisions like refinancing, and anything else that might affect the community. "It's more hands-on than we expected," says Perez, but "they give us firsthand feedback on the challenges of how to operate this thing."

Event business. Even with frequent events booked by Changing Hands and Southwest Gardener, the gathering spaces—the Commons and two smaller meeting rooms—were still only partially booked. Event planners who toured the space told Perez that it filled a niche for smaller groups (from 10 to 180 people) that would otherwise be relegated to uninviting hotel ballrooms. In-house events then became the fifth tenant at The Newton: Venue Projects hired a full-time events manager, who works on site, and the ownership group purchased furniture, audiovisual equipment, and acoustical upgrades. The space has attracted many literary-themed events, from university-sponsored author talks to a vintage typewriter "type

Making tenants co-owners "aligns your interests. It was a sign of commitment [to lenders] that they were all in with us—but other developers do question your sanity."

off," as well as off-site business meetings, a concert series, and community group and association meetings. Unexpectedly, The Newton has even proved popular as an unconventional venue for weddings, particularly remarriages and same-sex marriages.

First Draft can cater beverages and snacks, and the restaurant can cater meals—the smaller meeting rooms have doors directly into the kitchen's back hallway. The event business is off to a strong start; Perez's goal is to have it carry the cost of the common areas, so that the retail tenants are not underwriting the spaces via common area maintenance fees. Events have also become a marketing vehicle for The Newton and its tenants. "The more events we have, the more traffic we're seeing," Perez reports. "It's an incredible vehicle for driving awareness and discovery."

LEASING AND PERFORMANCE

Once the two anchor tenants had signed on, the question remained about what to do with a space in the back corner of the building. The then-new concept of coworking seemed a good fit; it could use the site's common spaces during the day, and the location was near transit, restaurants, and existing offices and residences. A letter of intent was signed with a startup called Livelyhood, which then backed out because of family troubles.

A steady stream of commercial brokers had toured the space during construction, either out of sheer curiosity or an attempt to drum up listing business, so

Perez knew that interest existed even though "it breaks all the rules for retail." Hearing that they might be looking for a new location, Perez called up a retailer he had courted in the past, Southwest Gardener.

"They were a little skeptical at first," says Perez. "It was an interesting time for them—their current lease was up, and they were even thinking of shutting down. But they loved the partnership, a lot of their customers lived in the north central area, and most importantly they do a ton of events"—arts and crafts classes, gardening workshops, pop-up trunk shows, and plant sales. Moving to The Newton would bring their classes indoors and draw a complementary clientele.

One office tenant did end up in The Newton, though: Christofolo Schermer LLC, a pair of lawyers who started a strategy and leadership consulting firm. They came to love the project while advising Changing Hands, especially compared with their sublet in a nondescript office tower several blocks away, and so one meeting room in the back corner became their new office.

Although the project has met its internal financial goals, a problem arose when it came time to convert to permanent financing with a life insurer: the appraisals came in lower than expected. Some of that was likely due to lingering stigma over the location west of Central; the comparable properties selected were lower-value retail centers in the suburban West Valley, rather than urban properties in the denser, more fashionable neighborhoods just a few blocks east. In addition, the rent escalation clauses did not flatter the early income statements. Even though locally owned retailers like those at The Newton may have established operating histories and loyal customer bases, appraisers do not view them as "credit tenants" and thus discount their value.

None of that materially hurt Venue Projects, which intends to hold the property and still got favorable terms on a second loan with LISC. However, Perez sees the appraisal as indicative of a broader "disconnect between what society wants and what our finance system gives us. We were penalized for not doing just another armchair investment."

"Community banks and independent businesses are more likely to stay with" a landlord, he continues, "since these people realize that they also have a lot to lose both financially and emotionally." So-called credit tenants, on the other hand, can easily walk away and leave behind a dark box. Big banks, loan syndicators, and merchant builders have to work at such large volumes that they often cannot spend the time it takes to craft unique and thriving places.

OBSERVATIONS AND LESSONS LEARNED

Capture value. "Right when we purchased The Newton, Kitchell and I insisted that we also buy the vacant lot directly to the east," remembers Douglas. "I was afraid we would create a wonderful environment, and then someone would build a check-cashing store right across from us." Although the lot is currently used for overflow parking, it will eventually be incorporated into a broader district development plan.

Venue Projects followed up on The Newton by purchasing two open-gallery midcentury modern office buildings immediately west of The Newton. The office buildings are a chance to respond to a demonstrated demand for creative office space in the area. Offices' usage patterns and demand for meeting and dining spaces would complement the existing uses. Additional food and beverage options and art uses are also planned, including murals and a gallery documenting the neighborhood's midcentury modern heritage. The block also has a vintage hotel and numerous courtyard apartment buildings, which offer more opportunities for cross marketing.

Bringing the tenants into the deal as capital partners ensures that they benefit financially from the value of the place that they have helped create. It also gives them a stake in working hard to ensure that the place is successful.

Adjacencies matter. "We curate our tenants like art," says Perez—especially in an era when retail is driven by events, experiences, and "third places" that can appeal across the demographic spectrum. He

has been pleased to see the sheer variety of people and events that have been drawn to The Newton, from families and retirees to singles and students. Adding more dining options in future phases will further improve those adjacencies, says Perez. Even within The Newton, two smaller restaurants with two complementary menus could have worked better than one large restaurant.

Alcohol service. The event spaces are part of First Draft's alcohol-serving premises. At first, its liquor license was limited to beer and wine, which limited its appeal for some parties. By contrast, the restaurant has a full bar. Because the boundary between the two premises must be enforced, the door from the restaurant to the Commons is locked in the evenings. That division limits the flow and cross-pollination potential among the various businesses.

By contrast, Venue's newest project has a single operator and a single liquor license, which allows patrons to move through the property more easily. An umbrella-license approach, though, brings potential concerns about liability spreading to other businesses.

Parking. Some of the larger events held at The Newton can draw audiences from far afield, easily filling the small on-site parking lot. The sight of a full parking lot deters customers from visiting during the event; even though the Commons might be full, the restaurant might be empty. To manage the situation, The Newton encourages event-goers to use transit when marketing on social media and brings in parking lot attendants during events to direct arriving cars to the parking lots across the street. (In addition to the overflow lot that Venue Projects owns across Third, the transit authority owns park-and-ride lots across Camelback.)

Expanding with complementary uses on the adjacent parcels not only will increase the parking field—especially during the evenings and on weekends that are prime times for The Newton—but also will make it easier and more attractive to walk or take transit to The Newton.

Adaptability. Creative urban retail projects often have a unique character, so "you have to live with them for a few years to truly understand how they operate," says Perez. One key is to listen to new ideas and to be open to changing course: switching from office to retail, and switching from meeting to office, were changes that others suggested that ultimately paid off.

The Newton also shows that even cities as young as Phoenix have stories, buildings, and traditions to preserve, and these can, through effort and creativity, adapt to fit new needs.

ABOVE: The Commons during an informal event, with the window to the First Draft bar open. *(Venue Projects LLC)*

financing adaptation

AF BORNOT DYE WORKS | PHILADELPHIA, PA

AF BORNOT DYE WORKS IS A LOFT APARTMENT and retail project in central Philadelphia that involved the adaptive use and restoration of three timber and concrete factory buildings. Located along Fairmount Avenue, one mile north of Philadelphia's City Hall, the surrounding Art Museum area is one of Philadelphia's hottest submarkets, accounting for one-fifth of Center City's new housing in 2015. The four-story buildings include 17 rental residences on the upper levels and 13,210 square feet of retail space across two lower levels, which was preleased to neighborhood-serving tenants. The $10.7 million development was funded through a combination of conventional loans, federal and state historic tax credits, city incentives, partner equity, and a $375,000 mezzanine loan from an online crowdfunding platform.

THE SITE

The site includes three contiguous industrial loft buildings that fill almost half the block. Four blocks west is the Eastern State Penitentiary, a historic former prison that is now a popular tourist attraction.

The buildings were erected between 1900 and 1925 for a variety of industrial users. From west to east, the four-story AF Bornot Dye Works at 1644 Fairmount Avenue is a prominent end-cap for the block, with frontages on Fairmount to the north, 17th to the west, and Melon on the south. Its curved corner, large arched windows, and heavy timber frame make it a neighborhood landmark from the days when the Bornot company dyed and cleaned clothes on the premises. Behind it, and also running through the block, is a two-story concrete building at 1632 Fairmount Avenue that once housed the Security Elevator Company. To its east is a shallow (averaging only 50 feet in depth) three-story, concrete-framed factory built for Gaul Derr and Shearer Company, an auto brake manufacturer, with an address at 1615 Melon Street. The team refers to the last building as "the concrete building" because concrete-framed buildings were not common when it was built in 1925.

MMPartners, the project's developer, is simultaneously redeveloping a fourth building on the site:

a three-story, 7,500-square-foot factory on Melon Street, between the Security Elevator and concrete buildings. Because the 60-foot by 40-foot building was too small to be effectively partitioned into rental apartments, the architects suggested dividing it into two 30-foot-wide loft homes instead. These units are being developed for sale, rather than rental. Only rental units are eligible for the historic tax credits, so those credits were used to underwrite the renovation of the three larger buildings.

THE NEIGHBORHOOD CONTEXT

The site sits at the border of four different neighborhood contexts. Immediately to its south is the Spring Garden neighborhood, an area of elegant Victorian rowhouses that were built in the 1850s to house factory owners and managers just beyond the rapidly industrializing central city. To its north is the Francisville neighborhood, an area of more modest rowhouses whose skewed street grid was laid out at an earlier time. To its west is Fairmount, a neighborhood long anchored by the grand art museum along its western flank.

East of the site is a precinct of industrial lofts that sprang up along Broad Street, founded to take advantage of a railroad line that ran along the street. When the rail line was removed and replaced with a

---

OPPOSITE: MMPartners renovated nearly three-quarters of a block of factories to create AF Bornot Dye Works. *(Cope Linder Architects)*

wider street, the industries pivoted from manufacturing locomotives to making automobiles: Packard, Cadillac, Ford, and Studebaker set up factories along what was called Gasoline Alley. Smaller workshops that supported these factories, such as Gaul Derr and Shearer Company, sprang up nearby. After World War II, industrial change buffeted North Philadelphia's manufacturing-based economy, and by the 1990s both the industries lining Broad and the neighborhoods beyond had become severely blighted.

In the 1990s, residents of the Spring Garden neighborhood organized multiple revitalization efforts that laid the groundwork for the AF Bornot Dye Works adaptive use project. The Spring Garden Civic Association launched a sister community development corporation (CDC) to directly combat blight and to spur revitalization. The CDC purchased vacant lots and buildings and assembled them for resale, complementing the area's stock of spacious older homes with scores of new rowhouses that combined modern amenities and new construction in a central location.

One of the blocks targeted for the new rowhouses was Melon Street immediately south of the Bornot site. Unusually for Philadelphia, the neighbors along the street formed a homeowners association that

In recent years, the decades-long transformation of Center City Philadelphia from a nine-to-five office core to a thriving, 24-hour urban environment began to foster significant new demand for housing in adjacent areas such as North Philadelphia. A February 2016 report from the Center City District found 17 new apartment developments completed within four blocks of AF Bornot Dye Works in 2015 alone. These 17 developments accounted for one-fifth of the 986 rental apartments delivered in central Philadelphia that year, a feat that is particularly notable considering that the largest had just 34 units.

THE IDEA AND THE DESIGN

Among the properties that the CDC purchased were the four that became the Bornot site, which had fallen into disuse and abandonment. Yet the CDC's expertise lay in large single-family houses, not in commercial or multifamily development, so the properties remained empty for over a decade. In 2012, sensing that the recovering multifamily market was ready, the CDC retained Cope Linder Associates to evaluate the feasibility of renovating or demolishing the properties and to draw up a basic concept of what a renovation could look like. That initial schematic, with few alterations, became the basis of MMPartners' ultimate development.

Cope Linder has experience converting buildings into luxury lofts: it recently designed the penthouses now being built within Two Liberty Place, one of Philadelphia's most iconic office towers.

Residents of the Spring Garden neighborhood organized multiple revitalization efforts that laid the groundwork for the AF Bornot Dye Works adaptive use project.

purchased the street itself from the city in 2004 and gated it at both ends. The association also launched historic preservation efforts, adding the Fairmount Avenue Historic District to the National Register of Historic Places in 2002. The historic district comprises several blocks of mixed industrial and residential urban fabric at the northeast corner of the Spring Garden neighborhood, including the Bornot site.

More important in this case, however, principal Ian Cope lives on Melon Street, across from the site, and has been active with the CDC for decades.

The structures' existing windows and columns suggested the final layout. None of the buildings had floors that lined up, so the structures would have to stand alone. Cope saw "the juxtaposition of four different buildings, of different sizes and scales, from

different eras, for different purposes" as an interesting design challenge.

The Security Elevator building has a very deep footprint 115 feet by 65 feet and lacks windows except at its two narrow street edges, which ruled out residential use. Instead, it was designed with a ground floor that is principally parking and a shallow storefront behind its 34-foot-wide glass storefront on Fairmount Avenue. On the building's upper floor, an athletic club and yoga studio seemed to be the right uses for a space that has 40-foot beams and a dramatic skylight, but few windows. A small vacant lot on the Fairmount side provides access to the garage, plus a few surface spaces for retailers. Ironically, the Security Elevator building lacks an elevator, so a passage was cut to the Bornot building to permit wheelchair access via its elevator.

The four-story Bornot building at the corner lent itself well to three to four well-lit loft residences per floor, each with 11-foot ceilings. Most apartments have two bedrooms and two baths and range from 1,180 to 1,640 square feet; two units have three bedrooms. Unusually for a loft building, shallow floor plans mean that all bedrooms have ample exterior windows. On the ground floor, the two prominent corners along busy 17th Street could house two storefronts.

A windowless box with walls right at its outer lot lines, the concrete building was a greater challenge. Opening up the south-facing Melon Street frontage with "tremendous glass expanses," as Cope says, made fitting six loft residences on the building's two upper floors possible, which are serviced by a single-loaded corridor along the back walls. The ground floor houses six parking spaces plus storage. These lofts vary from 925 to 1,300 square feet, with two one-bedroom, three two-bedroom, and two three-bedroom units. Because only one side of the building has windows, these lofts have interior bedrooms.

The Spring Garden Civic Association expected the apartments to complement the upscale setting it had cultivated. The association insisted on off-street parking for each unit, a relative rarity in a neighborhood of narrow rowhouses, and barred a common roof deck so loud parties would have to stay inside. Spacious loft apartments with parking would complement the neighborhood's grand rowhouses and offered the developer a market niche.

David Waxman, managing partner of MMPartners, calls the units "really generous-sized loft homes" that appeal to "a niche market of people who don't want a cookie-cutter rental—young professionals, empty nesters." To make the luxury price point work, units

---

ABOVE: *Left:* The Fairmount Avenue frontage before construction. *(Cope Linder Architects) Right:* The building's curved corner entrance (after renovation) is a prominent landmark along Fairmount Avenue. *(Payton Chung)*

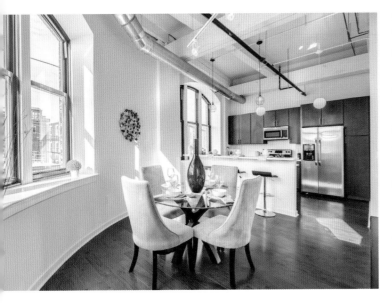

certed and continuing effort, so far involving more than $50 million invested in over 50 properties, to revitalize the Brewerytown neighborhood.

In 2001, Waxman returned to Philadelphia after working for a few years in New York and Miami for large developers. Central Philadelphia's housing market was just starting to take off, and Waxman saw an opportunity in Brewerytown: it was perched above Fairmount Park and I-76, just a mile beyond anchors such as the art museum and 30th Street Station, but it was isolated from the rest of North Philadelphia by Girard College and railroad tracks. Its urban fabric was torn but mendable, with a retail spine remaining along Girard Avenue. Large developers had begun redeveloping some of the old breweries into townhouses and lofts, leading to some trepidation about development.

Most important, Waxman says it was "where a 24-year-old could buy an entire block of shells" without a significant capital outlay. The 16 apartments and two storefronts carved out of the houses created enough of a critical mass to transform that block while respecting the broader neighborhood fabric. Waxman saw that further investment in the neighborhood would accrue even greater returns, as new amenities built upon and increased the value of existing projects. This organic, incremental approach also kept the pace of neighborhood change more manageable and less threatening for neighborhood residents.

Waxman realized that access to "retail drives residential [demand] in the city" and sought to reconstitute Girard Avenue's three shop-lined blocks with "retail for everyone," so that Brewerytown residents "can walk to everything [they] need—or at least what [they] can't order online—on a daily basis." Girard had once been a dividing line between neighborhoods, but rebuilt infrastructure and dozens of new retailers "tie together the neighborhoods," says Waxman.

That retail experience served MMPartners well when it bid on the AF Bornot Dye Works site. That the CDC wanted 13,210 square feet of retail space at AF Bornot Dye Works did not seem like a daunting task,

have the high-quality finishes and well-appointed kitchens and baths that such renters expect.

The site also presented an opportunity to stretch Fairmount's retail energy east into Spring Garden, an area with few other retail options. Local residents sought to have more neighborhood services within walking distance, such as restaurants, a bank, or a gym. The narrow storefronts along Fairmount are home to an eclectic mix of small retailers, but few could fit large–floor plate tenants like gyms.

In 2013, the Spring Garden CDC invited a group of prescreened developers to bid on the Bornot parcels, together with the plans developed by Cope Linder and a contract detailing exactly what the CDC expected from the final product. The city's Department of Commerce, knowing that MMPartners was familiar with retail/residential mixed use, historic rehabilitation, and North Philadelphia, introduced the CDC to MMPartners.

DEVELOPMENT TEAM

David Waxman started what became MMPartners in 2001, with the rehabilitation of eight abandoned brownstones along West Girard Avenue, 16 blocks northwest of AF Bornot Dye Works. These eight buildings were the genesis for MMPartners' con-

---

ABOVE: The apartment interiors have high-end finishes. (*PLUSH Image Corp.*)

Waxman says. "When we were brought in, we put a big value on the retail. Every other developer thought the retail was the albatross for the project, but we felt that this retail had a lot of value, and we were able to pay more. We knew we could land quality retail."

APPROVALS

The Spring Garden CDC keeps close watch on the ongoing development, with approval rights over matters such as retail leases and construction staging.

No zoning changes were required for the development. One strange complication arose during permitting: when Melon Street was privatized, the parcels along it were orphaned without addresses on a public street. These parcels had to be replatted as flag lots, with a tiny slice of frontage onto the outside of the block, before permits could be pulled and utilities connected.

The historic review process with the State Historic Preservation Office and the Department of the Interior went smoothly. Cope says that the reviewers accommodated the biggest change to the building's appearance: lowering the corner building's window sills so large retail display windows could be installed.

DEVELOPMENT FINANCE

The capital stack assembled for AF Bornot Dye Works is unusually complex for a project of this scale, partly because of its unusual mix of uses, its location outside the Center City core, and the challenges posed by historic rehabilitation. Waxman is particularly proud that a $10.5 million investment was leveraged with an equity investment of less than 5 percent of the project budget.

Although bringing together this capital was a tremendous learning experience, Waxman notes that "if we did this project today, we would have done this much more traditionally." Lenders have become much more savvy about urban residential and with historic tax credits in particular. Some lenders now do "one-stop" lending for historic projects, pairing a senior construction loan with a junior bridge loan that is repaid from the pending credits.

Conventional loans. Most of the $10.7 million project budget for AF Bornot Dye Works was funded with a conventional $7 million construction loan from Susquehanna Bank, a regional bank that has since been merged into BB&T. The loan period was 24 months at an interest rate just over 4 percent, with a six-month option to delay repayment of the interest reserve. The lender was comfortable with the local apartment market but was more skeptical of the market for neighborhood-scale retail and required that 50 percent of the retail be preleased. That hurdle was easily achieved, with over 90 percent of the retail leased by the time the loan closed.

The construction lender was located through a broker, although Waxman notes that "Philadelphia is a big city, but it's a small place," where most deals happen through a handful of regional banks that are active in development lending.

Tax credits and incentive loans. Over $2 million in equity funding resulted from historic preservation tax credits available to the project. Because it involves substantial rehabilitation of income property located within a National Register–listed historic district, the development qualifies for a federal income tax credit equal to 20 percent of the cost of construction. PNC Bank syndicated the federal tax credit, resulting in net proceeds of $1.9 million.

In addition, Pennsylvania is one of 33 states that offer state income tax credits for historic preservation. Unlike the unlimited federal program, this relatively new program is funded at just $3 million for a state with countless old buildings. Nonetheless, MMPartners beat the odds and was one of 15 recipients of Pennsylvania's state historic tax credits in 2015, winning a lottery for a $250,000 allocation that net the project $215,000 in equity.

Financing the remainder of the project meant turning to some unexpected lenders. Although Susquehanna Bank was more comfortable with lending for the project's residential component, the Philadelphia Industrial Development Corporation (PIDC) was happy to lend for the project's substantial retail component. MMPartners' previous work developing office and retail properties, in particular the renovation of a mill in the Manayunk neighborhood, into offices and several restaurant fit-outs, had introduced them to PIDC's incentive financing for job-creating developments like retail, office, and industrial buildings.

PIDC's capital project loans provide up to $750,000 in junior-lien debt, with a minimum of one new job created for every $35,000 loaned. The loan terms are attractive, with an interest rate of half of prime rate (2.75 percent, in this instance) and a loan term of up to 15 years. Because much of PIDC's loan funds come from government sources like the Small Business Administration, its upfront documentation requirements can be daunting. "Once you've gone through their process once," though, "it becomes very easy," says Waxman.

Crowdfunded mezzanine loan. MMPartners also used crowdfunding to finance the project. Fundrise, an online crowdfunding platform, made a $375,000 unsecured mezzanine loan to AF Bornot Dye Works. Crowdfunding, the practice of raising capital online via a large number of small sums, has transformed the business models for industries

One of the fastest-growing segments in crowdfunding is real estate: the $2.5 billion raised for real estate ventures in 2015 was almost three times more than in 2014, according to Massolution. Over 100 startups are vying for the market, including Prodigy Network, Patch of Land, Realty Mogul, and RealtyShares. Within the broader context of real estate finance, this is still a drop in the bucket; consultancy RCLCO estimates that it accounts for less than one-quarter of 1 percent of total investment flows.

The crowdfunding market did not exist until 2012, when legislation first permitted crowdfunding sites to market equity securities to "accredited investors" (i.e., high-net-worth individuals), and is poised for further growth now that the Securities and Exchange Commission (SEC) has adopted regulations permitting the sale of equity to the broader public. In addition, most states have passed their own regulations, which are usually more permissive than the SEC's. Because crowdfunding has been around for only a few years, the first ground-up development projects funded through the model are just now coming to fruition.

Washington, D.C.–based Fundrise is one of numerous startups that apply the online crowdfunding model to commercial real estate. Fundrise was established in 2011, and so far it has deployed $75 million in capital from 80,000 investors into nearly 100 projects. As at AF Bornot Dye Works, Fundrise typically makes mezzanine debt or preferred equity investments on development projects but also makes investments on stabilized projects and for predevelopment expenses.

Fundrise acts as an intermediary and market maker between investors and project sponsors. It prescreens accredited investors and provides an online marketplace to match projects (and project sponsors) with investors. Sponsors are encouraged to post a portfolio on the site and to recruit investors to a "network" that's notified when new projects are posted. When Fundrise accepts a

> *Marketing deals through crowdfunding helped the firm meet investors who have been great to work with, especially as it graduates to larger deals that might be attractive to private equity firms.*

from board games to presidential campaigns. Massolution, an advisory firm, estimated that more than 1,000 crowdfunding sites around the world raised $34 billion in capital in 2015, with almost 90 percent flowing into established markets like peer-to-peer consumer lending and reward-based projects.

project for funding, it syndicates the deal by issuing "project payment dependent notes," backed by a trust that receives the loan's interest payments, to the ultimate investors. Investor servicing, distributions, and tax compliance are handled by Fundrise.

For the AF Bornot Dye Works loan, MMPartners promised Fundrise investors a return of 18 percent annually over the loan's three-year term: an 8 percent current return that is paid out quarterly and a 10 percent annual return that is accrued and paid out either at maturity or if the loan is prepaid. The project was marketed to investors on Fundrise in mid-2014.

In July 2014, the deal was fully funded and closed, with 12 investors contributing a minimum of $5,000 toward the loan. More than half the investors put in the minimum, but the average contribution was $28,000. Fees paid included a 2 percent origination fee and a $5,000 due diligence fee. (Since December 2014, Fundrise prefunds all of its investments, so marketing to investors now takes place after the loan closes.)

Waxman "read about [Fundrise] before they launched" and reached out to get set up on the platform. Waxman wanted to "put up a deal that we knew we could get done," as a way to build goodwill and a track record with the platform's investors. That first project was already under construction, with all funding already secured, but allowed MMPartners to cash out some of its equity before permanent financing.

Ben Miller, cofounder of Fundrise, calls MMPartners "the quintessential Fundrise developer. Our sweet spot has been in the space too big for people, too small for large funds." This often means projects with budgets between $5 million and $50 million and particularly projects that involve complicated (but relatively small) urban infill sites. As Waxman found, construction lenders can be leery of projects that involve less-proven product types, like the upper-floor retail space at AF Bornot Dye Works, and a funding gap can result.

Typically, Fundrise buys out about half the sponsor equity as a preferred-equity or mezzanine-debt position in the capital stack, which can bring a project's loan-to-cost ratio up to 85 to 90 percent. Preferred equity caps both the upside potential and downside risk, but unlike senior debt the Fundrise position is typically not secured. Miller notes that this funding "looks like equity to the [construction lender], but it's senior to the developer. It results in less risk than [common] equity."

As with AF Bornot Dye Works, most of Fundrise's development deals pay out half the return from an interest reserve as current yield, with the other half of the return accrued and paid out at the end of the term, which usually occurs after permanent financing has been secured. This structure maximizes returns to investors while further leveraging the return on equity. As Waxman says, "You, the developer, keep all the upside. If the project can afford the higher interest rate, it's a way to own more of the project and offer a high return to the [Fundrise] investor."

Fundrise usually targets 12 to 14 percent returns for its investors. Miller contends that taking preferred equity provides "a better risk-adjusted return" than the common equity pursued by typical private equity funds. For retail investors, Fundrise's service and custodial charges are 0.5 percent of assets annually.

From a developer's standpoint, the due diligence documentation required and underwriting criteria applied are largely similar to a submission for a private equity firm. Miller says that developers who first submit their projects for review "are surprised by how intense we are with due diligence. We're conservative, value-centric investors. . . . It confounds people that we act like any other private-equity fund, except we are not as bureaucratic." The company's due diligence process rejects about 95 percent of submitted projects.

Waxman notes that marketing deals via the platform has helped him "meet some investors who have been great to work with," especially as his firm graduates to larger deals that might be attractive to private equity firms.

CONSTRUCTION

Like all rehabilitation projects, the AF Bornot Dye Works buildings had their share of surprises lurking underneath the skin. "Once you start opening up walls, you find hidden conditions," says Waxman. Water had infiltrated the Security Elevator building's front facade, which required replacing 30 courses of brick between the two windows. To fix the problem, Waxman says, "We had to pull off the brick facade and go back in with new brick. We found brick from the same brickyard—but because it's new brick, it's not as dirty" and had to be treated to fit in. Moreover, "it was winter, not the ideal time to lay brick. We had to tent it, heat it, and lay the new brick."

Cope, the architect, regrets that the arched windows could not be restored inside the Bornot building's elevator shaft. Despite extensive prior survey work, this fact was not apparent until demolition crews opened up the old elevator shaft. As a result, new windows could not be installed in seven of the original arched window openings along the prime Fairmount frontage, which remain bricked in.

Not all the surprises were unpleasant. In situ testing showed that the Bornot building's concrete floors transmitted less sound than expected. This meant that a subfloor sound blanket could be used instead of obtrusive ceiling insulation, allowing more of the building's striking wooden beams to remain exposed.

The biggest challenge that arose during construction involved replacing the project's general contractor several months into the project. The original general contractor was not making sufficient progress and agreed to leave the job. The project schedule was set back by almost a full year because of the changeover and power company delays. William Bostic, president of Axis Construction, recalls that nearly a month was spent "analyzing what they had done and what needed to be done, figuring out anomalies in the contract," redoing and reapproving drawings, sorting out unpaid invoices, and ultimately agreeing on a price.

Managing logistics on the very tight site also proved difficult. Because the neighbors on Melon Street technically own the street, "There's no access to that side of the building, other than what's basically someone else's front yard," says Bostic. Keeping the tiny street clear of subcontractors' trucks required constant vigilance.

MARKETING AND LEASING

MMPartners launched apartment leasing in April 2016, touting the units' spacious floor plans and in-building services comparable to luxury downtown high rises. Waxman is optimistic about lease-up, given the press and social media attention around the property. At above $2 per square foot, rents have been set at the high end for the Fairmount area but below what a comparably sized apartment would cost downtown.

Instagram has become central to MMPartners' marketing strategy over the past few years. MMPartners first tried marketing through social media in 2008, when its marketing budget had otherwise

ABOVE: The corner of 17th and Melon streets shows the large windows restored to the AF Bornot building's facades. The ground floor at this corner was intended to house a coffee roaster. *(Payton Chung)*

evaporated, and its early embrace of Instagram has paid off. "Real estate is visual," says Waxman, and especially within the Brewerytown and Fairmount communities, Instagram "helps keep up the excitement about the transformation around the neighborhood. It provides a window into the development process—people can see how the sausage is made." Even though few of their nearly 3,000 followers are in the market for an apartment at any given time, having a constant presence reminds users who to call when they do need a new space.

The broad following also helps with cross-merchandising. Staging companies have decorated model apartments for free, knowing that photos of their work will go to thousands of potential clients. Retailers in MMPartners' buildings can rely on a steady stream of publicity.

The project's retail space has been entirely preleased, largely to regional retailers, at rates exceeding pro forma, a feat that Waxman credits to working with the CDC and with local broker MSC Retail. "The process" of pursuing retailers, Waxman says, "was pretty seamless, because we share the same vision. [The CDC] wanted a gym, bank, café, yoga studio. [MSC is] really attuned to urban retail, and they nailed it."

Even the more unusual spaces were preleased. The rear of Security Elevator's second floor was briefly shopped around as office space, because its lack of visibility makes it less than ideal for retail use, but in mid-2015 Anytime Fitness signed a lease. A shallow, 975-square-foot space on the building's ground floor will house a second location for a boutique that was looking to open a second store on Fairmount Avenue, just three blocks down Fairmount from the existing store. A local coffee shop took the back corner of the Bornot building, attracted in part by an unusual basement storage area with 20-foot-high ceilings.

OBSERVATIONS AND LESSONS LEARNED

Local stakeholder engagement was not limited just to the approvals phase for AF Bornot Dye Works. Rather, neighbors defined the project's parameters from the very beginning. MMPartners stuck to that vision and constantly communicates its progress to neighbors—through both formal channels such as presentations at civic association meetings and informal channels such as social media. Neighbors' enthusiastic support helped with retail leasing, given that the CDC has already identified a ready market for the retailers it specified.

Rehabilitation work requires additional contingency planning and very careful attention during predevelopment. "You have to approach it with the mentality that you'll get there, that there's no problem you can't solve," says Waxman, adding, "Once you're in construction, it's going too fast to change course."

Close and early coordination between designers and builders can minimize surprises. AF Bornot Dye Works had an unusual history, because it was designed long before it was built. Bostic urges developers to have "construction expertise on board early, to vet the costs, the means, the methods" and notes that Axis has been involved early on for its next project for MMPartners.

Developing residential in urban neighborhoods can be tremendously rewarding—but neighborhoods revolve around retail, which needs careful cultivation. The synergies between urban residential and retail markets usually occur at the neighborhood scale, which is difficult (but not impossible) for a single small developer to influence. In-building retail amenities can build value even for small-scale residential projects but will depend on a broader customer base.

Emerging urban neighborhoods and medium-sized projects stand to benefit most from gap financing, because these kinds of projects are often appealing to the public sector and less appealing to conventional lenders. Nearly one-third of the project budget for AF Bornot Dye Works was funded through historic tax credits, PIDC, and Fundrise, because the conventional lender was skeptical about the market success of retail development at this location. Public incentive funding and crowdfunding can help address and expand the opportunity for mixed-use development where it may not otherwise be financeable.

innovation catalyst

TOMORROW BUILDING | CHATTANOOGA, TN

THE TOMORROW BUILDING IS A FOUR-STORY, 40,000-square-foot building in downtown Chattanooga, Tennessee, that was originally built as a hotel in 1888. After a $9.5 million transformation, it houses 39 furnished micro-unit apartments, shared social and work spaces, and four locally owned retailers. The building's developer is part of an incubator for early-stage companies, which has found that the co-living concept has helped with retaining employees.

THE SITE AND NEIGHBORHOOD

What is now the Tomorrow Building was erected in 1888 as the Delmonico Hotel, at the corner of Georgia Avenue and Patten Parkway in downtown Chattanooga. The hotel and an adjacent city market were built during the 1880s as downtown expanded south and east from Market Street, its historic spine. In 1925, the hotel reopened as the Ross Hotel, and after World War II the market was replaced with a war memorial. The hotel closed in 1979, but for years its ground floor was home to the Yesterday's nightclub.

Back in 1986, during Yesterday's heyday, leaders from the Lyndhurst Foundation and several local banks launched the River City Company (RCC). This nonprofit developer was initially tasked with implementing a 20-year regeneration plan for 130 acres of derelict industrial land along the Tennessee River.

Three recent plans that the RCC undertook set the stage for the Tomorrow Building. A 2013 City Center Plan envisioned a mixed-use future for downtown's central business district, a Downtown Chattanooga Market Study found a pent-up demand for new rental apartments downtown, and a parking study found plentiful existing parking resources. The plan identified specific "properties that could jump-start the middle of the city," says Kim White, president and CEO of the RCC, notably the Ross Hotel.

The Benwood Foundation, keen on catalyzing the implementation of the plan, pledged to support the RCC in the purchase of the Ross Hotel if the nonprofit could get the building under contract. The building's longtime family owners had rebuffed offers from many other developers over the years, and it took numerous entreaties from White to "get the whole family on the same page with what the vision could be." One family member had lived there during the 1970s, and White appealed to "her dream of getting more people living downtown"; unlike a speculator, the RCC both shared that vision and could bring it to fruition.

"While the money would have talked, it also took a lot of visits to get the project to move forward," White continues. The RCC's resulting request for proposals

OPPOSITE: The Tomorrow Building sits at the key corner of Georgia Avenue and Patten Parkway in downtown Chattanooga.
ABOVE: Units are furnished with maximum efficiency.

(RFP) for developers was "very intentional about what we wanted the program to be," says Jim Williamson, vice president of planning and development for the RCC: per the plan, it should be rental apartments.

THE INITIAL IDEA

Not far away, the Lamp Post Group (LPG) was solving a different sort of problem: hiring and retaining employees for the early-stage companies it incubates. The group was launched in 2010 by three college friends and supercharged in 2014, when its founders sold (for hundreds of millions of dollars) a third-party logistics company that they had also founded. The group launched Lamp Post Properties (LPP) in 2016 as a real estate arm that built out a coworking space to house the group's ventures, capitalizing on downtown Chattanooga's terrific historic buildings and high-speed fiber-optic municipal broadband infrastructure.

LPP piloted a co-living concept within a small apartment building nearby, master-leasing 14 apartments and paying new hires a stipend to participate in the experiment. Tiffanie Robinson, then the group's chief operating officer, said that they were "having a hard time keeping talent . . . finding housing that was flexible and [that] connected [residents] with people outside of work," an often-overlooked bit of social infrastructure needed by new arrivals working long hours at small companies.

After a year of tinkering, LPP was ready to try the experiment on a larger scale, just as the RCC released

ABOVE: Each floor of micro units shares two full-size kitchens with dining areas, one laundry area, living and recreation spaces, and a workspace.

its RFP for the Ross Hotel, a block from its offices. At first glance, LPP saw the micro-unit concept as a perfect match for the old hotel, which was already divided up into small rooms and had larger common areas downstairs. It should be straightforward to repurpose much of the existing structure. Of the few RFP responses received, LPP's was the clear winner.

THE IDEA EVOLVES

After spending $1 million on what had been estimated as a $4 million project, an estimate came in: asbestos remediation alone would cost $1 million. "Oh my gosh, that's a lot of money," Robinson recalls. "Then, the construction team thought the exterior walls would fall over."

The project budget spiraled, eventually doubling the initial projected costs. Williamson says that in the end, "almost nothing was left except for the exterior walls—which was not the intention going in, and certainly not within the [original] budget." Even worse, the degree of reconstruction required jeopardized the team's initial plan to use historic tax credits (HTCs). Not only was additional money needed, but also more capital would be needed to backfill the lost HTCs. Mark Feemster, financial adviser at Pinnacle Bank, points out that it "probably would have been cheaper to start from scratch," but that the team was committed to rehabilitation.

LPP had to recapitalize the project to rescue the deal. Instead of the RCC receiving a fixed price to sell the building, it accepted an equity stake in the project. Additional equity came from New Markets Tax Credits (NMTCs) syndicated by a local community development financial institution. "Those were incredibly complicated," says Robinson, "but we decided to go for them once we figured out that our building would cost a whole lot more to rehab than we'd anticipated."

FINANCIAL OVERVIEW

The $9.5 million final project budget was funded with a $5.5 million construction loan, $1.5 million from syndicated NMTC equity, $1.5 million in sponsor equity, and $1 million in the value of equity that RCC contributed.

Senior lien. Lamp Post Group had a longstanding business banking relationship with Pinnacle Bank, so it was natural to turn to that bank for commercial real estate lending as well. Feemster says that the bank has had "a great working relationship with Lamp Post for about 10 years now. We've done a couple of other buildings for them, but none that required this much attention."

As with any other novel product, Robinson put considerable effort into helping the lender understand "how viable the project was, since people were just starting to do multifamily projects again in downtown." Co-living was especially unusual, since its all-inclusive prices were higher than market rents. Feemster says that the bank "had to look at it outside the box." Robinson recalls, "I spent time helping the appraiser understand our rents, and everything

> *"Almost nothing was left except for the exterior walls, which was not the intention going in—and certainly not within the [original] budget."*

that was included." It certainly helped that LPP had its own experiment to point to, as well as guarantors.

RCC also contributed with its downtown market study. White says that she "went to local banks and gave presentations to make sure they felt comfortable" with the idea of new rental apartments, priming their loan committees for future projects. Williamson says that "it helps bankers get over their apprehension, if they can see a third party that's done a study that supports" the developer's idea.

The coaxing paid off, with the building "appraising right at what we needed it to appraise at" to close the loan, says Robinson. Feemster also is pleased with the end result: "When I toured it, I was surprised that they could make it as functional as they did with the limited space. . . . It's unbelievable what they've accomplished."

Equity. "Getting [LPG's principals] to buy into a historic rehab project wasn't as hard as you think," says Robinson, adding that "this building impacts their greater investment in these [early-stage] companies—which creates a better return for them"

> *It was so important that the project take place, instead of selling the building for a fixed acquisition price, that it was exchanged for an equity stake in the development entity, thereby improving the project's debt-to-equity ratio.*

across the entire portfolio. From the perspective of a venture capitalist, this was the natural next step after launching a successful prototype. Its investors also have a long-term focus, Robinson says. "We have a

mentality of a 10-year hold for all of our properties. . . . It has to do better than break even, but [our projects are] a long-term play."

As the capital stack was rearranged to accommodate construction cost overruns, RCC's role in the project changed. White says, "It was more important for us to see the project take place than to get a cash return." Instead of selling the building for a fixed acquisition price, RCC contributed the building as an 8 percent equity stake in Ross Hotel Partners LLC, improving the debt-to-equity ratio.

That investment has already paid off in another regard, White says. "It got so much recognition" from the national press for downtown's burgeoning startup ecosystem and RCC's efforts to develop a downtown innovation district. The Tomorrow Building has also been useful in establishing comparables, White continues: "We could tout that they don't have parking, which gets developers a little more comfortable with not having one parking space per apartment. They also have great unique local retail, which has been really successful at animating the street."

Public financing. RCC also introduced LPP to BrightBridge (River Gorge Capital), the largest community development entity in Tennessee, which made an NMTC equity investment in the building's ground-floor commercial component. Feemster says that "the NMTC enhancement took a project that maybe doesn't make sense the traditional way, allowed them to keep the history and the building in place, and allowed us to underwrite the deal."

However, Feemster warns that the NMTC has its drawbacks. "This was probably about the smallest deal we could have done based on the legal cost" of complying with its varied requirements, and that compliance costs valuable time as well: "Be prepared for a very deliberate and calculated closing process."

In this case, an extra two months of reviews were needed before closing.

The retailers also received signage grants available for small businesses in the area, and will benefit from a $2 million streetscape project underway on Patten Parkway.

LESSONS LEARNED

Patient, local partners. RCC and its foundation partners have strategically and patiently cultivated a decades-long regeneration of downtown Chattanooga, in collaboration with developer partners like LPP. Robinson points out that LPG's local founders share that commitment: "Local wealth is definitely what's going to keep recycling in your local ecosystem."

Selling the vision. RCC's City Center Plan made sure that everyone was on the same page regarding reusing the Ross Hotel as rental apartments—from its foundation partners, to the building's sellers, to its new buyers. The plan and its accompanying market study also helped sell the same vision to local lenders. Amy Donahue, RCC's director of communications, says that "providing these tools that help a developer do something" has had a tremendous impact on downtown's regeneration, even though RCC's facilitation of individual projects gets more attention.

Market intelligence. Both Lamp Post Properties and the River City Company had laid extensive groundwork for the Tomorrow Building, between the RCC's feasibility studies and LPP's prototype. These provided LPP with the confidence to forge ahead with the project even as it met difficulties. The property leased up in just six months and "met the intangible goals we were hoping for on the retention side," says Robinson.

OPPOSITE: Shared living rooms encourage residents to socialize. **ABOVE:** Each micro unit includes a kitchenette and a separate sitting area.

notes

Preface

1. Christine McClaren, "Toward an Uglier Architecture: Can We Keep Building and Keep the Mess?" Guggenheim Blogs, July 13, 2012, https://www.guggenheim.org/blogs/lablog/toward-an-uglier-architecture-can-we-keep-building-and-keep-the-mess.

Part I

1. Jane Jacobs, *The Death and Life of American Cities* (New York: Vintage Books, 1961).

2. Jacobs, *Death and Life of American Cities.*

3. Andrew Price, "Fine-Grained vs. Coarse-Grained Urbanism," Strong Towns, October 30, 2017, https://www.strongtowns.org/journal/2017/10/31/fine-grained-vs-coarse-grained-urbanism.

4. Price, "Fine-Grained vs. Coarse-Grained Urbanism."

5. Julia Levitt, "Preservation Green Lab's Liz Dunn on the Economics of Urban Grain," *Atlantic*, Dec. 1, 2011, www.theatlantic.com/national/archive/2011/12/preservation-green-labs-liz-dunn-on-the-economics-of-urban-grain/248190.

6. Victor Dover, CNU Council Montgomery, Alabama, October, 2011, YouTube video, October 2011, www.youtube.com/watch?v=gi5idjDna24.

7. Christine McClaren, "Toward an Uglier Architecture: Can We Keep Building and Keep the Mess?," *Guggenheim Berlin Lab, Lab|Log* blog, July 13, 2012, https://www.guggenheim.org/blogs/lablog/toward-an-uglier-architecture-can-we-keep-building-and-keep-the-mess.

8. Edward T. McMahon, "In Building Size and Age, Variety Yields Vibrancy," *Urban Land* online, August 7, 2014, https://urbanland.uli.org/planning-design/variety-building-size-age-yields-vibrancy.

9. ULI, "What Is Resilience?," About Resilience, https://developing resilience.uli.org/about-resilience.

10. Price, "Fine-Grained vs. Coarse-Grained Urbanism."

11. Giuseppe Moscarini and Fabien Postel-Vinay, "The Contribution of Large and Small Employers to Job Creation in Times of High and Low Unemployment," *American Economic Review*, 102 (October 2012): 2509–39, https://www.aeaweb.org/articles?id=10.1257/aer.102.6.2509.

12. Ross Chapin, *Pocket Neighborhoods: Creating Small-Scale Community in a Large-Scale World* (Newtown, CT: Taunton Press, 2011).

13. Joseph Minicozzi, "The Smart Math of Mixed-Use Development," Planetizen, January 23, 2012, https://www.planetizen.com/node/53922.

14. ABA, Civic Economics, and Local First, "Indie Impact Study Series: A National Comparative Survey with the American Booksellers Association, Salt Lake City, Utah," Summer 2012, http://localfirst.org/images/stories/SLC-Final-Impact-Study-Series.pdf.

15. Author interview with Kimber Lanning, October 20, 2017.

16. Local First and Civic Economics, "Local Works! Examining the Impact of Local Business on the West Michigan Economy," September 2008, http://nebula.wsimg.com/c9188c7a61817fd6dc3826b3f4df1ede?AccessKeld=8E410A17553441C49302&disposition=0&alloworigin=1.

17. Kimber Lanning, "When Cheaper Isn't Always Better (or Cheaper)," *AZCentral*, Dec. 26, 2014, https://www.azcentral.com/story/opinion/op-ed/2014/12/27/shop-local-arizona/20856649.

18. John G. O'Leary, "It's ONLY Rock & Roll?" *Business Lessons from Rock* (blog), Feb. 25, 2015, http://businesslessonsfromrock.com/notes/2015/02/its-only-rock-roll.

19. Daniel McCue, "Number of U.S. Households Projected to Increase by 12.2 Million in the Next Decade," *Housing Perspectives,* Joint Center for Housing Studies of Harvard University, December 20, 2018.

20. Belden Russonello Strategists, *Americans' Views on Their Communities, Housing, and Transportation*, Analysis of a national survey for ULI, March 2013, uli.org/wp-content/uploads/ULI-Documents/America-in-2013-Final-Report.pdf.

Part II

1. Incremental Development Alliance website, www.incrementaldevelopment.org.

2. Urban Land Institute Multifamily Housing Councils, *The Macro View on Micro Units* (Washington, DC: Urban Land Institute, 2014), http://uli.org/wp-content/uploads/ULI-Documents/MicroUnit_full_rev_2015.pdf.

3. Sarah Susanka, *The Not So Big House: A Blueprint for the Way We Really Live* (Newtown, CT: Taunton Press, 2001).

4. The Cottage Company, "Helping Communities Plan for the Future," www.cottagecompany.com/consulting/innovative-land-use-code.aspx.

5. The waterfall is a system of payment by which senior lenders are paid principal and interest first, and subordinate lenders are paid in turn.

6. Dave Biggs, "Is Face to Face Community Engagement Dying Out?" *Planetizen*, blog post, March 28, 2016.

7. Partnership for Building Reuse, *Untapped Potential: Strategies for Revitalization and Reuse* (Washington, DC: National Trust for Historic Preservation, October 2017). Available as PDF from https://forum.savingplaces.org/viewdocument/un-tapped-potential-strategies-for.

8. Congress for the New Urbanism, *Enabling Better Places: Users' Guide to Zoning Reform* (Sept. 15, 2018 draft), https://www.cnu.org/sites/default/files/Enabling_Better_Places_Jan_2018.pdf.

9. Richard Florida, "Parking Has Eaten American Cities," *CityLab,* July 24, 2018, https://www.citylab.com/transportation/2018/07/parking-has-eaten-american-cities/565715/.

10. Originally published in "Revitalization through Reuse: Learning from the Partnership for Building Reuse" (Preservation Green Lab and the Urban Land Institute, 2017).

small and the pandemic of 2020

In March 2020, after a long effort, *Building Small* was finally coming into reality. I was excited by what this book had become and pleased that the stories and explanations might help others think differently about how we build.

Then the pandemic that was COVID-19 surfaced. I wondered whether the stories and messages of *Building Small* could survive this once-in-a-generation disruptor. I spoke to colleagues with whom I had grown close through the SSDFs, and we commiserated about the impending challenges we, and our tenants, faced. This was not just an academic discussion—it was deeply personal. Having recently opened my own first small business (a shared workspace), I worried that all I had postulated in this book, and all I had invested in the business, was about to be bankrupted.

Nearly a year into the pandemic, I am emboldened to say not only is *Building Small* still relevant—it is even more so. The "stress test" presented by COVID-19 was countered by an outsized showing of community

support for local small businesses. Through duress, everyday citizens realized the importance of small businesses to their community's identity, authenticity, and

---

ABOVE: The pandemic that began in 2020 required businesses to close indoor seating space, leading to potentially devastating economic impacts. This meant the gatekeepers for barriers to *small*—from public works departments to alcohol control boards—had to adapt and become much more nimble in applying legacy regulations. What resulted was a more active and animated public realm that helped businesses stay alive while hopefully ushering in a new way of thinking about the value of *small*. *(All images ©2020 CRAFT Development)*

economic health. Websites blossomed overnight to bail out local small businesses. GoFundMe campaigns emerged to pay the staff of shuttered local businesses. And the refrain of "How can I help?" was heard again and again through social media or in person as local, loved businesses navigated an uncertain and constantly changing landscape.

I watched with awe as the federal government committed, then deployed, half a trillion dollars at lightning speed and with very low-friction underwriting to small businesses. (At the time it didn't feel like it, but reflecting back, it was an amazing show of fintech prowess.) If anyone had told me at the end of 2019 that the federal government would open its checkbook and send $500 *billion* to small businesses in less than 60 days, I would have laughed. But government did, because it realized that small businesses are essential to the health and well-being of our economy and our communities.

In fall 2020, I watched my fellow small business owners open their doors, move their furniture outside, and greet their returning and supportive customers with a smile—while having no idea how it would all turn out. Agility and positivity is the DNA of *small*. So are creatively adapting to whatever gets thrown at you, unbridled nimbleness to move quickly, and grit and determination to make it through another day. These are the qualities that define my favorite hashtag of the COVID experience: #toosmalltofail.

As spring nears and vaccinations begin, the pandemic at some point will be only a memory. Despite the challenges of this moment, I am now convinced *small* will endure. Because, in an increasingly homogenized, standardized, and institutionalized world, *small* is the soul of our communities; it is how we build places that people love and sustain. More important, it creates something our communities want to ensure not only survives—but thrives. COVID-19 will not be *small*'s undoing. It was its affirmation.

J.H.
February 2021

acknowledgments

Like some of you, I have always been intrigued by the idea of writing a book. Throughout my career, many colleagues and friends have offered sage advice. "Write every day." "Don't try to make it say everything." "When you think you are done, you are really just getting started."

Most of their advice went unheeded. I didn't write every day. I did try to make it say everything. But yes, when I thought I was done, I was really just getting started. And while it took much longer than anticipated, it is finally in your hands.

More than just storytelling, the raison d'être for this book is to elevate the conversation about how and why we build. It is also meant to inspire those seeking a different path in real estate development. Consistent with this vision, *Building Small* is a repository of the excitement, passion, and impact—and key lessons—I have seen and heard firsthand in countless projects and cities since 2012.

Gratitude is a noble goal, and a project as complex as this deserves a lot of recognition for those who helped make it real.

First and foremost are the people who gather around the ideas and principles that constitute the Urban Land Institute. Without that organization, I would never have had the opportunity to explore the subject matter that informed this book.

There is the "small posse"—the group of developers, designers, and socially minded builders who crisscrossed the country with me over the years in search of great ideas, inspired places, and personal stories of impact. Their camaraderie, curiosity, and enthusiasm powers me to create a new tour every six months and drove me to want to share the story of how *small* can transform the built environment and bring new meaning to one's career.

While I was encouraged to seek a single, institutional underwriter for this project, I felt that would be the antithesis of this story. If building *small* is

> *The raison d'être for this book is to elevate the conversation about how and why we build. I hope it will convey the excitement, passion, and impact I have seen and heard firsthand in countless cities since 2012.*

about incremental, boot-strapped change, why shouldn't funding for the book reflect that same approach? And when it came time to ask for support, many showed up to donate, large and small.

Behind the scenes was the team that helped bring this to closure: the collaborating authors, editors, designers, and those who prodded, poked, and distilled my thoughts. It was their professional skill and dedicated efforts that helped forge my observations into a cohesive text.

To everyone who had a role in *Building Small*, I give many thanks. I hope our collaboration and hard work will catalyze informed conversations and new attitudes that will make *small* really big.

SPECIAL THANKS TO:

David Mulvihill, the former vice president for education at ULI, who offered me the opportunity to create the Small-Scale Developers program. Ed McMahon, who has been a key collaborator for over two decades as we extol the virtues of development done differently. Patrick Phillips, who as CEO of ULI at the time this book was evolving, threw the weight of his role and his personal financial pledge to support the concept. Adrienne Schmitz, who reluctantly came out of retirement to quietly and skillfully guide this book into something real. Colleagues and early donors Alan Razak and Jeff Johnston, who demonstrated early financial commitment, which told me this was an idea worth pursuing. Partners Dan Carroll and Stasia Obremskey, Robert Eu and Betsy Hambrecht, who offered support that allowed me to to "walk the talk" and take theory into practice, living both the dream—and struggle—of building *small*. As we headed into production, the incredible skills and true collaboration of Jim Mulligan, senior editor, and John Hall, book designer, brought the subject matter to life.

And finally, my family—Marty and Maddie—who came to accept *Building Small* as my quixotic journey that may or may not materialize someday. But they nodded politely, offering support and moments of quiet time when I could write—never suggesting it would not happen. And so it has.

THE "SMALL POSSE"

Candace Baitz, Pivot Project, Oklahoma City, Oklahoma
Colin Brice, Mapsos, New York, New York
Devon Caldwell, Inkwell, Detroit, Michigan
Jonathan Dodson, Pivot Project, Oklahoma City, Oklahoma
Liz Dunn, Dunn & Hobbes, Seattle, Washington
Damian Farrell, Damian Farrell Design Group, Ann Arbor, Michigan
Andrew Frey, Tecela, Miami, Florida
Eric Garrison, TBG, Fort Worth, Texas
Hector Jimenez-Caballero, Central Barrio Development, Tucson, Arizona
Jeff Johnston, Cathartes, Boston, Massachusetts
Miles Kamimura, Pacific Property Group, Honolulu, Hawaii
Shawn Kichline, Oxide Development, Pittsburgh, Pennsylvania
Michael Lander, Lander Group, Oakland, California
David Light, Long Beach, California
Steve Mackey, Mack Industrial, Boynton Beach, Florida
Doug Moss, Holzman Moss Bottino Architecture, New York City, New York
Lorenzo Perez, Venue Projects, Phoenix, Arizona
Richard Ramer, Ramer Architecture, Portland, Oregon
Ben Sellers, Pivot Project, Oklahoma City, Oklahoma
Hal Shapiro, REAL Properties, Kansas City, Missouri
Sam Tuttle, Streetcar Properties, Richmond, Virginia
David Wanzer, Pivot Project, Oklahoma City, Oklahoma

ABOVE: Attendees of SSDF 14 listen as local developer and entrepreneur Sherman Ragland explains how his hometown of Baltimore has leveraged the power of small to assist in its regeneration of key neighborhoods. *(©2019 Jim Heid)*

DONORS

CATALYSTS: $5,000–$10,000
Jeff Johnston, Cathartes
Patrick Kennedy, Panoramic Interests
National Trust for Historic Preservation
Patrick Phillips, ULI (retired)

TRANSFORMERS: $2,500–$4,999
Liz Dunn, Dunn & Hobbes
Heartland LLC
Michael Lander, Lander Group
MIG Inc.
Mithun

BUILDERS: $1,000–$2,499
BUILD
Joe Hruda, Civitas Design
LOCUS
National Main Street Center
Pivot Project
Alan Razak, Athenian Razak
Seifel Consulting
Hal Shapiro, Real Property Group
Venue Projects
Women's Development Collaborative

MAKERS: $500–$999
Teri Behm and John Clawson
Miranda Fausto
Andrew Frey
John Hearin
Howard Kozloff
Linda Lea
Ted Lieser
Eve Picker
Frank Starkey
VITA

BOOTSTRAPPERS: $50–$499
Pavel Abaev
Rob Brewster
Amy Bridge
Katherine Gunderson
Damian Farrell
Gail Jennings
Hector Jimenez-Caballero
Marty Jones
Chris McCormack
Richard Ramer
Deb Schmucker
Matt Teresi

COLLABORATING AUTHORS

Samantha Beckerman is a development manager for Brookfield Properties Development in San Francisco, where she works on Pier 70, a 28-acre mixed-use development along San Francisco's central waterfront. She leads the design of Pier 70's nine acres of parks and helps manage the project's public/private partnership between Brookfield and the Port of San Francisco. Before joining Brookfield in 2018, she was a consultant working on projects related to small-scale real estate development and affordable housing. Beckerman has a BA in anthropology and environmental studies from Kenyon College and a master's in city planning from the University of California, Berkeley, where she focused on the intersection of equitable development, land use, and urban sustainability. An active member of ULI, she is vice chair of ULI's Public/Private Partnership Council, Blue Flight.

Margaret O'Neal is director of programs at the Congress for the New Urbanism (CNU), where she helps shape the organization's programmatic work, develops programming for the Annual Congress, and manages the Legacy Projects. Before joining CNU, O'Neal spent over a decade advocating for the preservation and reuse of older buildings in various positions at the National Trust for Historic Preservation, most recently managing on-the-ground projects, strategic partnerships, and communications for the National Trust's Research and Policy Lab. She holds a BA in political science from Clemson University and a master's in community planning from the University of Maryland.

Adrienne Schmitz is a freelance writer specializing in real estate development and urban planning. She was on the staff at the Urban Land Institute for nearly two decades, serving as project manager on numerous publications, and was also the primary author and coauthor of several ULI books. Before joining ULI, she was a real estate market analyst. Schmitz holds a master of urban planning degree from the University of Virginia.

resources and references

PROJECTS

	Location	Use	Type
200 West Center **www.specializedreg.com/projects/200-west-center**	Fayetteville, AR	F&B, office	Adaptive use
3535 Grand Avenue	Minneapolis, MN	Residential	New build
38 Harriet Street	San Francisco, CA	Residential	New build
761–771 NW First Street	Miami, FL	Residential	New build
Alumina Apartments	Oklahoma City, OK	Residential	New build
Amped Kitchens **www.ampedkitchens.com**	Los Angeles, CA	Maker	Adaptive use
Ankeny Alley	Portland, OR	Civic	Adaptive use
Avalon Hayes Valley	San Francisco, CA	Residential	New build
Bella Grace Hotel **www.goffdantonio.com/work/showcase/detail/** **hospitality/bella-grace-hotel**	Charleston, SC	Hospitality	New build/adaptive use
The Belt **www.thebelt.org**	Detroit, MI	Civic/art	Adaptive use
Biergarten **https://biergartensf.com/**	San Francisco, CA	F&B	New build
Chophouse Row **www.chophouserow.com**	Seattle	F&B, office, residential	New build/adaptive use
Circle City Industrial Complex/Ruckus **www.circlecityind.com**	Indianapolis, IN	Industrial/maker/office	Adaptive use
CraftWork **www.craftworkhbg.com**	Healdsburg, CA	Coworking	Adaptive use
Cultural Trail **https://indyculturaltrail.org**	Indianapolis, IN	Civic	New build
Edmund Oast	Charleston, SC	F&B	New build
El Moore Lodge	Detroit, MI	Hospitality	Adaptive use
The Fair-Haired Dumbbell	Portland, OR	Office	New build
Garden Theater	Pittsburgh, PA	Retail, residential	Adaptive use
Good Weather **www.goodweatherinseattle.com**	Seattle, WA	Retail	Adaptive use
H2	Healdsburg, CA	Hospitality	New build
Half Mile North	Charleston, SC	F&B	New build
Harmon Guest House **https://harmonguesthouse.com**	Healdsburg, CA	Hospitality	New build
Hotel Healdsburg	Healdsburg, CA	Hospitality	New build
Katrina Cottages **https://leanurbanism.org/publications/** **the-katrina-cottage-movement-a-case-study/**	Mississippi	Residential	New build
Laneways	Melbourne, Australia	Civic	Adaptive use
Melrose Market **https://melrosemarketseattle.com**	Seattle, WA	F&B	Adaptive use
Modern General	Santa Fe, NM	Retail, F&B	New build
The Newton **www.thenewtonphx.com**	Phoenix, AZ	F&B, retail	Adaptive use
The Ocean	Portland, OR	F&B, residential	Adaptive use
Open Works **www.openworksbmore.org**	Baltimore, MD	Maker	Adaptive use
The Orchard	Phoenix, AZ	Phoenix	Adaptive use
Oslo	Washington, DC	Residential	New build
Pacific Box and Crate	Charleston, SC	Coworking, F&B	New Build/adaptive use
Pine Street Market **www.pinestreetpdx.com**	Portland, OR	F&B, office	Adaptive use